Joseph J. Tobin
David Y. H. Wu
Dana H. Davidson

Preschool in
Three Cultures

*Japan, China, and
the United States*

Yale University Press
New Haven and London

Portions of chapter 2 first appeared as "Class Size and
Student/Teacher Ratios in the Japanese Preschool" by
Tobin, Davidson, and Wu in *Comparative Education Review*
31: 4.

Designed by Jo Aerne and set in Garamond no. 3 with
Goudy Old Style for display. Printed in the United States
of America by Vail-Ballou Press, Binghamton, New York.

Library of Congress Cataloging-in-Publication Data
Tobin, Joseph Jay.
Preschool in three cultures: Japan, China, and the United
States / Joseph J. Tobin, David Y.H. Wu, Dana H.
Davidson.
       p.   cm.
Bibliography: p.
Includes index.   21.50
ISBN 0–300–04235–3 (cloth)
        0–300–04812–2 (pbk.)
1. Nursery schools—Japan—Case studies.   2. Nursery
schools—China—Case studies.   3. Nursery schools—
United States—Case studies.   4. Educational anthro-
pology.   I. Wu, David Y. H.   II. Davidson, Dana H.,
1949–   .   III. Title.
LB 1140.25.J3T63   1989   88–20904
372'.21'0951—dc 19   CIP

10   9   8   7   6   5   4   3

60472

Contents

Preface

The approach we take to studying preschools in this book reflects our diverse backgrounds and interests. David Wu, a Taiwanese cultural anthropologist, has studied child rearing, mental health, and social organization in overseas Chinese communities as well as in Taiwan and the People's Republic. Dana Davidson has a degree in early childhood education and experience in preschool teaching, administration, and teacher training. I have a degree in human development with training in anthropology and psychology and fieldwork experience in Japan.

In 1983 I came to Honolulu to work with David Wu of the East-West Center and Wen-Shing Tseng of the University of Hawaii's Department of Psychiatry on a National Institute of Mental Health postdoctoral fellowship in Asian/Pacific Culture and Mental Health. I had been living and working in Japan, where my elder son, Sam, had been enrolled for a year in a Kyoto nursery school. The experience of being the parent of a child attending a Japanese nursery school had been so interesting to me, and so unlike my previous experience of being the parent of a child enrolled in an American nursery school, that I arrived in Hawaii ready to change my research focus from intercultural images to Japanese preschools.

At the East-West Center I soon found myself involved in discussions with David Wu about the role preschools in China and Japan are being asked to play in child socialization and cultural transmission. David Wu at that time was in the midst of research and writing on parenting and mental health in China. In the spring of 1984 he and Wen-Shing Tseng invited Dana Davidson and me to serve as discussants for a conference they organized in Hawaii on Chinese child rearing and mental health. At the conference several of the participants from the People's Republic spoke about the single-child family policy, about spoiling, and about preschools; this served to heighten our interest in doing a comparative study of preschools and the changing family in China and Japan.

Following the conference, David Wu and I agreed to work collaboratively on a comparison of Japanese and Chinese preschools. Six months later, having decided to include the United States in our study to avoid the overemphasis on differences inherent in a two-country comparison, we invited Dana Davidson to join us and add to our expertise in cross-cultural fieldwork and the study of culture her expertise in preschool education and the study of children.

We decided early on that we would use an approach to studying Japanese, Chinese, and American preschools that would give parents, teachers, and administrators a chance to speak directly. In chapter 1 we describe the method we developed for using videotape to stimulate a multivocal text. In chapters 2, 3, and 4 we present insiders' and outsiders' explanations of Japanese, Chinese, and American preschools. Chapter 5 is a comparative discussion of the ways people from each of the three countries conceptualize the purpose of preschools.

We worked collaboratively on the book as a whole, each taking primary responsibility for one of the three countries in our study. David Wu and his wife, Wei-lan Wu, did all the fieldwork and videotaping in the People's Republic of China, and David, with Wei-lan's assistance, wrote the first draft of the China chapter. Dana Davidson helped with the fieldwork in Japan and the United States, organized the quantitative data, and researched and wrote the first draft of the U.S. chapter. I took responsibility for the chapter on Japan, for the introductory and comparative chapters, and for reworking our stylistically dissimilar first drafts into a more coherent whole.

This book is multiauthored in several other ways. In each chapter, preschool teachers, administrators, and child-development specialists are quoted not just as informants but as authorities on their culture's preschools. Principal Yoshizawa, Assistant Principal Higashino, and teacher Fukui Masako in Japan; Comrades Xiang, Wang, Li, and Chang in China; and Barbara Culler, Cheryl Takashige, Colleen Momohara, and Linda Rios in the United States, among others, do not have their names on the cover of this book, but in an important sense they are coauthors, the true authorities behind our text.

Other friends and colleagues also made significant contributions. Andrew Jacobs prepared many of the photos in this book and also helped us clarify theoretical and methodological issues in visual anthropology. Dick Hinze, Janet Murakami, Susan White, Kathy Williams, Kathy Fagan, Janet Crescenzi, Bobbi Ribel, Nancy Berry, and Yu Xiao-ming also contributed photographs. Joe O'Reilly coached us in categorizing and analyzing our quantitative data. Zhou Nan and Zhou Li Jiu of Beijing Normal University, visiting scholars at the Institute of Culture and Communication of the East-West Center, made invaluable contributions to our understanding of Chinese preschools. Drs. Chien Xinzhong, Cui Yoeli, Wan Wenpeng, and Liu Jiequ, Madame Yang Qun, the late Madame Tian Ying, and professors Shen Yucun, Lin Bing, Yang Zhiling, and Zhang Shifu graciously facilitated our research in the People's Republic. The Kumagais of Senzan Yōchien in Kyoto, the Fujimotos of Chiba, the Nagamis of Hiroshima, Janet Murakami, Miki Lewis, Hayato Yamanaka, and Toshihiko Kishi helped in many ways with our fieldwork in Japan. Bea and John Whiting, Yasuko Nainan, and Irving Lazar watched our tapes with us and alerted us to issues we otherwise would have missed. Early on in the project Phil Altbach encouraged us to produce a book-length report of our research. Takeo Doi, Francis L. K. Hsu, Keith Brown, Michael McTear, Mary Martini, John Kirkpatrick, Beth Tobin, Richard Hinze, Stephanie Feeney, Diana Bethel, Fumi Nitta, and Mamoru Tsukada read drafts of one or more chapters and made corrections and suggestions, some of which we were sensible and open-minded enough to follow.

Victor Li, Mary Bitterman, and Leejay Cho of the East-West Center lent support to the project. Edith Yashiki and Dean Nagasako, among others, helped in the physical preparation of the manuscript. Gladys Topkis and Cecile Watters of the Yale University Press edited our unwieldy drafts. To each of these friends and colleagues, to Beth Tobin and Dan Davidson, and especially to Wei-lan Wu, who not only provided aid and insight but also carried our camera across China, we offer our thanks.

Joseph Jay Tobin
Honolulu, June 1988

Preschool in
Three Cultures

Chapter One

Introduction

In Japan, China, and the United States preschool is an increasingly common solution to the problem of how to care for, socialize, and educate children between infancy and the start of formal schooling. Approximately 95 percent of the four-year-olds in Tokyo, 80 percent of the four-year-olds in Beijing, and 65 percent of the four-year-olds in New York are enrolled in nursery schools, day-care centers, or group-care homes.

In other eras most young children in these societies were cared for in settings other than preschools. They were raised in their homes by full-time mothers, taken to the fields by parents who farmed, or cared for by hired country girls, mother's helpers, maiden aunts, grandmothers, or older siblings (Whiting and Edwards, 1988). In this book we explore the implications of this shift away from family and kin-centered child rearing toward institutionalized group care of young children in cultures as different as Japan, China, and the United States.

This book is a study not only of three cultures' preschools but also of three cultures as seen through their preschools. In addition to describing contemporary Japanese, Chinese, and American preschools, we relate the rise in the number and importance of preschools in these countries to larger social and cultural concerns. We view preschools as complex institutions serving children, parents, and, indirectly, the wider society. Embedded in communities, nations, and cultures, preschools both reflect and affect social change. For example, in China preschools are expected to provide an antidote to the spoiling that Chinese fear is inevitable in an era of single-child families. In Japan the increasing nuclearization and gentrification of the family brought on by a shrinking birthrate, an ongoing migration of young people from extended households in the country to single-family apartments in large cities, and the rise of the middle-class *sarariman* (salaried employee) life-style (Vogel, 1971) have led Japanese parents to believe that preschools offer their children their best chance of

learning to function in a large group and of becoming, in Japanese terms, truly human. In the United States, preschools are being asked to respond to changing patterns of men's and women's work, a high divorce rate, and a growing concern for the needs of single-parent families. As perceptions of work, marriage, and the family change in all three societies, they look to preschools to provide stability, richness, and guidance to children's lives.

Method

Our research methods are unlike those used in most comparative research in early child education.* We have not tested children to determine the

*For a fuller discussion of the theoretical foundations and implications of our method, see Joseph Tobin's "Visual Anthropology and Multivocal Ethnography: A Dialogical Approach to Japanese Preschool Class Size" (1989).

efficacy of various staffing patterns or pedagogical approaches. We have not measured the frequency of teacher-student interaction or computed dollars spent per student per hour in school or tabulated how many minutes a day students spend on reading readiness exercises. Although we touch on all these issues and others in this book, our focus instead has been on eliciting meanings. We have set out not to rate the preschools in the three cultures but to find out what they are meant to do and to be.

Multivocal Ethnography

Early in this project we were struggling to find an appropriate approach for studying Japanese, Chinese, and American preschools when we attended a screening of a pair of ethnographic films by Linda Connor, Timothy Asch, and Patsy Asch (1986). In the first film, *A Balinese Trance Séance* (Asch et al., 1983a), Jero, a medium, enters a trance state in order to help a grieving family contact their dead son. The second film, *Jero on Jero: A Balinese Séance Observed* (Asch et al., 1983b), shows Jero seeing *A Balinese Trance Séance* for the first time. While Jero watches herself on film, the anthropologist Linda Connor, watching with her, asks Jero how she feels about the film and encourages her to explain her actions and to recall what was going through her mind during each stage of the séance. The use Asch, Connor, and Asch made of ethnographic film to stimulate a second, reflexive level of discourse (Ruby, 1982) gave us the idea of using videotapes of preschools to stimulate a multivocal text (Clifford, 1983).

The structure of this book is dialogic. Each of the central three chapters is a series of theses and antitheses, a telling and retelling of the same event from different perspectives—an ongoing dialogue between insiders and outsiders, between practitioners and researchers, between Americans and Chinese, Americans and Japanese, and Chinese and Japanese. In each chapter, the voices, besides our own, are those of Japanese, Chinese, and American preschool teachers, administrators, parents, children, and child-development experts.

We begin each chapter with a description of a twenty-minute videotape we made of one preschool in each country in our study.* These written descriptions of videotapes provide our first level of narrative. Next, in each chapter, we introduce the voices of preschool teachers, parents, and administrators, who tell their own stories, creating their own texts that

---

*We have included in this book, in addition to standard photographs, photos made from our videotapes. Although these photos lack sharpness, we believe they will help readers better picture the three preschools in our study and give something of the feel of our visually centered research method.

discuss, deconstruct, and criticize our account of their schools. Each of these texts reacts to earlier texts while never entirely replacing, subsuming, or negating them.

Visual Ethnography

The visual ethnographies we describe at the beginning of each chapter are videotaped scenes of preschool everyday life, recordings of the daily routines and little dramas that compose the world of the preschool. Our videotapes are basically old-fashioned ethnography combined with new technology. As in any other ethnographic venture, we traveled to a foreign culture, asked and received permission to observe an important cultural institution (a preschool), and made extensive field notes (in our case using videotape in addition to pen and paper and tape recorder). Choices of when, where, and what to observe and document, as in any other such study, were the result of negotiation between ourselves and our hosts, a compromise between what we had come to the field hoping to film and what our hosts felt was most important and appropriate for us to see. Considerations of time, money, distance, and, not least of all, lighting also were important factors in determining the look of our films.

Before leaving for the field we had made some preliminary decisions about what we wanted in our videotapes. We knew we were looking for good (as opposed to mediocre) middle-class (as opposed to elite or impoverished) preschools in urban areas of China, Japan, and the United States. We wanted to tape throughout what we hoped would be a more or less typical day, including scenes of arrival and departure, of play both indoors and out, of children and teachers, children and parents, and children and children. In each school we hoped to get shots of free play, of more structured learning activities, and of lunch, snack, bathroom, and nap times. We hoped to film examples of parents and children saying good-bye, of children fighting and cooperating, and of teachers instructing, comforting, and disciplining children.

We were able to accomplish most of these goals in our videotapes, although the compromises we had to make were many. We chose preschools where the administrators, teachers, and parents seemed relatively free to enter into dialogue with us. We say "relatively" free because what preschool teachers, administrators, parents, and children feel free to say to visiting anthropologists is itself largely culturally determined. Notions of what it means to speak honestly, of what to show and say to a guest, of how frankly to criticize oneself and others vary widely from culture to culture and reflect changing political climates. For example, Chinese teachers and administrators appeared to consider carefully what they should show

us and to weigh the implications of their words before they spoke. But this is not a uniquely Chinese phenomenon: several American and Japanese preschools we approached were also hesitant to participate.

Our choice of classrooms in each preschool followed a similar logic. In each school we asked for permission to film primarily in a four-year-old children's classroom. When more than one were available we asked the preschool director to select a class with a teacher who would be comfortable letting us spend a day videotaping in her class and willing and able to meet with us several times during the next year to discuss her teaching strategies. All other factors being equal, we asked to film in the classroom with the best lighting and camera angles and with convenient corners for us to stand in, out of the way.

Our choice of where and what to videotape reflected our desire for comparability across cultures. We hoped to record comparable situations, with children of comparable ages, in comparable institutions, in three different cultures. But this desire for comparability was tempered by our knowing that comparability across cultures can be only approximate at best. We wanted, for example, to videotape at least one fight scene in each culture and one scene showing a teacher disciplining a child. But what constitutes a fight and what constitutes teacher discipline turned out to be hard to define and highly variable culturally.

To make our videotapes more interesting and accessible to viewers, we decided to focus on two or three children in each class. In retrospect we realize that this decision was itself highly culture-bound, mirroring American preschool teachers' thinking about how best to allocate their time and energy in the classroom. When the American members of our team (Tobin and Davidson) were in control of the camera, we unconsciously tended to focus on misbehaving, aggressive, and highly verbal children. When the Chinese members of our team (David and Wei-lan Wu) were taping and editing, the footage tended to be more of large groups and less of individual children.

The result is three videotapes that are very subjective, idiosyncratic, culture-bound—and yet consistent with our method. In our taping and editing we looked for emotional and dramatic interactions because with our visual ethnographies we were trying not to portray a nation's preschools but instead to begin a dialogue. Like psychologists selecting pictures for projective tests, we selected images that were ambiguous, that opened up rather than closed down possibilities for discussion and interpretation.

Insiders' Explanations

Insiders' explanations—Japanese, Chinese, and American preschool administrators', teachers', and parents' explanations of and reactions to the videotapes we shot in their schools—are the second voice we introduce in each chapter. We elicited these insiders' explanations by taking edited versions of our tapes back to the schools where they were filmed and showing them to children, parents, teachers, and administrators. As they watched our visual ethnographic accounts, we engaged these people in discussion, asking them, first, if the videotapes succeeded in reflecting their schools as they saw them, and if not, how not? We assigned the classroom teacher the task of providing a running commentary, a post-hoc play-by-play analysis of her actions as shown in our tapes. When the insiders' talk was spontaneous, we remained silent and let it flow. When they grew silent, we prompted them with questions and with our outsiders' hunches about what was going on. We asked parents, "Are you surprised to see how your children behave in school?" We asked a teacher, "Why did you wait so long to break up that argument?" We asked children, "Do you remember when we came to your class to make this movie? Does this look like a usual day in your school?"

The Problem of Typicality

Clearly, one preschool cannot be assumed to represent the preschools of a nation. We do not claim that Dong-feng is representative of all Chinese preschools or that the explanations parents, teachers, and administrators at Komatsudani gave us are typical Japanese views. There is no one Chinese view about how to care for children, no one typical American preschool, no one Japanese approach to disciplining children who misbehave.

To address the problem of typicality and to give a sense of the great range of preschool practices and beliefs to be found in each country, we showed our videotapes to audiences associated with other preschools in the same country, in other cities. For example, we showed our videotape of Kyoto's Komatsudani Day-care Center to audiences in Osaka, Hiroshima, Tokyo, and Chiba. We showed our Dong-feng tape in Beijing, Shanghai, and Kunmin. Our videotape of St. Timothy's Child Center of Honolulu was seen by audiences in State College, Pennsylvania; Nashville, Tennessee; Chicago, Illinois; and Claremont, California. In each city we asked preschool parents and staff, and students and faculty at university early child education programs, to tell us in what ways the preschools we videotaped were typical or atypical of others in their country.

These responses to our videotapes provide a third voice in our book, a narrative strain that contextualizes both our videotapes and the insiders' explanations of the tapes. If Dong-feng is not a typical Chinese preschool, we could count on the preschool teachers and education specialists in Beijing who watched the Dong-feng video to tell us exactly what is unusual and, in their minds, good or bad about the way people in the provinces care for young children. Similarly, audiences in Tokyo and Hiroshima told us what they found lacking in Kyoto's Komatsudani Hoikuen, and audiences associated with preschools on the U.S. mainland criticized St. Timothy's Child Center of Honolulu, as seen in our videotape, for giving either too much or too little emphasis to academic readiness and for being either too strict or not strict enough with children who misbehave.

Altogether, we recorded the reactions to our videotapes of approximately three hundred parents, teachers, administrators, child-development specialists, and university students from each of our three countries. In this book we present what we learned in these screenings statistically as well as descriptively. We generated quantitative results by asking audiences to fill out rating sheets following the screenings of our videotapes.

These rating sheets called for respondents to make judgments about the preschool from their country as seen in our tape. We asked respondents, for example, to rate how well or poorly the teachers in the tapes dealt with discipline: "Were the teachers too strict, just right, or not strict enough?" We also asked in this way about curriculum, equipment, pace, safety, and a dozen other issues. On questionnaires we also asked these informants their views of the most important reason for a society to have preschools, the most important thing for children to learn in preschool, and the most important characteristics of a good preschool teacher.

Outsiders' Judgments

Following an idea first developed by Robert A. LeVine in his 1966 paper "Outsiders' Judgments," in this book we empower preschool teachers, administrators, and parents to speak as anthropologists. Ethnographic judgments, whether rendered by a layman or by an anthropologist, reflect an intermingling of the culture being described and the culture doing the describing. Thus statements by American preschool parents and staff about a Chinese preschool have something to teach us about both American and Chinese beliefs and values.

The outsiders' judgments we weave into this book are intended to make our project more truly intercultural (rather than merely cross-cultural) than are most comparative multinational studies. Our book is not only *about* three cultures; it also contains perspectives *from* three cultures: Japanese, Chinese, and American interpretations of themselves and of each other.

We stimulated the production of outsiders' judgments by showing audiences in cities across China, Japan, and the United States our videotapes of the other two cultures' preschools. Once again we recorded their judgments and analyses both by taping the discussions we held with them following the screenings and by asking them to fill out the same rating sheets we used to record their reactions to tapes of their own country's preschool.

Contexts: Time, Place, and Social Class

Ethnography as a method of research and a mode of representation is vulnerable to the accusation of being static, ahistorical, ideal-typical, and conservative in its reification of the status quo. Ethnography tends to find order, function, and symmetry in institutions while missing conflict and dysfunction; ethnography highlights ritual, belief, and ethos while giving less attention to the issues of social class, politics, and power.

Our videotapes of preschools, like other ethnographic narratives, freeze people and institutions in time and isolate them from their larger contexts. Our introduction of insiders' judgments of their own preschools and of outsiders' judgments of each others' schools widens the perspective, but our narratives as a whole remain at risk of being essentially timeless and contextless. To counteract this tendency, we have in each chapter tried to introduce a sense of place, time, and social class.

Place matters: we made our videotape of a Japanese preschool in Kyoto, a city with a long history of Buddhism and a more recent tradition of socialist sympathies, especially in the school system. Time matters: we filmed in China five years after the beginning of the single-child family policy, at a time when parents, teachers, and child-development experts were struggling with the question of how best to socialize this first cohort of children growing up without brothers and sisters. Class matters: in the United States we taped in a middle-class preschool in a suburban neighborhood of Honolulu, a city with a very high cost of living, a high percentage of working mothers, and a tradition of private education.

We have tried to privilege those contexts that insiders in each culture see as being most important. When, as in the case of Japan, social class emerges in discussions with teachers and administrators as an important contextual issue for understanding the meaning of preschool, we provide an analysis of the historical and contemporary tension between Japan's working-class day-care centers and middle-class nursery schools. When, as in our research in the United States, teachers and parents speak of changes in women's work, parenting, and sex-role expectations, we offer feminist analyses of the relationship between the changing American family and the changing American preschool. When, as in the case of China, the issue of population control spontaneously arises in discussions with parents and child-development specialists, we explore the connection between the structure of the Chinese preschool and the shrinking of the Chinese family.

Learning about Ourselves and Others

The study of foreign cultures, in addition to its explicit mission of documenting the diversity of human beliefs and institutions, also functions, in Marcus and Fischer's words (1986), "as a form of cultural critique for ourselves." In other words, the study of other cultures, in addition to making the exotic familiar, also can work to make the familiar exotic. In this book we have tried to achieve both of these goals. We hope our work will help scholars as well as preschool teachers, administrators, and parents find something familiar and perhaps even attractive and useful in foreign preschools. And we also hope that reading about a preschool from one's own culture alongside descriptions of parallel institutions in foreign cultures will encourage a process of cultural defamiliarization, a realization of the essential arbitrariness and culture-boundedness of taken-for-granted beliefs and practices.

Chapter Two

Komatsudani:
A Japanese Preschool

Komatsudani Hoikuen, a Buddhist preschool located on the grounds of a three-hundred-year-old temple on a hill on the east side of Kyoto, has 120 students. Twelve of these children are infants, under eighteen months, who are cared for in a nursery by four teachers. Another 20 Komatsudani children are toddlers, under three years of age, who are cared for in two groups of 10 by three teachers and an aide. The rest of the children are divided into three-year-old, four-year-old, and five-year-old classes, each with 25 to 30 students and one teacher. Each class has its own homeroom within the rambling old temple.

A Day at Komatsudani

The school opens each morning at 7:00 A.M., and soon after, children begin to arrive, brought to school by a parent or grandparent on foot, by bicycle, or, less commonly, by car. By 9:00 most of the children have arrived, put their lunch boxes and knapsacks away in the cubbyholes in their homerooms, and begun playing with their friends in the classrooms, corridors, or playground. Some of the older children stop by the nursery to play with the babies or to take toddlers for a walk on the playground. At 9:30 the "clean-up" song is played over loudspeakers audible throughout the entire school area. As the children put away toys, balls, and tricycles, the music changes from the clean-up song to the equally lively exercise song, and, with their teachers' encouragement, the children form a large circle on the playground and go through ten minutes of stretching, jumping, hopping, and running together in a group.

12

Taisō (morning exercise) complete, the "end-of-exercise-go-to-your-room" song comes over the loudspeakers, and the children, led by their teachers, run in a line into the school building, class by class, each child removing his or her shoes in the entranceway. Inside, the twenty-eight four-year-olds of Momogumi (Peach Class) enter their homeroom, which is identified by pictures of peaches on the door and the word *momogumi* written in *hiragana* (the phonetic alphabet). The Momogumi room has four child-sized tables, each with eight chairs that are covered with gaily embroidered seat covers the children have brought from home.

The *Momogumi-san-tachi* (Peach Class children) come in and stand behind their chairs while their teacher, Fukui-sensei, a twenty-three-year-old university graduate, plays the morning song on a small organ and the two *toban* (daily monitors) lead the class in singing:

Sensei, Ohayō (Teacher, good morning)
Minna-san, Ohayō (Everyone, good morning)
Genki ni asobimashō (Let's play happily)
Ohayō, Ohayō (Good morning, good morning)

After attendance is taken by roll call, a counting song is sung to the tune of "Ten Little Indians" to determine how many children are in school that day. Fukui-sensei then leads the children in recitation, each of her words echoed by the children's choral response:

Today . . . *today* . . . is May . . . *is May* . . . twenty-sixth . . . *twenty-sixth* . . .

today . . . *today* . . . twenty-eight children . . . *twenty-eight children* . . .

have come to school . . . *have come to school* . . .

today . . . *today* . . . is a fine spring day . . . *is a fine spring day.*

These housekeeping chores and morning ceremonies completed, the children begin a workbook project which lasts about thirty minutes. Under Fukui-sensei's direction, they color in boxes indicating how many pigs are riding bicycles in a picture, how many foxes are riding motorcycles, and how many rabbits are riding in cars.

Throughout this workbook session there is much laughing, talking, and even a bit of playful fighting among tablemates. As the workbook pages are completed, the children grow increasingly restive; some leave their seats to talk and joke with friends or visit the bathroom. Fukui-sensei makes no attempt to stop them, but forges ahead with the task at hand, "How many rabbits are there? Color in one of these boxes for each rabbit you see in the car."

Workbooks completed, Fukui-sensei puts a sticker on each child's finished pages as the books are brought to her. After they turn in their workbooks, the children begin to play loud chasing games, *janken* (paper-rock-scissors), and to engage in mock karate and sword fights. After twenty minutes or so of this free and raucous play and trips to the bathroom, the children, heeding their teacher, grab their *bentō* (box lunch) from their cubbies and take their place at the table, arranging their lunch and cups and placemats in front of them. The food from home is supplemented by one warm course provided by the school and by a small bottle of milk. All the children sing in unison, under the direction of the daily toban and to the accompaniment of the organ:

> *Obentō o tabete iru toki* (As I sit here with my lunch)
> *Okāsan no koto kangaeru* (I think of mom)
> *Oishii na* (I bet it's delicious)
> *Nan daro ka* (I wonder what she's made?)

After the song the children stand, bow their heads, put their hands together, and recite:

> *Hotokesama* (Buddha)
> *Arigatō* (Thank you)
> *Otōsama* (Honorable Father)
> *Okāsama* (Honorable Mother)
> *Arigatō Gozaimashita* (We humbly thank you)

Lunch itself is loud and lively, each child eating at his or her own pace, which varies from less than ten minutes for some to forty-five minutes or more for others. Fukui-sensei sits with the children at one of the four tables each day (the children keep careful track of whose turn it is), talking quietly to the children near her and occasionally using her chopsticks to help a child snare a hard-to-pick-up morsel from his bentō.

When children finish eating they wrap up their chopsticks, placemats, and lunch boxes. Some girls ask Fukui-sensei for help in properly tieing up their lunch things in the large cloth *furoshiki* they have brought from home.

By this time children who have finished with their lunch have gathered on the narrow covered porch adjoining their classroom. Four girls stand in a cluster, talking and laughing. Several boys are singing songs from television cartoon shows, engaging in more mock-fighting, and playing a game with flash cards meant to teach the hiragana syllabary. One especially energetic boy, Hiroki, who has been much the noisiest and most unruly child in the class throughout the day (though it must be said that no one has tried very hard to control or quiet him), becomes increasingly raucous in his play, his mock karate blows becoming by the moment more like actual punches. While Fukui-sensei is quietly exhorting children still in the classroom to finish their lunches and clear and wipe off the tables, Hiroki has been throwing flash cards off the porch balcony. Midori runs inside to tell the teacher of Hiroki's misconduct and is encouraged by Fukui-sensei with a "go get 'em" sort of pat on the back to return to the balcony and deal with the problem herself. After sweeping up rice and other detritus from underneath the tables in the classroom, Fukui-sensei comes out to the porch, announcing to the children that it is clean-up time. Catching sight of Hiroki pounding on the back of another boy, Fukui-sensei chooses to ignore the ruckus and returns to the classroom to help stragglers wrap up their lunches. Out on the porch Hiroki and the other children continue to throw cards, sing, and fight. When Fukui-sensei returns to the balcony ten minutes later to urge the children to finish cleaning up the flash cards they've been playing with, she again finds Hiroki involved in a fight and again does little to break it up.

Eventually the fighting ceases, the cards are cleaned up (with Fukui-sensei's help), and the children settle in at their desks, where they sing the after-lunch song ("Thank you. It was delicious . . .") and then rest with their heads on the table for five minutes or so while Fukui-sensei plays a soothing tune on the organ.

Rest time over, a major origami project begins, the children led by their teacher through a twenty-step process resulting in the production by each child of an inflatable ball. ("Can you make a triangle? Good, now take these two ends of the triangle and make a smaller triangle, as I'm doing. . . .") The project takes about thirty minutes, with another ten minutes spent by Fukui-sensei on repairs to improperly folded balls that refuse to inflate. Soon the children, paper balls in hand, run laughing and screaming from the classroom to the playground for an extended period of outdoor play.

Back inside later in the afternoon, Fukui-sensei reads a story to the class, using not a book but a *kami shibai* (literally, a paper show), a series of a dozen or so large cards, each with a picture on one side and the narrative to be read by the teacher on the back. A song and a snack round out the schedule. After singing the good-bye song ("Teacher, good-bye, everyone, good-bye . . ."), the children go outside to the playground once more to play until their parents come for them between 4:30 and 6:00 P.M.

Interpreting Komatsudani: Insiders' Perspectives

In these first pages we have provided a description of a day at Komatsudani as recorded in our videotape. Now we turn to Komatsudani's teachers' and administrators' explanations of our videotape, focusing on the issues of structure versus chaos, class size and student/teacher ratios, sex role differentiation, and definitions of the good child.

Dealing with a Difficult Child

On the day we videotaped at Komatsudani, Hiroki started things off with a flourish by pulling his penis out from under the leg of his shorts and waving it at the class during the morning welcome song. During the workbook session that followed, Hiroki called out answers to every question the teacher asked and to many she did not ask. When not volunteering answers, Hiroki gave a loud running commentary on his workbook progress ("now I'm coloring the badger, now the pig . . .") as he worked rapidly and deftly on his assignment. He alternated his play-by-play announcing with occasional songs, entertaining the class with loud, accurate renditions of their favorite cartoon themes, complete with accompanying dancing, gestures, and occasional instrumental flourishes. Despite the demands of his singing and announcing schedule, Hiroki managed to complete his workbook pages before most of the other children (of course, those sitting near him might have finished their work faster had they a less distracting tablemate).

Work completed, Hiroki threw his energies wholeheartedly into his comedy routine, holding various colored crayons up to the front of his shorts and announcing that he had a blue, then a green, and finally a black penis. We should perhaps mention at this point that penis and butt jokes were immensely popular with four-year-old children in nearly every school we visited in all three countries. The only noticeable difference was that such humor was most openly exhibited in Japan, where the teachers generally said nothing and sometimes even smiled, whereas American teachers tended to say something like "We'd rather not hear that kind of talk during group time," and in China such joking appeared to have been driven largely underground, out of adult view.

As the children lined up to have Fukui-sensei check their completed work, Hiroki fired a barrage of pokes, pushes, and little punches at the back of the boy in front of him, who took it all rather well. In general, as Hiroki punched and wrestled his way through the day with various of his male classmates, they reacted by seeming to enjoy his attentions, by becoming irritated but not actually angry, or, most commonly, by shrugging them off with a "That's Hiroki for you" sort of expression. The reaction of Satoshi, who cried when Hiroki hit him and stepped on his hand, was the exception to this rule.

During the singing of the prelunch song, Hiroki, who was one of the four daily lunch monitors, abandoned his post in front of the organ to

Lunch monitors lead singing (Hiroki at right)

Hiroki runs off to wrestle

Hiroki steps on Satoshi's hand

Midori comforts Satoshi

wrestle with a boy seated nearby. While eating, Hiroki regaled his class-mates with more songs and jokes. Finishing his lunch as quickly as he had his workbook, Hiroki joined other fast diners on the balcony, where he roughhoused with some other boys and then disrupted a game by throw-ing flash cards over the railing to the ground below. The other children seemed more amused than annoyed by these antics, although one girl, Midori, ran inside to tattle to the teacher, who was by now sweeping up under the tables. Fukui-sensei sent Midori back to the balcony with some instructions. A few minutes later Fukui-sensei walked out to the balcony, looked over the railing, and said, "So that's where the cards are going." Soon several of the children, with the conspicuous exception of Hiroki, ran down the steps to retrieve the fallen cards. This proved to be a losing battle as Hiroki continued to rain cards down upon them. It was now that Hiroki (purposely) stepped on Satoshi's hand, which made him cry. Sato-shi was quickly ushered away from the scene by Midori, the girl who had earlier reported the card throwing. Midori, arm around Satoshi's neck, lis-tened very empathetically to his tale of woe and then repeated it several times with gestures to other girls who came by: "Hiroki threw cards over the balcony and then he stepped on Satoshi's hand, and then he punched Satoshi like this." The girls then patted Satoshi on the back, suggesting that in the future he find someone other than Hiroki to play with.

Lunch over and the room cleaned up, Fukui-sensei returned to the balcony where, faced with the sight of Hiroki and another boy involved in a fight (which consisted mostly of the other boy's being pushed down and climbed on by Hiroki), she said neutrally, "Are you still fighting?" Then she added, a minute later, in the same neutral tone, "Why are you fighting anyway?" and told everyone still on the balcony, "Hurry up and clean up [the flash cards]. Lunchtime is over. Hurry, hurry." Hiroki was by now disrupting the card clean-up by rolling on the cards and putting them in his mouth, but when he tried to enter the classroom Fukui-sensei put her hand firmly on his back and ushered him outside again. Fukui-sensei, who by now was doing the greatest share of the card picking-up, several times blocked Hiroki from leaving the scene of his crime, and she playfully spanked him on the behind when he continued to roll on the cards.

The rest of the day wound down for Hiroki in similar fashion. At one point in the afternoon Komatsudani's assistant principal, Higashino-sensei, came over to Hiroki and talked softly but seriously to him for three or four minutes, presumably about his behavior. During the free playground period that ends the day, Hiroki played gently with a toddler and more roughly with some of the older boys. He was finally picked up shortly before 6:00 by his father, making him one of the last children to go home.

When we showed Fukui-sensei and her supervisors the film we made in her classroom, we were most curious to see if Fukui-sensei would be at all defensive about the way the film depicted her dealing with—and seeming not to deal with—Hiroki's misbehavior. Both Fukui-sensei and her supervisors told us they were very satisfied with the film and felt that it adequately captured what they are about. Indeed, they said, the way Fukui-sensei dealt with Hiroki in the film, including ignoring his most provocatively aggressive and exhibitionistic actions, reflected not negligence but just the opposite, a strategy worked out over the course of countless meetings and much trial and error.

Japanese preschool teachers and, to a lesser extent, preschool administrators generally are pragmatists rather than ideologues, and thus their discipline and classroom-management techniques tend to be eclectic, focusing on what works. And for most Japanese teachers, for most situations, what seems to work best is a nonconfrontational, energetic, friendly, yet affectively neutral approach. After viewing the tape, we discussed their strategy:

> Higashino: Dealing with Hiroki is really a problem. We've had him here two years now, since he was less than three. You should have seen him before if you think he's something now. We've tried just about everything we could think of to deal with Hiroki. But we've found that especially for a boy like Hiroki the techniques you saw Fukui-sensei using in the film work best. Hiroki has one more year here in our school, so we have one more year to help him straighten himself out, to get over his problem, before he begins primary school.

> Tobin: Do you ever punish Hiroki?

> Higashino: What do you mean? Like tie him up or hit him or something?

> Tobin: Well, no. I was thinking of time-outs—for instance, making him sit alone on a chair in a corner for a while.

> Higashino: We've tried that sort of approach a bit and some other approaches as well, but with Hiroki, he misbehaves so often we must overlook the little things or we'd be yelling at him and making him sit in the corner all day. He's got pride. He gets easily offended; his pride gets hurt a lot when we punish him. He gets [physically] punished at home.

Komatsudani's teachers are careful not to isolate a disruptive child from the group by singling him out for punishment or censure or excluding him from a group activity. Similarly, whenever possible, they avoid direct confrontations with children. As Higashino-sensei told us, "The moment a teacher raises her voice or begins to argue or plead with a child, the battle is already lost." Catherine Lewis (1984) suggests that Japanese teachers think their most powerful source of influence over children is their being viewed unambivalently as benevolent figures; teachers are therefore careful to avoid interacting with children in unpleasant, stressful, emotionally complex ways. (Of course this is an ideal: teachers in Japan, as in other countries, occasionally lose their tempers and say and do things they later regret.) Lewis also suggests that teachers maintain order without intervening directly in children's disputes and misbehavior by encouraging in various ways other children to deal with their classmates' troubles and misdeeds.

Fukui-sensei's approach to dealing with Hiroki illustrates each of these Japanese strategies of discipline and classroom management. She scrupulously avoided confronting or censuring Hiroki even when he was most provocative. (Indeed, she remained composed even during those moments when it was all we could do not to drop our camera and our posture of scholarly neutrality and tell Hiroki to cut it out.)

Fukui-sensei encouraged the other children in the class to take responsibility for helping Hiroki correct his behavior—for instance, when she told Midori to go do something herself about Hiroki's throwing cards. And Fukui-sensei diligently avoided excluding Hiroki from the group in any way. In fact, she insisted he participate in the balcony clean-up to the bitter end, though his presence clearly made the others' task much more difficult.

Another strategy Fukui-sensei employed to remain a benevolent figure to Hiroki was to allow Higashino-sensei to play the role of heavy and give Hiroki a stern talking to (by Japanese preschool standards). This is a strategy we observed in many Japanese preschools; for example, the teacher would tell the children that if they did not clean up, the principal would be cross. Principals, who are often men in this world of women and children, generally appear to be willing and well suited to play this role. They periodically give assembled groups of children lectures on comportment, on the need to work and play hard, to wake up early during vacation just as they do during the school year, to eat well and get plenty of exercise, and to be respectful of their elders and mindful of the feelings of others.

Intelligence and Behavior

Why does Hiroki misbehave? Dana Davidson, who has a background working in assessment and in gifted and talented programs, speculated

that Hiroki's behavior problems might be related to his being intellectually gifted and easily bored. When we returned to Komatsudani to talk
with the staff about our tape, Davidson suggested to Fukui-sensei and
Higashino-sensei that Hiroki might be quicker and smarter than the other
children and that this "giftedness" (which proved to be a very difficult
concept for us to express in Japanese) might provide at least a partial explanation for Hiroki's behavior in the classroom. Fukui and Higashino looked
a bit confused and even taken aback by this suggestion:

> Higashino: Hiroki's intelligence is about average, about the same as
> most other children, I would say.

> Davidson: But he finishes his work so quickly. And he looks like he
> knows the words to so many songs. He just seems so bright, gifted.

> Higashino: What do you mean by "gifted"?

> Davidson: Well, by "gifted" in the United States we mean someone
> who is exceptionally talented in some area, like intelligence. Like
> Hiroki who seems to be so smart, so quick. He has such a bright
> look in his eyes. We would say that a boy like this has a lot of energy
> and is so bright that he is quickly bored by school. To me, it seems
> that his incidents of misbehavior occur when he has finished his work
> before the other children. He provokes his teacher and the other
> children in an attempt to make things more exciting, better matched
> to the pace and level of stimulation he needs.

> Higashino: It seems to me that Hiroki doesn't necessarily finish his
> work first because he is smarter than the other children. Speed isn't
> the same thing as intelligence. And his entertaining the other chil-
> dren by singing all those songs is a reflection not so much of intelli-
> gence as it is of his great need for attention.

The different perspectives that are apparent in this discussion suggest important cultural differences between Americans and Japanese, not only
in definitions of and attitudes toward intelligence, but also in views of
character, behavior, and inborn dispositions and abilities.

One possible explanation for Higashino's insistence that Hiroki is of
only average intelligence might lie in the great value Japanese teachers
and contemporary Japanese society place on equality and on the notion
that children's success and failure and their potential to become successful versus failed adults has more to do with effort and character and thus
with what can be learned and taught in school than with raw inborn
ability. Thus, even if we were to assume, for the moment, that Hiroki is
in fact of exceptional intelligence, his Japanese teachers would be hesitant

to acknowledge this special gift because of their reluctance to explain or excuse behavior in terms of differences in abilities. We suspect that many Japanese preschool teachers and administrators we talked with found our questions about giftedness hard to understand in part because of their distaste for the notion of inborn abilities and their suspicion that the identification of children as having unequal abilities would inevitably lead to an unequal allocation of educational effort, resources, and opportunity.

The Japanese do, of course, recognize that children are born with unequal abilities and that some children have special gifts, but Japanese society in general and teachers in particular view the role of education and perhaps especially of primary and preschool education as to even out rather than sort out or further accentuate these ability differences. Thus one Japanese preschool teacher responded to our description of programs for gifted children in American preschools by saying, "How sad that by age three or four a child might already be labeled as having less chance for success than some of his classmates."

In his book *Education and Equality in Japan* (1980) William Cummings argues that in Japanese society teachers tend to be the most insistent advocates of equal opportunity and the most strident and consistent supporters of social and educational egalitarianism. It is true that preschool teachers, who by and large are not unionized and are younger and less career-oriented than the primary school teachers Cummings discusses, are far less likely than they are to be socialists and to be part of political struggles. And yet this belief in egalitarianism goes beyond political ideology. Our hunch is that Japanese preschool teachers no less than their public school colleagues have a strong intuitive commitment to equality of educational opportunity and to what they believe to be the inequality and even the potential tyranny of an emphasis on inborn individual differences in ability. Working with younger children, they are perhaps especially sensitive to what they see as the injustice of providing children with an unequal educational beginning.*

Since Japanese pedagogy, from primary school on, stresses the need for children to be able to work productively and harmoniously in large mixed-ability classrooms and in smaller mixed-ability work groups (*han;* see M. White, 1987, pp. 114–115), preschool teachers see as one of their chief tasks encouraging children to see themselves as like others in fundamental ways. This includes an effort by teachers to speed up and encourage slower learners and at times to slow down more talented members of the

*We should mention that since Cummings's research, like much of ours, was done in Kyoto, which tends to be more leftist than other parts of Japan, the findings of both of us tend to emphasize egalitarianism in Japanese education and to downplay competition.

class. Teachers do not view as a disservice this holding back and slowing down of the more capable students because they believe that students benefit in the long run by developing an increased sensitivity to the needs of others and a sense of security that comes from being a member of a seemingly homogeneous group.

When Japanese preschool teachers do talk about inborn differences in ability, it is usually in the context of praising a child of less than average ability for struggling to keep up with his classmates. For instance, on school sports days it is not unusual to hear a teacher say: "Look at him go! His legs are shorter than everyone else's, but he sure is trying hard." When Fukui-sensei watched the section of our film that shows Kuniko, a pudgy, slowish sort of girl, struggling to make an origami ball with her fat, uncooperative fingers, the teacher said, "Things never come easily to Kuniko, but she really gives it her best."

The Japanese, in contrast to Americans, seldom view intelligence in a young child as a value-free trait that can be used to good or bad result (LeVine and White, 1986). Rather, Japanese tend to view intelligence as closely linked to moral action and to associate the terms *orikō* (smart) and *atama ga ii* (intelligent), when applied to young children, with traits such as *kashikoi* (obedient, well behaved), *erai* (praiseworthy), *ki ga tsuku* (sensitive to others), and *wakareru* (understanding). Intelligence or smartness in a child in America is just as likely to be associated with asocial (naughty) as with desirable behaviors, as can be seen in such expressions as "smart-alec," "too smart for her own good," and "don't get smart with me, young man." But in Japan misbehavior is more likely to be associated with being not smart enough (lacking understanding). Lewis gives the example of the teacher who explains her young charges' misbehavior on an outing (throwing rocks at carp) by saying, "If they *understood* it was wrong, they wouldn't do it" (1984, p. 77).

One often hears Japanese preschool teachers and Japanese adults in general use the word *smart* to compliment preschool-aged children for a variety of socially approved actions, including behaviors Americans might consider indicative of intelligence but also behaviors that to Americans have little or nothing to do with intelligence, such as helping to clean up. In these situations the words *smart* and *intelligent* are used more or less synonymously with the words *well behaved* and *praiseworthy*.

These linguistic and cultural factors make it difficult for Hiroki's teachers to think of him as especially intelligent. Their reasoning would go, "If he is so smart, why doesn't he understand better? If he understood better, he would behave better."

Misbehavior as a Dependency Disorder

Many of the Chinese and American parents, teachers, and administrators who watched "A Day at Komatsudani" were bothered by Hiroki's misbehavior and Fukui-sensei's failure, in their minds, to respond adequately to his provocations. Our respondents offered various explanations of Hiroki's problem. Many of the Chinese respondents called him spoiled. For example, one teacher asked: "Why are the teachers so easy on a boy who is so spoiled, a boy so used to having his own way and monopolizing so much of his class's energy and attention?" Higashino-sensei responded:

> I suppose you could say in a sense that Hiroki is spoiled, but we believe that his problem is really just the opposite. To me spoiling implies getting too much care and attention, and Hiroki's problem is that he hasn't really received enough of the right kind of care and attention and doesn't know how to receive care and attention. Hiroki, you know, is a boy without a mother. He has been cared for since his birth by his father, who had him while still really just a boy himself, and by his father's mother. Without a mother things have of course been hard for Hiroki. He wants attention and to be cared for [*amae*], but he asks for it in the wrong way. We would only make this problem worse by yelling at him.

Higashino-sensei's description of Hiroki's problem as an inability to know how appropriately to solicit, receive, and respond to care and attention is consistent with Doi Takeo's work on *amaeru* (a Japanese word meaning to presume on the benevolence of others, to be dependent) and specifically with Doi's discussion of common disorders of amae: "*Tereru* describes the behavior of a child or an adult who is ashamed of showing his intimate wish to *amaeru*. . . . *Hinekureru* describes the behavior of a child or an adult who takes devious ways in his efforts to deny the wish to *amaeru*" (1974, p. 148). It is believed in Japan, as Doi explains, that amae, dependence, is not something an infant is born with, but something that must be learned and developed, and thus something that must be taught. Following this logic we can see that a child like Hiroki, who is diagnosed as being awkward in the ways of amae, must be given help to overcome this problem.

From a Japanese perspective Hiroki's problems have both an emotional and a cognitive component, as he suffers from an inability to amaeru (to be dependent) and an inability to wakareru (to understand; White and LeVine, 1986). But this inability to understand and thus to know how to be more obedient and more sensitive to others is attributed by his teachers to his lack of a mother and thus to his emotional problem, his inability to be dependent.

Some Japanese (including Doi) would reason that even if Higashino is wrong and Hiroki's outbursts do not stem from a disorder of amae, nothing would be lost and much might be gained by approaching Hiroki as if frustrated, misguided dependency urges were the core of his problem. Fukui-sensei and the other teachers at Komatsudani often diffuse children's anger and overcome their stubbornness by assuming that behavior problems such as these are at heart problems of amae and responding with concern and sympathy rather than anger or criticism.

Lois Peak (1987), focusing more on the coercive than the nurturant dimensions of preschool teachers' management of difficult children, suggests that at times teachers purposely use their affectively neutral nonresponse to frustrate a misbehaving or crying child, forcing him into more extreme misbehavior or more desperate crying before he finally breaks down in rage and frustration. At this point the teacher, having forced the child into an undisguised demonstration of dependency, comforts him and helps him regain his composure.

Developing Self-Control

The staff of Komatsudani believes that children best learn to control their behavior when the impetus to change comes spontaneously through interactions with their peers rather than from above (Lewis, 1984). Thus Hiroki's best chance to learn self-control lies not in encounters with his teachers but in play with his classmates.

> Fukui: I told Midori and the other children that if they felt it was a problem, then they should deal with Hiroki's throwing the cards. If I tell Hiroki to stop, it doesn't mean much to him, but if his classmates tell him, it affects him.
>
> Tobin: But he kept throwing the cards even after Midori told him to stop.
>
> Fukui: Because he's so proud. He won't ever change his behavior if someone orders him to. He'll always do the opposite in the short run. But in the long run, his classmates' disapproval has a great effect on him.

We saw an example of the effect of social opprobrium on Hiroki when we visited Komatsudani nine months after making the original videotape. On this day we were surprised to find Hiroki, now five years old, sitting

Hiroki in a quiet moment

alone at the front of the classroom, eating his lunch, while the other children ate at tables of six and seven.

Tobin (to a group of children eating lunch): Why is Hiroki eating alone up there?

Several children: [We] don't know.

Tobin (to Hiroki): Why are you eating up here in front of the room alone?

Hiroki: Because I'm the leader of the class!

Tobin (to some other children): Is that why? Is Hiroki the leader of the class?

Yasuko (laughing): He thinks he's the leader, anyway.

Kenichi (on his knees, bowing toward Hiroki): O Honorable Leader.

Tobin (quietly, to Fukui): Is Hiroki really up there because he's the leader? Did you put him up there?

Fukui: No, no one told him to sit there. It just kind of evolved. I guess the other children gradually got tired of sitting next to him during lunch because he is so irritating. Everyone eventually decided they didn't like sitting next to him, and he's very proud, so he came up with this idea on his own of eating in the front of the room as the leader. It seems to be working out, so I'm letting him sit there.

We asked Fukui, Higashino, and Yoshizawa, Komatsudani's director, if it was not a problem for the other children that Hiroki causes so much chaos in the classroom and uses up a disproportionate amount of staff time and energy.

Yoshizawa: No, I'd say it's just the opposite. The children in that class are lucky to have Hiroki there. [Laughing] He makes things interesting.

Higashino: It's hard on Fukui-sensei, but I wouldn't say it's hard on the other children. By having to learn how to deal with a child like Hiroki, they learn to be more complete human beings.

When we returned to Komatsudani and showed the children in the peach class a twenty-minute version of the tape we made in their class, Hiroki at first was proud and excited, dancing in front of the monitor, making peace signs and pointing to himself on the screen. But halfway through the screening, as Hiroki could be seen on the monitor stepping on Satoshi's hand, and as the children in the class shouted out, "Look at what Hiroki is doing to Satoshi!" Hiroki grew agitated, then visibly embarrassed, and he covered first his ears, then his eyes, with his hands. Hiroki stood for a moment in front of the monitor and tried to distract his classmates with a silly song, but children shouted at him to get out of the way so they could see. Hiroki then pulled Kazumi to his feet, and led him off to play outside while the video continued inside.

Childlike Children

The answer given most frequently at Komatsudani to our question, "What kind of child are you trying to produce in your preschool?" was a "*kodomo-rashii kodomo*" (a childlike child). What, then, is a childlike child? Irene Shigaki (1983) polled Japanese teachers on this question and found the traits most highly valued by preschool teachers to be *omoiyari* (empathy),

Hiroki watches himself on videotape

yasashii (gentleness), *shakaisei* (social consciousness), *shinsetsu* (kindness), and *kyōchōsei* (cooperativeness). White and LeVine (1986) add to this list of traits *sunao* (obedience), *akarui* (enthusiasm), *genki/hakihaki* (energy, liveliness) *gambaru/nintai* (perseverance), and *yutaka* (openness, receptivity).*

Our interviews with Japanese preschool teachers generally corroborated Shigaki's and White and LeVine's descriptions of the Japanese concept of the ideal preschooler. We should point out, however, that in addition to these highly valued, traditionally Japanese traits, teachers and administrators also voiced appreciation for some values associated with the West, such as *dokoritsu* (independence), *kosei* (individuality), and *sōzō* (creativity).

Of the people we interviewed, we found preschool administrators who are Christian, Western-trained, or advocates of a particular philosophy

*For further discussion of sunao and other characteristics of the ideal Japanese child and for descriptions of Japanese parenting styles intended to maximize these traits, see M. White's *The Japanese Educational Challenge* (1987) and Hendry's *Becoming Japanese* (1987).

of preschool education (Montessori, Waldorf, and so on) most likely to emphasize the importance of these individualistic Western values and to criticize traditional Japanese values as old-fashioned, incompatible with creativity, and conducive to a revival of militarism or fascism. In contrast, conservative or traditional preschool administrators we talked with often disparaged creativity, self-actualization, and individuality as false values transplanted from the West that threaten to undermine Japanese character and culture. Most administrators, however, attempt to steer a path between traditionalism and Westernism and to stress the need to offer a curriculum and a teaching style that balance the values of group harmony, interpersonal sensitivity, and obedience with creativity, independence, and self-confidence. And nearly all preschool teachers, who tend to be more pragmatic and less concerned with issues of pedagogy and ideology than their bosses, espouse a balanced approach mixing traditionally Japanese and Western values.

Japanese preschools thus strive to produce children who are obedient, energetic, persevering, gentle, and group-oriented with a dash of self-confidence and individuality. But on this list of clearly attractive traits we must also find a way to include behaviors such as the fights we observed so often in Japanese classrooms among boys like Hiroki and his friends. Our informants were careful to explain to us that fighting, especially among boys, is inevitable and even (within bounds) desirable, as it represents a display of age-appropriate behavior that is part of the human condition and thus part of the developmental curriculum of the childlike child.

Yoshizawa-sensei views misbehaving, including fighting, as a lost art for today's sheltered, nuclear-family-raised children:

> I worry more about some of the other children who never misbehave than I worry about Hiroki. He'll be okay. It's easier to teach a mischievous child to behave than to teach a too-good child to be naughty. In the old days children had more chance to play freely, without adults always peering over their shoulders. These days, children don't know how to play, to play like children, which includes being mischievous, right?

When we asked Fukui-sensei why she had not made more of an attempt to break up Hiroki's fights with the other boys the day we filmed, she responded:

> Of course there are times I do intervene, depending in part on whom Hiroki is fighting and under what circumstances, but in general I let them fight because it is natural for boys of that age to fight and it's good for them to have the experience while they are young of what it feels like to be in a fight.

Yoshizawa-sensei, who had experience teaching in a junior high school in Kyoto before taking over the directorship of the preschool, went so far as to link a lack of fighting in preschool to junior high school violence:

> If there were no fights among four-year-old children, that would be a real problem. We don't encourage children to fight, but children need to fight when they are young if they are to develop into complete human beings. As you may know, in Japan we now have a growing problem of violence in our junior high schools. Not just fair fights between two boys, but I'm talking about real violence, gangs beating up one boy, attacks on teachers with baseball bats, even cases of rape and murder. I have a theory about this. Ten or fifteen years ago, when the junior high students of today were in preschool, the prevailing trend in preschool education and in child rearing became too sweet. No, that's not quite the right word. The children were pampered in the wrong way; their school world became too safe, too calm. These children were never given the chance to fight. When children are preschool age they naturally fight if given the chance, and it is by fighting and experiencing what it feels like to hit someone and hurt them and to be hit and be hurt that they learn to control this urge to fight, that they learn the dangers of fighting and get it out of their system. These junior high school kids of today are big and strong like adults, but they never experienced fighting when they were young, so now they fight when they are too big, too strong, and violence results.

Many Japanese would not completely endorse Yoshizawa's theory of junior high violence (everyone in Japan these days seems to have his or her own theory on this topic), but most Japanese teachers and administrators we talked with agreed that fighting is natural and has a place in the informal preschool curriculum. For example, Assistant Principal Kumagai of Senzan Yōchien told us, "as the year progresses we put fewer and fewer toys out during free-play time to give children additional opportunities to learn to share and to deal with the conflicts which arise." To Japanese educators of young children, a child like Hiroki, who provokes fights, serves the function of giving other children a chance to experience a range of emotions and to rehearse a variety of strategies both for resolving their own disagreements as well as for mediating conflicts among others.

Gender

When Komatsudani's staff say that they allow children to fight and encourage other children in the class to intervene, what they leave unsaid is that the children they let fight are almost always boys and those they encourage to intervene are almost always girls. Although we observed girls in Japanese preschools involved in arguments and in wild physical play, we saw no actual physical fights involving girls, and we were told by Fukui-sensei and Higashino-sensei that girls rarely fight. When they do, their fighting is not viewed as positively as it is in boys. If fighting is part of the unofficial preschool curriculum intended to teach boys how to become men, how are girls in Japanese preschools taught to become women?

At Komatsudani we rarely observed teachers directly admonishing boys and girls in their classes to behave in sexually differentiated ways. In our discussions, teachers seemed hesitant to admit to treating boys and girls differently or unequally. For example, Fukui-sensei responded to our questions on this topic by saying, "Boys and girls at this age are still more or less the same, so we try to treat them the same way." Higashino-sensei told us, "Boys and girls are all children, so we treat them all the same—as children." We believe these sexually egalitarian sentiments reflect to a small extent a recent surge in feminist thought among young, educated, working women (such as preschool teachers) and to a much larger extent, the more generally egalitarian, anti-innate-difference values we have already described as fundamental tenets of Japanese preschool education.

If the teachers believe that boys and girls are more or less the same and should be treated alike, why do we observe such dramatic differences in the behavior of boys and girls in Japanese preschools? The answer, of course, must be complex, but we believe it lies in part in the considerable sex-role socialization that takes place in Japan (and, of course, not only in Japan) before the child reaches preschool age and in part in the myriad ways in which Japanese adults, including preschool teachers and administrators, give boys and girls unconscious and sometimes unintended cues and expectations to behave differently.

Japanese preschool girls appear ready and willing to assist their teachers to mediate disputes and to minister to the needs of younger children. If boys in Japanese preschools are warriors, girls are peacemakers, healers, and counselors. Although staff members rarely use the manifestly gender-specific words *otoko-rashii* (masculine) and *onna-rashii* (feminine) to praise children, they often encourage boys to be *takumashii* (brave, strong) and girls to be *yashashii* (gentle, nice). Children in general and girls in particular are praised by teachers for their displays of *omoiyari* (empathy).

In Komatsudani we frequently witnessed four- and five-year-old girls (and, less often, boys), helping the one- and two-year-old children take off or put on their shoes and outdoor clothing and get up and down stairs. Higashino-sensei explained that the older children often "adopt" one of the babies or toddlers as their special charge and visit the nursery several

Older children play with toddlers

times a day to play with or help change or feed the infant. When we commented that such attention must be great for these nursery-reared infants, Higashino-sensei replied:

> Not just for the infant. We believe it is good for the infants, of course, but we also believe it is just as important for the older children because it gives them a chance to experience what it feels like to take care of another person. These days most of our children do not have younger siblings, and we feel this contact with babies and toddlers gives them a chance they might not otherwise have to develop empathy [*omoiyari*] and to learn to know and anticipate the needs of another [*ki ga tsuku*].

Komatsudani was unusual among the preschools we visited in Japan in the amount of contact allowed and encouraged between older and younger children, but in all the *hoikuen* (day-care centers) and *yōchien* (nursery schools) we visited, teachers and administrators stressed the importance of helping children develop compassion and empathy. In each of these schools we saw children helping and being praised by their teachers for their help. Older children learning to care for the dependency needs of younger children and girls learning to understand and deal with what is believed in Japan to be the naturally somewhat impulsive, brutish, and immature behavior of boys (and men) are, along with fighting, important features of the informal Japanese preschool curriculum.

Class Size and Student/Teacher Ratios

Many of the Chinese and most of the American preschool teachers, administrators, and parents who viewed "A Day at Komatsudani" were horrified by the size of the class and the 30/1 student/teacher ratio. A teacher in Honolulu said: "No wonder there is so much wildness and fighting. It's a wonder there's not more with that many kids in a class." A day-care administrator wrote on her response form, "The worst thing [about Komatsudani] by far is the ratios. 30/1! That's way, way, too high." A Chinese teacher commented, "I'm surprised their classes are so big. They are a rich country."

When asked why they have such large classes, Japanese teachers' and administrators' first response tends to be, "Because of money. With our low preschool tuition we cannot afford smaller numbers of students per teacher. We are barely getting by as it is." But why, then, do American and European preschools feel they cannot operate with student/teacher ratios of much more than fifteen four-year-olds to one teacher, while Japanese preschools, even in an era of growing wealth and great concern with education, choose to hold the line on tuition and maintain large student/teacher ratios?

When we asked teachers and administrators at Japanese preschools directly, "Would you like to have smaller classes?" they almost always replied affirmatively. Fukui-sensei, for example, answered without hesitation, "Sure, it would be much easier to teach a smaller class." Watching a tape of an American preschool that has a student/teacher ratio of about eight to one, a teacher at Senzan Yōchien in Kyoto sighed, "It must be great to teach in America. Such small classes!" Another Senzan teacher added that she envied the way the American teacher in the film played with the children in her class so happily, in what she called a "barefoot" (uninhibited) manner. But when we followed up by asking, "So you think it would be better to have a class size of ten or twelve instead of twenty-five or thirty?" Yano-sensei responded: "No, I wouldn't say better. Well, maybe you could say better for the teacher, but not better for the children. Children need to have the experience of being in a large group in order to learn to relate to lots of kinds of children in lots of kinds of situations." Tanaka-sensei, the teacher who had commented favorably about the uninhibited play style of the American teacher, then explained:

> I envy the way the American teachers, with such small classes and such low student/teacher ratios, have time to play so affectionately with each child. That's how I like to play with my nieces and nephews. That's a good way for aunts and uncles and parents to play with their children. But I don't think that's necessarily the best way for a teacher to relate to children. Teaching is different from being a parent or aunt or family friend to a child. Sometimes I feel like playing very warmly in a down-on-the-floor, barefoot sort of way with my students, and sometimes I feel like hugging some of my students or having an intimate chat with one of the little girls. And sometimes I do these things, of course. I'm a human being, as well as a teacher, and I'm not suggesting that teachers should be cold or formal by any means. What I am trying to say is that a teacher should relate to the class as a whole rather than to each student, even if this is a little harder or even a little bit sad for the teacher sometimes.

If money were not a consideration, many Japanese teachers and administrators would certainly prefer a smaller students-per-teacher ratio than is currently the rule in most of their schools. And many Japanese teachers and administrators, influenced either directly or indirectly by Western preschool pedagogy (such as those trained in Montessori centers) or by Western values (Christianity), take positions on class size, teacher/student ratio, and indeed on child rearing and education in general that are virtually indistinguishable from the views of American teachers and administrators. And yet, when asked, "Financial considerations aside, what would you consider an ideal class size and student/teacher ratio for four-year-olds?" few Japanese teachers and administrators say less than fifteen or, at the lowest, twelve to a teacher, whereas many Americans say ideally they would prefer to see no more than eight, or six, or even four students to each teacher.

In the eyes of Japanese preschool teachers and administrators, then, very small classes and low student/teacher ratios produce a classroom atmosphere that emphasizes teacher-student over student-student interactions and fails to provide children with adequate opportunities to learn to function as members of a group. A teacher in Tokyo said of our tape of an American preschool, "A class that size seems kind of sad and underpopulated." Another Tokyo teacher wondered, "In a class that size wouldn't a child's world be too narrow?" Yagi-sensei of Senzan Yōchien in Kyoto commented:

> I understand how this kind of small class size can help young children become very self-reliant and independent. But I can't help feeling that there is something kind of sad or lonely about a class that size. Don't American teachers worry that children may become too independent? I wonder how you teach a child to become a member of a group in a class that small?

We should note that class size and teacher/student ratio, though closely related, are not the same issue. A large preschool class can have a small student/teacher ratio if two or more teachers are assigned to the class. In general, Americans tend to focus on ratio as the more important factor, whereas Japanese teachers tend to stress the importance of class size. As we have noted, Japanese teachers believe in a large ratio of students to teachers to keep teachers from being too readily available to children, for they fear that an overly available and charismatic teacher, whatever her other merits, will tend to discourage children from forming friendships and reacting primarily to one another rather than, as at home, primarily to an adult. But to Japanese teachers and administrators group size is even more important because they believe that a large class better reflects the complexity of the outer world and gives each child a chance of getting to know and to deal with a wide variety of other children in a wide variety of situations. Even in university laboratory preschools, which have a large pool of teachers to draw on, class size is generally kept above thirty with three or more teachers assigned to each class.

Komatsudani's classes, then, are large not because Japanese are good at functioning in large groups; rather, Japanese get to be good at functioning in large groups in part by attending preschools with large classes. The levels of noise and chaos characteristic of Japanese preschools are not unfortunate side effects of large class size; rather, class size is kept large to ensure that the preschool experience will be optimally noisy and chaotic.

Group Life

Virtually all the Japanese preschool teachers who viewed our tape of an American preschool contrasted the individualism (*kojin-shugi*) they perceive as characterizing preschool in America with the groupism (*shuudan-shugi*) they believe characterizes their own society and schools. The more Westernized Japanese teachers and administrators thought the individualized educational style they associated with America a good thing; others thought a group approach better; and some said that a mixture of the two would be ideal. But virtually all agreed that groupism is the key distinguishing factor between Japanese and American preschools and, indeed, between the two societies.

By groupism these Japanese teachers and administrators did not mean, evidently, what they saw on our film of a Chinese preschool. Dong-feng, the Chinese preschool in our study, was rated as very group-oriented by Americans and Chinese—"too much" so by 65 percent of the American and 85 percent of the Chinese parents, teachers, and administrators who viewed "A Day at Dong-feng." Thus we were surprised to find that 60 percent of our Japanese respondents rated Dong-feng as having "too few group activities," especially since it looked to us as though the children in the Chinese school do everything in groups. Principal Kumagai of Senzan Yōchien explained, "Well, of course, I can't say for sure why you got the results you did, but I wonder if perhaps to Japanese viewers the Chinese school didn't lack a real group feeling. Everyone doing the same thing at the same time isn't the same as real group life, is it?"

Several other Japanese informants explained that the real problem they saw in the Chinese preschool film was not groupism but the manner in which group-oriented behaviors are taught to children. They felt that the best alternative to Chinese authoritarianism was not American individualism but a gentler, more joyful, more understanding, flexible, Japanese sort of groupism. Yano-sensei said: "What bothers me isn't so much that the Chinese teachers expect the children in their schools to do things in groups so much as that their group activities seem so joyless and unspontaneous, so lacking in human feeling." The key point here, we believe, lies in the Japanese teacher's assumption that groupism can and should be compatible with human feeling. This runs contrary to the assumption many of our American informants made that groups are necessarily unspontaneous, repressive, and antithetical to human feeling.

To teachers at Komatsudani groupism does not inhibit the expression of natural feelings and joyful behavior. Rather, it makes possible the fullest realization of something truly human, the experience of camaraderie, of fusion, of unity with something larger than the self. A child's humanity is realized most fully not so much in his ability to be independent from the group as in his ability to cooperate with and feel part of the group (M. White, 1987, pp. 184–185). Assistant Principal Kumagai of Senzan Yōchien, commenting on the Chinese preschool tape, said:

> The feeling I get from this tape is that to the Chinese, groupism means subjugating yourself to the group. But to us, in our preschools, we don't tell children they must be in groups, or they must participate in group activities, or that doing things alone is selfish or

bad. Instead, we just try to show them, to teach them the fun and the sense of belonging one can get only by being part of a group.

Most Japanese preschools attempt to steer a course between the loneliness and anomie they associate with individualism in the West and the tyranny and authoritarianism they associate with Chinese and, for some, with traditional Japanese forms of group organization. One teacher commented: "This film of the Chinese preschool reminds me of what Japanese education must have been like in the prewar period, when duty and sacrifice were stressed and teachers were expected to be very severe with children."

How is this supposedly gentler, more humane, more joyful sort of group feeling achieved in the Japanese yōchien and hoikuen? The first and most obvious signs of groupism are the uniforms worn by most yōchien students. Typically, a yōchien child goes to school wearing navy-blue, knee-length overalls or skirt, a white shirt with a round collar, a lightweight navy-blue coat, a felt or straw hat with a ribbon or tassel, and a blue or red knapsack. Each yōchien's uniform is distinctive, differing from the uniforms of neighboring yōchien most dramatically in the shape and color of the hat. Some yōchien uniforms are nautical in flavor. Some use capes instead of jackets, or they are maroon instead of navy blue. Uniforms in Tokyo and in wealthy areas of any city are likely to be fancier, those in rural and poor districts somewhat plainer and more functional (lightweight blue smocks instead of jackets and shorts). But nearly always the yōchien child goes to school dressed in clothes that clearly identify him to the outside world, to his classmates, and to himself as a preschooler and, more important, as a member of a particular preschool, a special group.

Children in hoikuen, where uniforms are usually not worn, wear badges on their shirts bearing their family and given names, their school's name, and the name of their class. Children at many yōchien are picked up by distinctive, brightly painted buses; others walk to school behind teachers carrying school flags. Some schools also issue children a pin or emblem in the shape of the flower or animal that has provided the name for their class. On school sports days children wear special sports uniforms and brightly colored caps, color-coded to identify them by their class. On field trip days hoikuen children wear special white, yellow, or red caps, which, besides making it easier for the teachers to round up runaways and strays, give the children a feeling of shared group membership while in the outside world.

Uniforms and other symbols such as pins, name tags, and signs over shoe lockers, cubbies, and classroom doorways emphasize the child's membership in a school and, within a school, in a class. Upon enrolling in preschool, a Japanese child receives not just a uniform but a group identity.

She becomes instantly *Komatsudani Hoikuen no Midori-gumi no Yoko* (Yoko of the Green Class of Komatsudani Day-care Center) or *Senzan Yōchien no Tampopo-gumi no Chiseko* (Chiseko of the Dandelion Class of Senzan Nursery School). Japanese children are referred to throughout their preschool careers not only by the name of their class but also by their school-year cohort, as, for instance, in such announcements heard at school during the day as "*Nencho-gumi-san-tachi* [Children in the oldest classes], please line up by the swings for morning exercise," or "*Onenshō-san-tachi* [the first-year students] will now entertain you with their version of 'Snow White and the Seven Dwarfs.'"

Competition among classes in a school is often used to encourage group effort and to promote a sense of group identification and pride. During morning clean-up time at Senzan Yōchien, for example, the assistant principal's voice can be heard over the loudspeaker in each room intoning, "Let's see which class can be first to clean up their room today." During school sports days (*undōkai*), vigorous competition between classes of children and even between the mothers or fathers of a class is enthusiastically encouraged by the teachers, principals, and spectators watching the races. In these events the feeling of group solidarity experienced by the losers, who commiserate with each other, "*Zannendakedo, gambarimashita* [It's too bad, but we did our best]" is perhaps even more keenly felt than is the collective sense of group accomplishment of the victors.

Japanese preschools achieve nearly 100-percent participation levels in group activities by making it extremely easy as well as attractive to be included. Indeed, the harder trick in a Japanese preschool would be to figure out a way not to be included in group activities. For example, during the schoolwide daily morning exercise period, though teachers hope that all the children will participate actively, no child is ordered or threatened or even very aggressively cajoled into running, jumping, or stretching with the others. Rather, children are included in the group simply by virtue of being in proximity during an activity. At Komatsudani the three-, four-, and five-year-olds perform their calisthenics in a large circle while the toddlers and infants are assembled in a smaller circlelike constellation in the middle. The nine-month-old babies are bounced about by the teachers to the rhythm of the exercise song, slightly older babies crawl or stumble around on their own with teachers or older children occasionally coming over to manipulate their arms through calisthenic motions, and the two-year-olds, if the spirit moves them and the flesh is willing, attempt to imitate the older children. The few children who choose to use the exercise period as an opportunity to stage a mock-karate battle, to discuss last night's television cartoon show, or just to watch are rarely pressured to do the exercises everyone else is doing. Thus each child in the school is given

Morning exercises at Senzan Yōchien

an opportunity to participate in his or her own fashion. Those who cannot or will not join in the activity are periodically encouraged to join in by teachers and other children, but usually they are allowed to refrain from active participation or, more accurately, to participate in their own way even if that way involves seeming not to participate actively.

By having very liberal, easy-to-satisfy criteria for what constitutes participation in group activities, a Japanese preschool like Komatsudani readily includes children from the youngest to the oldest and from the most easily distracted and badly behaved to the most attuned and energetic in daily group activities.

Classroom activities follow a similar form. During the thirty-minute origami session we taped, most of the children followed Fukui-sensei's step-by-step instructions and made origami balls, but two boys made paper airplanes instead, and one did not make anything at all, choosing to while away the time crumpling up and smoothing out his paper and talking and joking with his friends. The teacher encouraged all the children in the class to participate, and she asked the children who chose not to why they were not joining in, but the tone of voice in which she asked was neutral and inquisitive rather than supplicating or threatening, and she readily accepted their explanations, and even any lack of explanation, for not making origami balls with the other children.

Discipline is handled in much the same manner. Children in Japanese preschool can commit misdeeds of varying severity without being either emotionally or physically excluded from the group. We saw in Japan none of the time-out periods of forced isolation from the group that we so frequently witnessed in American preschools. By being extremely reluctant to label children's behavior as bad or beyond the pale, Japanese preschools reduce the number of situations that could potentially lead to confrontation and thus to a child's feeling ostracized or in any other way excluded from the group. Because group participation is so attractive and ubiquitous, the threat of not being included, when it does arise, is all the more frightening. As group membership becomes more and more the norm of social interaction and the primary source of identity for a Japanese preschool youngster, even the implicit threat of exclusion becomes terrifying, and explicit exclusion (for example, by *ijime*—scapegoating) a potentially dangerous problem.

Thus Fukui-sensei's gentle warning to a group of recalcitrant cleaner-uppers that if they did not finish soon the class would begin the next activity without them proved to be enough to get the children involved in their task. When this approach fails, the teacher may resort to a stronger and more dramatic threat, using a form of child management that has long been a favorite of Japanese mothers: the teacher simply calls, theatrically, over her shoulder to the children still in the sandbox as she begins to lead the children in line back inside, "*Ja, sayōnara* (well, then, good-bye)." This usually does the trick, but if the children in the sandbox are incorrigible offenders, as occasionally happens, other children in the class will run back to the sandbox and plead with their wayward classmates to come along quickly. These good children feel most acutely the misbehaving children's shame, imminent loss of teacher approval, and the risk they are running of isolation from the group, so they implore the stragglers to see the error of their ways and come back to the fold before it's too late. But, of course, it is rarely if ever too late to join or rejoin the group in the world of the Japanese preschool.

Little dramas of this type take place not just daily but many times throughout each day, but it is unusual (though by no means unknown) for the tone of these encounters to become strained or tense or for real confrontation to occur between teacher and student. As Lewis points out, emotional confrontations of any kind between teacher and student are usually avoided, both to allow the teacher to remain a benevolent and accessible

(though perhaps somewhat affectively neutral) figure and, equally important, to allow the child maximum room to stay within the boundaries of
group participation and membership (1984).

Is Komatsudani a Typical Japanese Preschool?

In the course of this study we visited preschools in Tokyo, Kyoto, Osaka,
and Hiroshima. Some of these schools appeared very Western in approach,
particularly some of the Christian and Montessori schools we visited.
Others, in some respects, looked more like Chinese schools. We chose to
focus on Komatsudani because it seemed to us at the outset to be a quintessentially Japanese preschool. We approach this question of its typicality by
reporting discussions we held with teachers, parents, and administrators
of other Japanese preschools following the screening of our tape.

Although we went to Japan expecting to find varied opinions about the
best approach to preschool education, we were surprised by the depth of
disagreement we encountered. In discussing the tape of Komatsudani with
parents, teachers, and administrators of six other Japanese preschools, we
gained awareness of the very deep rifts in ideology, religion, economics,
geography, and social class that characterize the range of Japanese feelings
about preschool education and, indeed, the discontinuity and heteroge-
neity of contemporary Japanese society.

Hoikuen and Yōchien

The Japanese word *yōchien* is most frequently translated into English as
"kindergarten" and *hoikuen* as "nursery," but this is misleading. Yōchien
usually serve three- through six-year-olds; hoikuen accept children from
six months in age to six years. The last year of both the hoikuen and
yōchien curricula are roughly equivalent to the American kindergarten; the
earlier years of yōchien are more like the American nursery school, and the
earlier years of hoikuen are like the American day-care center. Although
there are great variations within both categories of Japanese preschools,
yōchien, serving mostly the children of nonworking mothers, are usually
tonier and better equipped than are hoikuen, which serve the children of
working mothers. Komatsudani, a hoikuen (day-care center), looked to us
much like a yōchien (nursery school) in teaching style, curriculum, and
children's play. But to higher-status yōchien administrators, teachers, and
parents, the un-uniformed children of Komatsudani inevitably looked a
bit scruffy.

Our screenings of the Komatsudani film and the discussions that followed at preschools throughout Japan showed us that there are unspoken yet clear class and status distinctions between yōchien and hoikuen. These distinctions can readily be discerned in the way staff of the two kinds of preschool talk about their schools.

When asked to compare their program to that of a yōchien, hoikuen staff often betray a sense of inferiority in their eagerness to minimize the differences between the two kinds of school. For example, a Tokyo hoikuen administrator said: "I think that these days hoikuen and yōchien are really just about the same. Perhaps once there was more of a difference, but over the years we've gradually grown more and more alike. These days what we do, our curriculum, and what yōchien do—well, there's really not much difference between us, is there?" Conversely, a sense of superiority and even smug condescension is apparent in yōchien teachers' and especially administrators' suggestion that what they do in their preschools cannot be compared to what is done in a hoikuen. When asked to compare her school to Komatsudani, an Osaka yōchien assistant principal said:

> I think one really can't compare the two because they are so basically different in educational approach and goals and history. I've never actually been inside a hoikuen in any official capacity, so I can't really answer definitively, but I would have to say from watching your film and from what I've read and heard that yōchien and hoikuen are really two very different kinds of organizations. I think if you look into the history of the two and into their administration and regulations you'll be able to better understand the nature of these differences I am referring to.

The class and status differences between Japanese yōchien and hoikuen (much like the class and status differences between American nursery schools and day-care centers) are rooted in the clearly distinct and unequal constituencies they were established to serve. The first yōchien, opened in 1876, was Meiji Japan's self-conscious attempt to further the cause of modernization by offering a Western-style educational experience to children of the Japanese gentry (Shoji, 1983). Based on Froebel's theories of kindergarten education, the first yōchien taught children of the upper and middle classes the cognitive skills (including shape recognition, colors, and counting) that they would need to succeed in primary school. In 1899 the approximately two hundred yōchien in Japan were brought under the direction of the Ministry of Education. During the first half of the twentieth century the number of yōchien grew steadily, especially in urban, white-collar areas. Since the war the number has risen dramatically, from approximately two thousand in 1940 to six thousand in 1960 to fourteen thousand in 1976, and the percentage of Japanese preschool-aged children attending yōchien has gone from only 7 percent in 1948 to 44 percent in 1965 and 66 percent in 1977 (Shoji, 1983).

The first hoikuen in Japan opened in 1890 to serve poor children who might otherwise be cared for by older siblings forced to drop out of school to do so. The second hoikuen was opened in a textile company to serve working mothers. The third was established by American missionaries for children in a slum area of Tokyo. In 1919 the first public day nursery was established, in Osaka. Many other municipalities soon followed suit, opening hoikuen to serve poor families and working mothers in their districts. During this century the number of hoikuen has risen steadily; by 1921 there were one hundred hoikuen; in 1935, nine hundred; and in 1939, fifteen hundred. The proportion of Japanese young children attending has gone from fewer than 2 percent of five-year-olds in 1950 to 25 percent in 1977 (Shoji, 1983) and over 30 percent in 1985.

In 1947 the Diet passed legislation formalizing the class and status distinctions that had existed since the beginning. The School Education Law defined yōchien as educational institutions and formally placed them under the control of the Ministry of Education (Mombushō); the Child Welfare Law passed the same year defined hoikuen as welfare facilities and placed them under the control of the Ministry of Health and Welfare (Koseishō).

Mombushō and Koseishō have separate sets of guidelines and standards for preschool education. Each certifies teachers, for example, but certification from one does not carry over to the other, making yōchien and hoikuen teachers noninterchangeable despite very similar training. Japanese universities thus must offer separate programs for training prospective yōchien and hoikuen staff. Mombushō and Koseishō have similarly parallel but distinct regulations covering staff/student ratios (no more than thirty four-year-olds to one teacher in hoikuen, forty to one in yōchien), facilities and equipment, curricula, and health and safety standards.

The tuition and financial structuring of the two are also very different. Yōchien, whether public or private, receive national aid for building and purchasing equipment and a modest yearly subsidy per student from Mombushō. Yōchien generally charge parents a flat-rate tuition, with some limited tuition aid available to poor families. Public and private hoikuen, in contrast, receive large reimbursements per student from Koseishō: approximately 80 percent of hoikuen costs are covered by federal funds, 10 percent by local funds, and 10 percent by tuition payments. Many hoikuen parents pay a sliding-fee tuition based on their taxable income. Poor parents thus pay less on the average to enroll their children in a sliding-fee hoikuen than a fixed-fee yōchien, whereas wealthier parents find a fixed-tuition yōchien on the average less expensive. Middle-income parents usually pay about the same for yōchien and hoikuen—about a third of tuition in the United States.

Because hoikuen accept infants and are open for children of all ages from as early as 7:00 A.M. to as late as 7:00 P.M. six days a week, they are clearly the more convenient choice for working mothers, whereas yōchien attract children of *sarariman* (white-collar) families, in which the mother usually does not work. But the distinctions between yōchien and hoikuen families are not solely economic and work-related. A mother who for various reasons must work in the afternoons but who identifies herself more closely with sarariman than with working-class society will often enroll her child in a relatively less convenient yōchien, asking relatives or friends to help out with child care after school, rather than in a more convenient but lower-status hoikuen. Conversely, nonemployed mothers living in neighborhoods where there are hoikuen but not yōchien have been known to take part-time jobs just to qualify to enroll their children in hoikuen and thereby give them a group experience before primary school (Imamura, 1987). The class distinction separating yōchien and hoikuen is further muddled by the growing presence of children of dual-career, high-status professional parents (such as physicians) in hoikuen. The most basic distinction is that yōchien tend to serve the children of women who define themselves as full-time mothers and sarariman wives, and hoikuen serve the children of women who work and who for economic or ideological reasons are not involved in the sarariman family life-style described by Ezra Vogel in *Japan's New Middle Class* (1971).

Although well over 80 percent of Japanese identify themselves as middle class, there are in fact several middle classes in contemporary Japan (Fuse, 1984). One is that of the *kaisha-in* (company man) who graduates from a good university, moves into a white-collar job with lifetime security, a good yearly salary and biannual bonuses, has a wife who is a full-time mother, and sends his child to yōchien. Other middle-class mothers and fathers go to lower-status universities (or to none at all), work in blue-collar jobs or in white-collar jobs that offer little security, and, needing two full-time salaries to make ends meet, send their child to hoikuen. Yōchien and yōchien children tend to look more upscale than hoikuen and hoikuen children because yōchien are in the business of offering not just education and child care to children but also middle-class status and identity to mothers. The typical yōchien mother selects a preschool for her child that she believes will start him on the road to a kaisha-in life-style of his own. This usually means finding a yōchien where the other children come from "good" (meaning kaisha-in) families and where an enriched educational program is offered.

To attract these upwardly mobile mothers in a time of declining birthrates and diminishing cohorts of three-year-olds in many parts of Japan, yōchien must present parents with a package that includes appealing uniforms for the children (Peter-Pan–collar white shirts and English children's sailor suits with short pants), upscale programs including swimming, piano, and English conversation classes, and lavish special events such as school plays, graduation ceremonies, and sports days, where grandparents can be brought to see how well the child and thus his mother are doing.

Hoikuen in general have less need to compete for students. Since a much higher percentage of their costs are covered by government reimbursement (as opposed to tuition payments), hoikuen are freer of economic pressures to stay at full enrollment. And since hoikuen are usually associated with a local city ward office, most have a clearly defined catchment area of families to serve. Yōchien, in contrast, especially in urban areas, send their buses out farther and farther each year in search of children to fill their classrooms. Although propinquity is certainly a major factor in parents' choice of a yōchien, it is by no means the only or even the most important one.

Hoikuen staff and their overseeing organization, Koseishō, have worked hard to upgrade the hoikuen curriculum and close the gap in quality. But hoikuen such as Komatsudani still face the task of overcoming the class and status prejudices that make them appear to the Japanese public (and perhaps even to themselves) inferior to yōchien.

Hoikuen and yōchien, though traditionally serving very different clientele, find themselves, in an increasingly homogeneous middle-class Japan, competing for a dwindling cohort of young children. In 1987 approximately two-thirds of Japanese preschool-aged children attended yōchien; one-third, hoikuen. Mombushō would like to see preschool education made compulsory (under its direction, of course). But the long run may favor underdog hoikuen such as Komatsudani over the more glamorous, better-connected yōchien. The percentage of the population interested in following the full-time-mother life-style of the sarariman family may have peaked in the 1970s. With an increasing percentage of young Japanese women (including teachers) reluctant to stop working when they marry and have children (Holden, 1983; Carney and O'Reilly, 1983; Smith, 1987), hoikuen seem better positioned than yōchien to secure an increased share of the dwindling preschool market. Others suggest that the kinds of social change that have led women in the United States and China into the full-time work force are not occurring in Japan, that in fact it is the percentage of working mothers rather than of sarariman wives that has peaked, and that Japan's increasing wealth is leading to gentrification of the middle class, which will favor the long-term survival of yōchien over hoikuen.

Many Japanese preschools are working to protect themselves against these demographic difficulties by diversifying, offering, in addition to their traditional preschool services, after-school music lessons and tutoring for children, special academic coaching classes for mothers of elementary school children, and even, in some cases, gerontological services for Japan's rapidly aging population.

The turf battles between Mombushō and Koseishō for control of preschools obscure the very similar and complementary roles they play in the world of Japanese child education and socialization. Mombushō and Koseishō share the function of minimizing variations in the quality of preschools across the country. Yōchien and hoikuen in wealthy neighborhoods of Tokyo are better equipped and offer more diverse activities than the average preschool in rural Hokkaido, but Mombushō's and Koseishō's regulations and national standards for teacher training and certification control quality and limit diversity, making for much less variation on the average in preschools in Japan than one would find, for example, in the United States.

Komatsudani is typical of hoikuen across Japan in the training, career patterns, and salaries of its teachers, tuition levels, teacher/student ratios, facilities and materials, and the balance of curricular activities. And yet, as we will suggest in the next two sections, within the parameters set by the Koseishō system of nationwide regulations and standards, there is still room for variation in program emphasis, mood, and the flavor of teacher-student and student-student interactions.

Ideology

Preschools like Komatsudani, which self-consciously and deliberately reflect and cultivate traditional Japanese values, are praised in some Japanese circles, criticized in others. This difference of opinion in turn is a reflection of highly charged political and ideological public debate over Japanese versus Western values and also of a more subtle ambivalence in the hearts of all Japanese about how best to balance the old and the new, how to be modern while retaining the core of Japanese character and identity.

This battle between forces associated with the East and the West, between Japaneseness (*yamato-damashii, Nihonron*) and internationalism (*kokusaisei*), can be seen clearly in the ongoing war between the Ministry of Education (Mombushō) and the socialist-leaning Japanese Teachers Union (Nikkyōso) over such issues as teacher autonomy, textbook selection, the examination system, and the public school teaching of Japan's role in the Second World War. It can also be seen in Japan's long-standing educational stalemate: although nearly everyone in Japan seems to have something critical to say about how the Japanese educational system from the preschool to the university level stifles creativity, initiative, and individuality, the system nevertheless manages to endure partly because, despite its faults, it serves many interests and needs and partly because people fear what might be put in its place. Proponents of the current educational system and of traditional Japanese values tend to align themselves with conservatism and are accused by their critics of being associated with right-wing politics and with the kind of militarism, imperialism, ethnocentrism, and authoritarian groupism that led Japan into World War II. Supporters of educational reform and internationalism generally align themselves with liberalism and the left, while in the eyes of their critics they are associated with the kind of soft-headed, weak, feminine individualism that Japanese conservatives believe has led Western Europe and more recently the United States into an economic and moral decline.

Thus when we asked Japanese teachers, parents, and administrators what they thought of Komatsudani as depicted in our film, we turned out to be walking into an ideological and pedagogical battle being fought for the souls of today's Japanese children and thus for the shape of the future of Japan. Preschool teachers, who by and large are resolutely non-ideological and pragmatic in approach (their motto seems to be, handle every situation on a case-by-case basis), found Komatsudani unexceptional. Administrators and some parents, however, reacted very strongly to the videotape, either praising or condemning Komatsudani for its Japaneseness. The harshest and most adamant critics were administrators (who also were often founders or children of founders) of Christian and other Western-style preschools.

Missionaries have played an important role in the development of Japanese preschools. Early yōchien as well as hoikuen were established by American missionaries, Christian educators, and Japanese educated in the West (who often became Christian along the way). Although Christians make up only 1 percent of the Japanese populace, approximately 15 percent of Japanese preschools are Christian, and Christian, and more generally Western, values and notions about child development play a very strong role in Japanese preschool pedagogy.

Many Christian administrators and teachers were disturbed by what they felt to be the anti-individual, noncreative, group-dominated ethos of Komatsudani and particularly the laissez faire reaction of the staff to Hiroki's fighting with other children. The principal of a Hiroshima hoikuen commented,

> I would hate to think Americans will see this film and think this is
> what Japanese are like. Certainly there are schools in Japan, maybe

even many schools, maybe even most schools in Japan that are like the school you've shown us here. But there are other, much better Japanese schools you could have chosen that would have given Americans a much more positive image of Japanese education.

A head teacher added:

This school, by ignoring children's individual needs and personalities and emphasizing only doing things in groups, is an example of what's wrong with Japanese education and with Japanese society. This is the kind of approach that leads to fascism and blind following of leaders. There is no place in this kind of school for the soul and for individual self-expression.

A Japanese teacher in a Christian yōchien in Osaka explained why she objected to Komatsudani's approach to fighting:

We handle fighting and discipline in our school much more like the American school in your film than like the Japanese school in the film you showed us. If there is a fight between two children in our school, we quickly separate the children and tell them that fighting is wrong, that it doesn't settle anything, and encourage them to apologize and settle their problems without violence. Of course this kind of approach works better with the older children than the real little ones, who can't really understand the idea of an apology. But it just seems to me that it is cruel to let children hurt each other in fights without trying to do something to stop it.

This Japanese teacher was not alone in praising the American school in our film. We were surprised to hear many Japanese parents, teachers, and administrators—not all Christians—express a preference for St. Timothy's over Komatsudani. This may have been due in part to Japanese etiquette, to a reluctance when dealing with outsiders to seem to brag about themselves or their culture or even indirectly to criticize a guest, and in part to an inferiority complex vis-à-vis the West and an attraction to American ideas lingering from the days of defeat and occupation, especially among older Japanese, even in this period of Japanese cultural and economic resurgence. But most of the praise we heard from Japanese about American preschool education clearly reflected a genuine attraction to the creativity, energy, and excitement they saw in our film of a day at St. Timothy's. Even at schools as traditionally Japanese as Komatsudani, teachers and administrators found much to like about St. Timothy's. For example, Fukui-sensei praised her American counterpart's energy, warmth, and creativity. Higashino-sensei, admiring and even envying the varied activities, including cooking and field trips, which are part of the program of American schools such as St. Timothy's, commented, "I wish we could be free to be that spontaneous in our program."

Confused to find so many Japanese teachers and administrators seeming to prefer an American preschool to one of their own, we asked two articulate Japanese administrators—both, as it happens, Christians—to explain. Did they not think that the Japanese values of groupism, perseverance, and empathy, and the social and cultural identity stressed at Japanese preschools like Komatsudani were important?

Nagami Kengo, director of a five-school chain of yōchien and hoikuen in Hiroshima, responded:

> Of course, as Japanese, we think these values you mention are extremely important. We would not be Japanese without them. But as Christian educators we believe that children in Japan need more of a balance between these traditional Japanese values and other values such as individuality, self-confidence, a sense of right and wrong, and a knowledge of the teachings of Jesus. Living in Japan, Japanese children get the groupism, the obligation, and all the rest without us teaching it to them. We think preschools like ours are about the only chance these children will have to become creative individuals before they get into the public school system. That is the battle we are fighting here. Japan doesn't need more groupism. That's why in our schools here in Hiroshima we emphasize the need for developing what you are calling Western or Christian values. It's a matter of giving to children that which they do not have and thus need.

Okamoto Chiaki, a respected social worker and educator who directs the Jūsō community center and hoikuen in Osaka, tried to help us understand some of the nuances and subtleties we seemed to be missing in the Japanese reactions to our films.

> You asked why we Japanese seem to prefer the way discipline problems are handled in America to the way they are handled in Japan. Well, this is a complex but crucial point. You know in your film of the American preschool, where the teacher takes aside the boy who refused to clean up his toys, and she talks to him and really confronts him? That approach is very attractive to us as liberals and intellectuals and Christians because it seems much more humane and caring and, well, I guess, educational in the best sense of the word than the way the teachers in your Japanese film let the children fight and cry without intervening. Here at Jūsō we handle these kinds of problems on a case-by-case basis, depending on the teacher and the

temperaments and relative sizes and ages of the children involved, so in actual practice I suppose we are somewhere in between your American and Japanese schools and in some ways maybe a bit like your Chinese school.

But what I am trying to explain to you is that while I and others find something very attractive about the American psychological, personalized approach to discipline, I feel something about it isn't quite right or appropriate or feasible for Japanese. For my tastes there is something about the American approach, the approach you've shown us in your film, that is a bit too heavy, too adultlike, too severe and controlled for young children. The way Americans deal with children's disagreements by agonizing about motivation and guilt and atonement—it's all very Judeo-Christian in a way which is very foreign to most Japanese. It's based on a very different notion of original sin and conscience and guilt and individuality and especially of the efficacy of words than we have in Japan. Though it is all very attractive and familiar to me personally I also find it in a crucial way not really right for Japan.

Few Japanese parents, teachers, or administrators are as thoughtful or articulate as Okamoto Chiaki or Nagami Kengo in analyzing the complex ways Western and Japanese values interact in Japanese preschools. But even less articulate left- and right-wing ideologues usually acknowledge at least implicitly the need for some sort of balance between both traditional and modern values, between native and imported elements, in the preschool curriculum. Although conservatives blame the teaching of Western values to Japanese young children for the decadence they see in Japanese youth, and although liberals decry the authoritarianism they see in the preschool curriculum, which they believe will lead Japan back into the fascism and thought control of the prewar period, at the level of practice rather than ideology, all Japanese preschools from the most free to the most traditional mix Western and Japanese values and approaches. Our sense as outside observers is that Japanese preschools are much more alike in practice than they perceive themselves to be and much more alike than the heavily ideological statements of many of their directors might lead one to believe.

Play and Work

Japan is a very education-oriented country, and public debate over the costs and benefits of academic pressure at every level of the system is frequent and often acrimonious. Widely discussed issues—the role of education in Japan's national economic development, education-hell, exam-induced suicides, school phobias, the declining equality of educational opportunity, the rising importance of extramural educational institutions (*jukus* and *yobikō*), calls for tracking and more vocational education—all have effects that trickle down to the preschool level.

Given this climate of widespread ambivalence and discord over educational policy, it is not surprising that when we asked our informants what they thought of Komatsudani's curriculum some felt strongly that it was too narrowly academic and pressured, and others felt that it was not academically demanding enough. Parents and staff of several yōchien, for example, criticized Komatsudani, as seen in our tape, for putting too much emphasis on teaching academic readiness. A Hiroshima yōchien teacher commented:

> I get a sad feeling seeing the children in this school, in this film, sitting there at their tables working away at those workbooks. There will be plenty of time for that sort of book-oriented learning later on, when they start primary school. To me that kind of approach is too academic—it's forcing an elementary school kind of learning onto preschool children—and I'm not even so sure that elementary school children learn much that way.

An Osaka yōchien administrator added:

> You can see just by looking at the children's faces in that film that four-year-olds are not ready for that kind of curriculum. For the first few minutes of the workbook session—you know, when they were doing that exercise involving counting rabbits and raccoons and following directions and coloring in boxes—the children attended to the task. But they soon became restless, which should have indicated to the teacher the disinterest in what they are doing and thus the lack of age-appropriateness of the task. Children of this age should be engaged in more childlike activities. But I don't mean to single out or blame that teacher. It certainly is not her fault. The whole country is putting pressure on preschools these days to do more of that kind of thing, "more substance in the curriculum" is how they put it.

But other Japanese parents and teachers criticized Komatsudani's curriculum for being not academic enough. For example, one Tokyo hoikuen mother wrote in the general comment section of her questionnaire: "It is difficult to know how much time is spent at this hoikuen on academic skills in a given week from seeing only this film, but as a parent I would like to see more structured learning activities and less wild, free play." And a hoikuen administrator's comments were similar: "It seems to me that this school wastes a lot of opportunities to do more teaching. Children of that age, four and five, have an enormous thirst for learning and it's a crucial time in their cognitive development. This is the time to give them a good start."

Kyōiku Mamas and Education Escalators

Perhaps the key figure in the debate over the costs and benefits of academic pressure and achievement is the *kyōiku mama* (education mother), one of the best-known and least-liked pop-culture figures in contemporary Japan (Lebra, 1984). The kyōiku mama is Japan's version of those American stereotypes, the stage mother forcing her child onward to show-business success or the Jewish mother haranguing, self-sacrificing, and guilt-inducing her child into medical school (DeVos and Wagatsuma, 1973). The kyōiku mama is feared by her own children, blamed by the press for school phobias and youth suicides, and envied and resented by the mothers of children who study less and fare less well on exams.

Although parents, teachers, and administrators we spoke with complained of the ubiquity of kyōiku mamas and of their deleterious effects on Japanese education, no Japanese woman we interviewed answered yes to the question, "Are you a kyōiku mama?" Instead they typically said something like "Of course I take an interest in my son's education and I help him in any way I can with his work, but I try to keep things in perspective. I would like him to do well but I also want him to be happy and well adjusted."

In our interviews and observations in Japanese preschools we encountered not only no self-identified kyōiku mamas but also very few kyōiku-seeming mothers, relatively few explicitly academic-oriented activities, and little evidence of parental concern about their children's primary school admission. To be sure, kyōiku mamas, preparatory preschools, and heavily academic curricula exist in Japan. But they are relatively rare and largely concentrated in urban, wealthy areas of the country.

High-status, fast-track preparatory preschools can be divided into three basic categories. First in prestige come *esukareta* (escalator) or *fuzoku* yōchien, preschools attached to top universities that also run respected elementary, junior high, and high schools. These attached preschools, which use tests and interviews to select three- and four-year-old entrants from large pools of applicants, serve as an early-admissions route to academic and thus professional success, a first sure step up the education escalator (Vogel, 1971). Next come *eisai* (enriched) yōchien, private preschools offering demanding, academically oriented curricula aimed at preparing children to succeed on primary school admissions tests and in interviews. These eisai yōchien have widely envied reputations for placing their graduates in a handful of elite private elementary schools (which in turn have reputations for placing their graduates in prestigious junior highs, and so forth). Finally there are nontraditional preschools that offer an alternative curriculum mixing artistic, cultural, and cognitive activities that appeal to progressive parents. Some of these preschools specialize in teaching music appreciation, dance, and the playing of musical instruments, others in swimming or in English conversation. Some yōchien have programs modeled after various European alternative-education pedagogies (such as Waldorf or Montessori).

Although alternative and high-powered academic preschool programs together account for perhaps 5 percent of the preschools in Japan, they play a much larger role in the national imagination. Tales of young women who choose a maternity hospital on the basis of its reputation as an escalator institution able to place its alumni in prestigious yōchien abound in the Japanese press and contemporary Japanese folklore, although the number of women who actually make such arrangements for their as-yet-unborn children is actually extremely small. And although very few Japanese send their children to alternative schools, Kuroyanagi Tetsuko's account of her early years in a "free" school run by a director trained in French pedagogy and eurythmics (*Totto-chan: The Little Girl by the Window*, 1982) is among the best-selling books in Japanese history.

Both Mombushō and Koseishō officially encourage a middle road between academic achievement and social development at the preschool level. Both favor a balanced curriculum combining excursions, athletics, and play with the teaching of health awareness and grooming skills, social studies, nature, language skills, music, rhythm and dance, and arts and crafts.

Japanese preschools are unlike most American schools and more like programs in China in their emphasis on music in their curriculum. All preschool teachers in Japan can play the piano, and every preschool classroom has a piano or organ which is used frequently throughout each day. Musical cues announce and punctuate the beginning and end of activities. Children sing and perform on a variety of simple instruments, including small pianos and harmoniums, for school shows. At one yōchien we visited a class of five-year-olds played the "March of the Toreadors" on triangles, small accordions, tambourines, and drums. Physical education is also systematically taught at the preschool level. Children learn tumbling and rhythmic dance, and practice each summer for the school mini-Olympics (undōkai), which includes sprints, relays, hurdles (over thirty-centimeter barriers), and marathon races (once around the playing field).

Thus, despite the common American perception of Japan as a country where young children are driven academically at the expense of their happiness, physical well-being, and social development, there is relatively little explicit academic pressure in most Japanese preschools. In these respects Komatsudani appears about mid-range among Japanese preschools. There are preschools in Japan that cater chiefly to kyōiku mamas by offering a curriculum that is more academically rigorous than Komatsudani's, and there are also preschools that assiduously avoid all formal academic activities and scorn the kind of workbooks children at Komatsudani use several times a week. But these schools at the curricular and pedagogical extremes are clearly in the minority.

Teachers and Mothers

Who Teaches Japanese Children to Read?

International tests of math and reading achievement invariably show Japanese children outperforming their American peers not only in junior high and high school but even in the first grade (Stevenson et al., 1986), thus suggesting that at least part of Japan's educational success must be traced back as early as preschool. But the fact that Japanese children enter primary school reading better than their agemates in the United States does not necessarily mean that they learn to read in their preschools. Many, perhaps most, Japanese children learn to read at home (M. White, 1987).

Japanese parents feel that there are many crucial pre–primary school skills they cannot easily teach their children at home, including how to play, share, and empathize with other children, how to be a member of a group, and socialization to the role of student. But most parents feel they can teach reading at home.

Why in Japan, in contrast to America, is reading viewed as a skill that parents are competent to teach while character development is viewed as something that can best be learned at school? The answer has something to do with the way the Japanese language is written and read and something to do with Japanese character and culture.

Although it is far more difficult to learn to read and write the two thousand standard Japanese characters (*kanji*) used in newspapers and official documents than to learn to read and write English (Stevenson and Lee, 1986), it is much easier to learn to read the Japanese hiragana syllabary of forty-six elements than it is to learn to sound out and recognize the irregular English vocabulary. While a debate rages in the United States (and indeed throughout the Roman-character world) about how best to teach reading to young children, and while parents in the West feel incompetent to teach so technical and mysterious a skill as reading to their own children, there is no comparable pedagogical problem or controversy in Japan over how best to teach children to read *kana*. Japanese parents and grandparents find it almost as natural and nonproblematic to help their children learn to read as to help them learn to talk. For example, by learning to read and write his own name, a boy called Fujimoto Takahiro will already have learned eight of the forty-six basic hiragana characters. From seeing the names of their schoolmates written on their shoes, bags, and school badges and from seeing train stops and street signs written in hiragana, most Japanese children readily learn to read. Toys like blocks with the phonetic hiragana syllabary on the front and a simple picture of an object beginning with that character on the back facilitate the process.

Reading speed and comprehension grow rapidly as books written entirely in hiragana and aimed at prereaders are read at home with parents and grandparents. By writing the daily monitors' names on the blackboard in clear kana and pointing to the lyrics of songs written in large characters as they are sung by the class, preschool teachers facilitate rather than initiate or take the lead in this process. As Higashino-sensei suggested, in hoikuen, where children spend more time each day with their teachers than with their mothers, the teachers often feel a need to spend time systematically teaching reading. But even here the role of the teacher is less as reading specialist than as parent substitute.

Teaching Social Skills

Although reading can be readily taught at home most Japanese parents today feel that character can be properly developed only at school. To grow up exclusively in the bosom of a nuclear family is to risk not becoming truly Japanese, to risk being too self-centered and too dyadic rather than group-oriented in one's interpersonal relations. Japanese parents send their children to preschool not just for child care and not just so the children can learn to modify their behavior to conform to demands of society but, more profoundly, to facilitate the development of a group-oriented, outward-facing sense of self (Doi, 1986).

Traditionally, the process of growing up and becoming a person was thought to take place, metaphorically if not literally, on the road. The word *dō* (*michi*) has the meaning not only of road but also of way, as in *jūdō*. To learn to be a man a boy must venture outward, embarking on a journey where he will be forced to encounter and deal with strangers. Japanese proverbs such as "If you love your child, send him to the wide world," "Travel teaches friendship, life teaches compassion," "To become a [mature] person one must eat a stranger's rice," and "It's good to be made to endure hardship" suggest that there are dimensions of the Japanese self that cannot develop at home and cannot be taught by parents. These lessons can be learned only on the road, where one can experience the life of the outsider.

In earlier eras Japanese children were not literally sent out on the road, to dine with strangers. But in earlier eras Japanese children had more opportunities than they do today to spend time outside their homes and apart from their mothers, in interactions with children and adults in their community who, though not strangers, were also not immediate family.

In the past twenty-five years or so the world of the Japanese family has shrunk: nuclear families have become more common, as young people have moved to cities, leaving parents and grandparents behind. Extended family households have been replaced by urban condominiums and apartment complexes (*danchi*) and by suburban "bed towns" composed of single-family homes. Average household size dropped from 4.97 in 1955 to 3.32 in 1980 (Fuse, 1984), and fertility, from four children per family a few generations ago to fewer than two children per family today (Iritani, 1979; Lebra, 1984). The rise in the past twenty years in the number and significance of Japanese preschools can be understood not just in the context of a rising interest in education but also as a reaction to what most Japanese view as the shrinking world of the post-Meiji and especially post–World War II Japanese child. The contemporary Japanese preschool provides children with an institutionalized version of the extended family and face-to-face, mixed-age community (*kyōdōtai;* Imamura, 1987) in which Japanese children in the past are believed to have developed a group-oriented sense of self.

Principal Yoshizawa was among those who told us that the world of the Japanese child has become too sheltered: "Children's lives have become so narrow. Most of our children live in apartments, with just their parents, who tend to overindulge them and make things too easy for them." Our informants often used the word *narrow* (*semai*) to describe the world of contemporary Japanese children. Several Japanese parents told us that they fear their children are missing out on the spontaneous, unsupervised interactions with other children that they recall experiencing when they were growing up in larger families surrounded by a friendly sea of cousins, family friends, and neighbors. For example, a preschool parent in a suburb of Tokyo told us:

When I was a little girl I was outside all day. As soon as I woke up, I would be outside, playing with my friends until dark. But it is not like that these days. At least not here, in Chiba. I don't know my neighbors that well. People move in and out so much and we live so high up, we only really meet people who share this stairwell.

Some theorists argue that preschools exacerbate more than remedy this shrinking world. Hendry (1986) points out that "some adults lament the fact that kindergarten and other classes have severely reduced the number of hours children have available for such [unsupervised] play" (p. 60). She cites Yanagita Kunio, who argues that kindergarten is a middle-class phenomenon that deprives children of the chance to play with other children away from adult supervision and to develop a sense of equality and justice spontaneously, naturally. Whether they are part of the problem or part of the solution, preschools like Komatsudani self-consciously attempt to expand the child's world at school.

In Kyoto two years after our initial videotaping, we were treated to an example of Principal Yoshizawa's strategy of using the preschool to widen children's worlds. When we arrived at Komatsudani one overcast morning in the spring of 1987 with several visiting American educators in tow, Principal Yoshizawa told us, "Instead of having taisō [exercise] on the playground, as we usually do, today the older children will take a walk and have taisō at a different place." "A park?" we asked him. "Not a park, exactly," he responded. We assured the American educators that Yoshizawa must be planning to take the children and us to an especially beautiful setting for us to watch and film morning exercise. Perhaps we were heading to nearby Kiyomizu Temple or Okazaki Shrine.

At 10:00 A.M. the sixty four- and five-year-olds, their two teachers, and our delegation left the grounds of Komatsudani. We walked in a long line behind Principal Yoshizawa for nearly twenty minutes, through the city streets, past the turn-off for Okazaki, past the road to Kiyomizu, and finally past the grounds of Kyoto Women's College, where we momentarily thought (hoped) the exercises might be held. We doubled back two or three times across our path before finally arriving at an unpaved lot. The lot, marked for future construction, was covered with debris from houses that had previously stood on the site. Rain from the night before had settled into depressions across the gouged and pitted ground, leaving several mud puddles and ditches of standing water.

Under their teachers' direction the children formed a large circle, taking care to avoid the mud, the pools of standing water, and the piles of litter and construction debris. Without benefit of the recorded music they usually have to guide them through the morning exercises, the children and teachers seemed awkward and a bit at a loss, but they persevered through ten minutes of song and calisthenics. Taisō completed, the children, teachers, and the confused and a little disappointed American observers (this was not what we had anticipated videotaping) stood around apprehensively, looking to Yoshizawa to see what would happen next. Finally, a five-year-old boy asked, "Well, what do we do now?" "Play," answered Yoshizawa.

The children gradually began to break ranks. Some started games of "paper, rock, scissors." Several boys discovered empty soda cans and began to fill them with muddy water. Other children threw rocks and sticks at cans. Children trying to broad-jump small puddles often missed, muddying themselves and others. Some children continued to stand around, confused, while others grew bolder and more excited, making mud pies, purposely splashing each other, and collecting interesting litter and debris. Several children, muddied by others, ran to their teachers, who gave them a quick wipe-off, a pat on the back, and encouragement to enter the fray, "to play." After twenty minutes of play on the muddy, littered lot, the teachers got the children lined up and we returned, by a more direct route this time, to the school. Back at Komatsudani, over tea, Yoshizawa explained the morning's activity:

> Tobin: Why did you take the children to that place for taisō?

> Yoshizawa: These days children only know how to play if they are given special toys and playground equipment. We took them to that field so they could learn how to play without special equipment. The idea was for them to discover that they can have fun even on an empty lot.

> Tobin: Did you know it would be so muddy?

> Yoshizawa: It's because I knew it was muddy that I chose to take them there today. I went by there this morning and saw the mud and decided to bring the older children. You noticed that most of them were afraid of getting dirty? These days many children don't know how to be children. Especially hoikuen children like ours, who are in school all day, every day. They grow up not having the opportunity to play in the mud if we don't arrange for them to get it here with us.

Nonmotherlike Teachers

In the 1970s and 1980s preschools have come to play an increasingly significant role in the socialization and emotional and cognitive development of Japanese children. But Japanese mothers by and large do not feel threatened by the growing role of preschools in their children's development because the duties the preschools have come to take over are those traditionally performed less by mothers than by extended family and community. Although hoikuen must by necessity provide mothering to their infants and toddlers, hoikuen and yōchien teachers are rigorously nonmothering in the ways they relate to the older children in their care.

To a greater extent than in the United States (though perhaps somewhat less than in China) in Japan the roles of preschool teacher and mother are viewed as distinct. Although American preschool teachers also think of themselves as professional educators rather than mother-substitutes, teachers and parents in the United States nevertheless expect consistency between teachers' and parents' approaches to child care and discipline and between children's behavior at home and at school. In Japan, in contrast, teaching is viewed as completely discontinuous with parenting, and little consistency in approach or behavior is expected across the two domains. As the yōchien teacher pointed out to us after watching a film of an American preschool, "barefoot," intimate, motherlike, one-to-one play is good for children and satisfying for adults and children alike, but it is not the role of teachers to provide this kind of play. Teachers are not parents, and to the degree a Japanese teacher allows herself to slip into a maternal relationship with a child in her care she has failed in her role as teacher.

The key point is not that American teachers are observably more motherlike than their Japanese or Chinese counterparts (though this may be true). Rather, by emphasizing dyadic over group interpersonal relations in child development, in America any relationship between an adult female and a small child (as, for instance, between a preschool teacher and a student) cannot help but reflect the mother-child bond, whereas in Japanese preschools, where group relations are emphasized over dyadic relations, preschool teachers are less likely to play motherlike roles vis-à-vis the children.

The issue of teacher/student ratios can be understood in this context as a strategy used by Japanese preschools to keep teachers from becoming too motherlike in their interactions with students. Large class sizes and high student/teacher ratios are disliked by Americans because they make intense dyadic relationships between teachers and students more difficult. In Japan this loss of intensity, rather than being an undesirable outcome of large ratios, instead is an anticipated and intended effect. As the ratio falls below fifteen or so students to one teacher, she becomes more accessible to individual students, and this not only threatens the group ethos and interferes with children's play with peers but also makes the teacher more motherlike and thus encourages children to behave more like dependent sons and daughters. A clinical psychologist in Osaka, Dr. Sakuma Toru, put the point very strongly when we asked him why he thought therapists in Japan are seeing more cases of school phobia as early as the preschool level:

Sakuma: I believe many of the emotional problems we are now seeing in Japanese preschool and elementary schools are caused not by there being too many children per class but rather by there being too few. Some children may thrive with smaller classes, but other children do much better in classes of larger size.

Tobin: What kind of children do badly in a small class?

Sakuma: It's not that there are certain kinds of children who necessarily will do badly in a small class. If the teacher is sensitive and capable, these children can do fine in a small class. What I am saying is, if the teacher is mediocre, as some teachers are likely to be in any school anywhere, I suppose, in a larger class children more easily can find a kind of safety or haven in the group. If this same class with this same teacher is suddenly shrunk in half, from, say, forty students down to twenty, certain children may begin to feel more uneasy in school and to exhibit school phobia, for example.

Tobin: So you're saying that if the teacher, for example, is scary or mean, children will do better being in a larger class, where they can more easily avoid interacting directly with the teacher?

Sakuma: Well, that's close to what I am saying, but it's a little more complicated than that. In a smaller class the teacher's personality becomes more important as does her relationship to each student. This can be a problem for some students with some teachers.

The Japanese preschool facilitates the child's transition from the dyadic world of home to the more complex world of school and society by offering a program carefully structured to limit face-to-face, emotionally intense interactions between children and teachers, which would be painfully like and yet unlike mother and home.

Although, as we have seen, some Japanese parents and teachers praised the creativity and warmth they saw in the American teachers in our videotapes, a few wondered whether in preschools in the United States there might be too little chance for children to enjoy spontaneous, unsupervised child-child interactions. For example, a mother in Tokyo said of "A Day at St. Timothy's":

The teacher is so stimulating and creative. The children look happy and bright. Everything looks so exciting. But as I was watching I found myself wondering if it might sometimes not get to be too much. I wonder what it is like for a child to be in a class where the teacher is always so fun and creative and exciting and so important to the children. Wouldn't the children get to be too dependent on the teacher's always being there to organize their play and show them how to have fun?

Contact between Teachers and Mothers

In Japan contact between the domains of school and home is frequent but in general formal and stylized rather than spontaneous and frank. Mothers and teachers are not linked to each other by long acquaintance, shared tasks, or working under the same boss, factors that would tend to encourage the buildup of affection and mutual identification and thus facilitate frank, spontaneous communication. Rather, teachers and mothers usually are tied to each other only by role demands and socially defined mutual obligation, factors that require, especially in Japan, formality, ceremony, and restraint.

As a result, as Lois Peak suggests, it is rare for parents and teachers in Japanese preschools to discuss the problems a young child seems to be having in his adjustment to school or his general emotional development. Parents and teachers tend to view themselves as specialists with distinct and dissimilar roles to perform. For this reason and also because of a more general reluctance to tackle interpersonal problems head-on, Japanese teachers and parents rarely share their concerns about a child with each other (Peak, 1986, 1987). Teachers in many preschools visit the home of each child assigned to their class. Although these house calls may help teachers better understand the children, the visits are usually formal, and frank discussion is unwelcome and unlikely (Taniuchi, 1984).

In many preschools a contact book (*renraku cho*) in which mothers and teachers keep daily records of each child's mood, health, eating, and even elimination is sent back and forth between home and school each day. Mothers and teachers see each other when the children are dropped off and picked up, but unless the child is an infant a mother is unlikely to enter the classroom or to exchange more than formal greetings with the teacher. In general, unless something untoward or extraordinary occurs in the child's home or school life, communication between parents and teachers is brief and highly stylized. As Peak (1987) suggests, Japanese preschool parents and teachers are careful not to say anything to each other that could be construed in any way as a criticism or complaint. Mothers are hesitant to speak of unhappiness or difficulties their children might be experiencing at school for fear that their comments might sound like a criticism. Teachers are similarly reluctant to share concerns about children's behavior that could be taken as a suggestion that parents are deficient in their parenting.

Preschool administrators speak to groups of mothers during orientation, on special holidays, and at graduation, sharing platitudes about parenting

and sometimes giving direct but very general advice about child rearing ("During vacation don't let your child watch T.V. too much or stay under the *kotatsu* [electric blanket] too long").

Parents also have dealings with the school through the PTA, which is actually almost always an MTA—Mother-Teacher Association—or, more accurately, a Mothers' Preschool Booster Society (Higuchi, 1975; Imamura, 1987). Japanese preschool PTAs are service rather than administrative or watchdog organizations, as we learned by interviewing a yōchien PTA president in suburban Chiba:

Tobin: What would you do if there were a teacher in your school who was doing a bad job?

Nakao: Oh, our school has excellent teachers.

Tobin: But what would you do? How would you handle it if such a problem did arise?

Nakao: You mean what should be done?

Tobin: Yes, as the PTA president, don't you ever have to deal with this kind of situation?

Nakao: No. That kind of problem is the responsibility of the principal.

PTA mothers help set up chairs for graduation, arrange for pounding holiday ricecakes, paint sets for school plays, and organize projects to raise funds for new playground equipment. Some PTA mothers are kyōiku mamas who volunteer for PTA duty in the hope of facilitating their child's rise up the education escalator by being highly involved in all facets of his education. But most PTA board members need to be cajoled and pressed into service. Women with babies still at home find it easier to come up with an effective excuse not to serve.

Although PTA board members deny seeking office and complain goodnaturedly of having been arm-twisted into running, being an active PTA member can nevertheless be a source of friendships and of a modicum of status. It can serve as a step toward solidifying an identity for a young woman as a mother in her own eyes and in the eyes of family and community (Vogel, 1967; Higuchi, 1975; Lebra, 1984).

Supporting and Socializing Young Mothers

Japanese preschools, yōchien in particular, actively serve mothers as well as their children. They offer young women friendship, structure, and guidance in learning appropriate role behavior and in solidifying their identities as mothers (Imamura, 1987). Some yōchien mothers, like mothers of preschoolers in China and the United States and like most hoikuen parents, look to their yōchiens not for structure or meaning in their lives but simply for competent and convenient child care. They do not especially need or want the support and counsel and resent the political pressures to conform placed on them by yōchien. Nevertheless, for many others, the yōchien plays a central and important role in their lives.

The job of being a yōchien mother is challenging, time consuming, and even at times complex (Imamura, 1987). Yōchien schedules are variable in a way that demands a great investment of maternal time and attention, making it difficult for the mothers to hold down even part-time jobs. Yōchien, unlike hoikuen, are closed on many working days as well as on Sundays and holidays. Most yōchien designate a day each month for teacher preparation, a boon, no doubt, to harried teachers, but a burden to harried mothers. Yōchien are also closed for six weeks in the summer and two weeks each in the winter and spring.

Days requiring special maternal participation and preparation also abound at yōchien. Mothers are frequently asked to come to school on weekdays for PTA and other meetings, to accompany children on field trips, and to send to the school various kinds of art supplies, clothing, and the like. Many yōchien also invite (and expect) mothers to attend outings, talks, and luncheons, and even to play on the yōchien's "mamas' " volleyball team against teams from neighboring yōchien.

The making of the daily bentō (box lunch) is a good example of and metaphor for the earnestness and energy required of a dedicated yōchien mother. A simple sandwich will not do for a bentō. These lunches must be works of art—attractive arrangements of rice, leftovers from dinner, and freshly cooked delicacies. An American woman living in Kyoto with a son in a local yōchien explained the burden of lunch making:

> In America I just make a peanut butter sandwich and put in some chips and a piece of fruit and some carrot sticks. But here it is an entirely different story. One day my son came home from yōchien crying and told me that the Japanese kids had laughed at his sandwich, saying that his peanut butter looked like *unchi* [excrement]. At that time he was still having a hard time as the only foreigner in his school so I felt especially badly about his getting teased about his lunch. The next day I made him a Japanese lunch, a bentō. But he came home from school again unhappy, again about his lunch. I said, "Now what's wrong? I made you a Japanese lunch." He said, in tears, "But you didn't cut the apple slices so they look like bunny rabbits like the other mothers do." I was sure this was an exaggeration on his part. I thought, "All the other mothers can't be cutting apples to look like rabbits." But I checked around a bit and discovered that children's lunches really do look great—the apples and carrots are cut up like rabbits and flowers and whatnot. I just don't have the time to be a professional lunch maker. I'm lucky in the morning to get him dressed, fed, and out of the house with a peanut butter sandwich.

Mothers at many Japanese yōchien must not only make a fancy bentō and get their child fed and into his uniform each morning; they also must get themselves sufficiently dressed up and made up to meet the other mothers and the teachers. Especially in wealthy neighborhoods in urban Japan, groups of well-dressed young mothers and their sailor-suited children standing on corners waiting for the yōchien bus to arrive are a common sight.

Why do Japanese mothers work so hard to make the perfect school lunch? Why do they take pains to dress up so early in the morning just to meet other mothers? For many young Japanese mothers, as Merry White suggests (1987), preparing their children for school is their most important work; their children's education is the center of their interests. And meeting other yōchien mothers before and after school is, other than shopping, their only daily personal contact with the outside world (Imamura, 1987). They dress up for other preschool mothers because these are their most important reference group. They strive to make their children's lunches as good as the others' because the other mothers are their *seken,* the ever-watching, mutually concerned, supportive, and critical community, those who define what is normative, desirable, or deviant. The point is not that Japanese society as a whole is more limiting and restrictive for women than is China or the United States but rather that Japanese yōchien play a more central role, for better or worse, in defining mothers' identities and role demands than do preschools in the United States or China.

Teachers' Careers

Fukui Masako, the twenty-five-year-old teacher of the Momogumi class of the Komatsudani hoikuen, first worked there as a part-time, unpaid teacher's aide during six weeks of her senior year at a Kyoto women's college. A term of practice teaching was a requirement for her major in preschool education, as were courses in child psychology, music, health, science, and nature. Fukui-sensei graduated at twenty-two, got her license as a hoikuen teacher, and was immediately offered a full-time position as an assistant teacher at Komatsudani. After a year of filling in for the regular teachers during their breaks, illnesses, and vacations, she worked for another year alongside two other teachers taking care of twelve infants. In her third year Fukui-sensei was given her own class, the three-year-old Momogumis.

When we visited Komatsudani the first time, Fukui-sensei was in her second year of teaching the Momogumi children, who were now four years old. In most yōchien and hoikuen, children stay with the same teacher for three years. Fukui-sensei lived at home with her parents and younger sister during the years she taught. In the spring of 1986 Fukui Masako married a young policeman she had met through a family friend, and at age twenty-six, she retired after four years of preschool teaching.

Fukui Masako's career is typical of Japanese preschool teachers. The employment curve for Japanese women across occupations is M-shaped— most work for six or seven years after high school or three to four after college before retiring either when they marry or soon after, when they have their first child (Carney and O'Kelly, 1987). Many of these women return to the work force when their children are grown, but most, including preschool teachers, are unable to return to their previous positions.

Women's salaries are generally low in Japan; a hoikuen or yōchien teacher's starting salary of five to seven or eight hundred dollars a month plus twice-yearly bonuses makes this a relatively well-paid, high-prestige job for a young Japanese woman, although not nearly as well paid or prestigious as elementary school teaching, a job held by men as well as women (and one that, unlike most preschool teaching jobs, is unionized). A few preschool teachers rise to become administrators. One out of every five or so may stay on beyond the usual four to six years of teaching, choosing either not to marry or to marry and have children whom they place in a hoikuen. Directors usually are either men untrained in preschool education, who reign by virtue of owning the school or being Buddhist priests (like Principal Yoshizawa of Komatsudani), or older unmarried women who have moved laterally to a preschool directorship from social work or public school teaching. A few women rise through the ranks from teacher to head teacher to director by dint of long service and determination; more commonly these career-oriented women (like Higashino-sensei) fail to rise above the rank of assistant director.

Preschool teaching, especially in hoikuen, is an arduous job. Teachers arrive at school an hour or so before the children for a quick staff meeting with the principal and to prepare materials for the day. Some yōchien teachers, especially those with little seniority, are required to ride school buses both before and after school or to walk to and from school with groups of children who live nearby. Yōchien children are dismissed at 2:30 four days a week and at noon on Wednesday and Saturday, but teachers at most yōchien must stay at school until as late as 5:00 each day, cleaning, doing paperwork (of which there is a great deal), and preparing teaching materials for the next day. Hoikuen teachers usually begin work a little earlier than teachers in most yōchien, and the children in their care do not go home until as late as 5:00 or 6:00, six days a week. In deference to the heavier demands of this schedule hoikuen usually allow teachers one or two fifteen-minute breaks a day. Breaks at yōchien are more sporadic.

With long hours, large classes, and only average pay, it is no wonder that Japanese preschool teachers tend to burn out and retire after four or five years. Conversely, one could argue that the short average career span of preschool teachers allows the young, single yōchien or hoikuen teacher to expend more sheer energy per day and per year than her counterpart in China, who has a lifetime of preschool teaching ahead of her and thus must pace herself, or her counterpart in the United States, who is likely to have children of her own awaiting her return from work each night.

As changing social attitudes in Japan gradually make it more acceptable for middle-class, educated women such as preschool teachers to continue their careers after marriage and childbirth, and with salaries gradually rising, teachers may become less willing to walk away from their careers after four or five years. If preschool teaching continues to change in this direction, there may be profound and unintended (though not necessarily deleterious) effects on Japanese preschool education. The average age of teachers in the preschools participating in our study was twenty-five, as compared to an average age of thirty-one in the United States and thirty-seven in China. And it's a young twenty-five at that, as unmarried preschool teachers, like unmarried women in other occupations, are expected to act young—to be cute, energetic, unwifely, and nonmatronly (*buriko*). Preschool in today's Japan is thus a world of young children and still girlish teachers. If teachers' careers lengthen, the character of Japanese preschools like Komatsudani may change, the pace and mood growing subtly less frenetic and exuberant, a concession to the maturity of a more experienced, less energetic staff.

Conclusion

The Japanese preschool, which a hundred years or so ago did not exist and as recently as twenty years ago played only a marginal role in the care and socialization of young children, has become a core institution of contemporary Japan. Today over 95 percent of Japanese children attend yōchien or hoikuen before they begin first grade.

This rise in the ubiquity and importance of the Japanese preschool is a result not only of increased Japanese interest in early child education but also of the postwar nuclearization of the Japanese family. As family size has dropped and young people have moved from the country to cities and suburbs, preschools have gradually taken over child socialization and child-care functions traditionally performed by extended family, neighborhood, and community. Japanese mothers today, like those of a century ago, remain the chief caretakers of infants and toddlers and thus the chief source of training in dyadic relations. What has changed is that the teaching of social skills and the fostering of an identity as a member of a group have become primarily the responsibility of preschools.

Aspects of the Japanese preschool including teacher/student ratio, class size, teachers' career paths, and techniques of classroom management and instruction are all structured so as to promote the development of a group identity and group skills in young children and to preclude teachers from interacting with children in intense, emotionally complex, mother-like ways. Japanese preschools are set up to make clear to children the distinctions between school and home and between mothers and teachers.

All this seems to suggest that in contemporary Japan children learn dyadic relations at home and group relations at school, and that the role of schools is to transform dependent, selfish toddlers into group-minded youngsters ready to function in a group-oriented school system and society. But this is an oversimplification that underestimates the complexity of the Japanese preschool (and, for that matter, of Japanese character and society). To be Japanese is not to suppress or sacrifice the self to the demands of the group but rather to find a balance between individualism and groupism, between *giri* (obligation) and *ninjō* (human feeling). The task of the Japanese preschool is to help children find this balance, to help them integrate the individual and group dimensions of self, to teach them how to move comfortably back and forth between the worlds of home and school, family and society.

Chapter Three

Dong-feng:
A Chinese Preschool

Dong-feng (East Wind) Kindergarten is a preschool run by a city in southwest China for the children of municipal employees. Occupying the grounds of an old estate, the six red brick one- and two-story buildings of Dong-feng provide space for 270 three- to six-year-old children and sixty staff members. Three-quarters of Dong-feng's children are day (*ri tuo*) students, who attend school from about 8:00 A.M. to 6:00 P.M. Monday through Saturday. The other quarter are boarding (*quan tuo*—literally, "whole care") students, who go home only on Wednesday evenings and weekends.

A Day at Dong-feng

At 7:45 on a brisk Monday morning in early spring parents pull up to the school's front gate on bicycles, each carrying a brightly dressed child riding on the back. Inside the gate, in Dong-feng's front courtyard, two health-care workers (*bao jian yuan*), dressed in white, examine the arriving children one by one. "How are you feeling today, little boy? Open your mouth. That's good. Did you eat a lot of sweets over the weekend?" To the mother: "Has he had any stomachaches? How are his bowel movements?" The next boy, following his routine examination, announces in a loud voice, "I have a rash on my leg." The nurse, rolling up the boy's pants leg, smiles at his mother and says, "Don't worry. He's fine."

When four-year-old Li Aimei finishes her health check, her father, Li Chou, takes her by the hand and leads her down a corridor, past the day students' classroom, to the four-year-old boarding students' classroom and

dormitory in the rear of the complex. Martial music, played over loudspeakers, fills the courtyard. By the time Aimei and Mr. Li enter her classroom, a dozen children are already inside, sitting on benches and eating steamed buns. Aimei's grip on her father's hand tightens as one of her teachers, Ms. Xiang, approaches, saying good morning. With an affectionate but directive pat on the back, Mr. Li attempts to send Aimei off toward her teachers and classmates, but Aimei stamps her foot in protest and tugs on her father's hand, pulling his head near to whisper in his ear. Ms. Xiang waits attentively nearby, looking concerned while father and daughter talk. Aimei whispers earnestly to her father: "Don't forget to come and pick me up on Wednesday evening. Keep that thought in your

mind, Dad!" After a minute or two, Ms. Xiang approaches the pair, and Mr. Li, with a final good-bye and pat on the back, literally hands Aimei over to her teacher, who leads her to a spot on the bench.

As Mr. Li leaves the room, Ms. Xiang hands Aimei a bun, but Aimei refuses to take it, jumps up from the bench, and runs from the classroom, catching up with her father in the courtyard. Father and daughter speak intensely for two or three minutes while Ms. Xiang watches from just inside the classroom doorway, still with a look of concern on her face. At last, Mr. Li and Aimei again enter the classroom hand in hand. Mr. Li, trying to speak in a matter-of-fact tone, says to Aimei, "Well, I'm going to work now. See you later," and again sends her toward her teacher, turning on his heels and quickly leaving the room. This time Aimei accepts the offered bun and takes a seat on the bench between two classmates. Mr. Li, by now outside the room, furtively sticks his head back in, sneaking a last peek at Aimei. Seeing his daughter involved with her bun, neither crying nor searching for him, Mr. Li smiles, turns away from the room, and strides across the courtyard.

Aimei's father consoles her

Ms Xiang leads Aimei to class

By 8:30 all twenty-six children in the class have been dropped off by their mothers or fathers. This morning, only Aimei shows any signs of separation difficulty. With a pat on the back from a parent and a good-bye, the other students cheerfully run up the classroom steps and join their friends. Although many of the children have already eaten breakfast at home before leaving for school, they all seem to have a hearty appetite for the buns their teachers give them.

In marked contrast to the drabness of their parents' clothing, most of the girls wear red or blue slacks under brightly colored dresses and sweaters, with red or pink bows in their hair. The boys are less colorfully dressed, several of them wearing military uniforms and caps. The children keep their jackets and sweaters on inside the unheated classroom.

Two columns of desks, each with an attached bench large enough to seat two students, run down the middle of the classroom. In front of the room are a blackboard, a calendar, and a chart of Chinese characters. Above the blackboard is a mural of children playing in a field with forest animals. The walls and ceiling are gray. The floor is bare concrete. The temperature, inside as out, is fifty-five degrees Fahrenheit.

While forty-year-old Ms. Xiang and her coteacher, twenty-five-year-old Ms. Wang, arrange the children in a circle for morning exercise, their assistant (*bao yu yuan*), twenty-four-year-old Ms. Chen, takes the break-fast bowls and glasses away to the central kitchen to be washed. With Ms. Wang playing an up-tempo song on a small organ, Ms. Xiang leads the children in calisthenics. All of them participate with enthusiasm and surprising grace. Dancing and singing follow calisthenics. Ms. Wang an-nounces, "Let's do the 'Little Train Friendship Song.'" The children smile and clap, a few jumping in anticipation. Ms. Wang, inside the circle of children, begins to dance and sing: "I'm a little train, looking for some friends. Who will come and ride on me?" Chugging across the circle, she stops in front of a little girl, and then, facing each other and patty-caking, they dance and sing in unison: "Good friends, come quickly! Come and join us! Come ride our little train!" With her conductor now aboard (be-hind her, holding onto her waist), Ms. Wang, dressed in gray slacks and jacket, with pigtails trailing far down her back, chugs back across the cir-cle, stopping in front of a boy, and the song and dance continue as the engine and the conductor invite him to get on board. Eventually, all the children are hooked up, snake-dancing around the room, singing along with their teacher.

After singing another song (about ducklings), the children are told to sit down at their desks. Once they are seated, the teachers distribute wooden parquetry blocks to each child. The blocks come in a small box, which

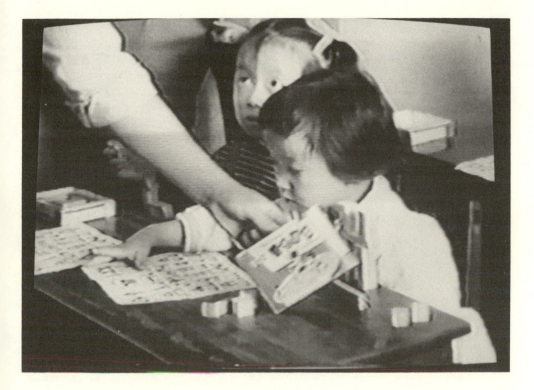

also contains pictures of several structures that can be made with them. Ms. Xiang says to the students:

> We all know how to build with blocks, right? Just pay attention to the picture of the building and build it. When we play games like this, we must use our minds, right? Once you are done, raise your hand and one of us will come by and check to make sure you've done it correctly. Begin. Do your best. Build according to order.

The children begin to work in silence. Those who are working in a nonorderly way are corrected: a child whose box is placed askew on her desk has it placed squarely in the desk's upper right-hand corner by Ms. Xiang. After three minutes one little girl, who apparently knows the blueprints by heart, completes construction of a multistoried house. Raising her right arm in the air, she calls in a soft voice, "Teacher, I'm done." But the teachers do not hear her as they are busy helping less able builders. Finally, Ms. Xiang comes over and says to the little girl, "You're done already?

Bathroom time

Well, take it apart and build another." After ten minutes most of the children have completed their structures. The teachers come over to check their work. If a building has been constructed properly (that is, exactly as in the picture), the child is told to take it down piece by piece and then rebuild it. If the teacher spots an error, she tells the child to correct it. After fifteen minutes of building, tearing down, and rebuilding, some of the children grow a bit restive, squirming in their chairs and whispering to their deskmates. Ms. Wang says: "Keep still! There is no need to talk while you are working. Let's work quietly." After twenty minutes the children are told to put the blocks back in their boxes. A boy and a girl, today's monitors, collect the boxes of blocks and put them back neatly in a cupboard. The other children face the front, hands on their desks.

It is now 10:00, time for the children to go to the bathroom. Following Ms. Wang, the twenty-six children walk in single file across the courtyard to a small cement building toward the back of the school grounds. Inside there is only a long ditch running along three walls. Under Ms. Wang's direction and, in a few cases, with her assistance, all twenty-six children pull down their pants and squat over the ditch, boys on one side of the room, girls on the other. After five minutes Ms. Wang distributes toilet paper, and the children wipe themselves. Leaving the toilet, again in single file, the children line up in front of a pump, where two daily monitors are kept busy filling and refilling a bucket with water that the children use to wash their hands. Several boys in the back of the line indulge in some mock kung fu while other children talk and laugh.

After washing their hands the children line up for a game of tag. After being divided into two teams and hearing a brief description of the rules, the children are soon running about the playground, laughing and calling to one another in the excitement of the game.

At 10:45 the children come inside. It is bath time for the boarding students. With their teachers' assistance, the children get clean clothes from their "pigeon holes" in the dormitory room, which adjoins the classroom. Three or four at a time, the children bathe in large tubs. Most of them are able to dry off and get dressed with minimal help from their teachers.

Bathed and changed into clean clothes, the children return to the classroom and take their seats. Ms. Wang drills them in addition and subtraction. As she pins hand-painted paper apples onto a large piece of cardboard, the children count out loud in unison. With their teacher's encouragement, children raise their hands to answer problems Ms. Wang poses by adding or subtracting paper apples from the board. The students participate enthusiastically, each correctly answering at least one problem.

As the arithmetic lesson draws to a close, lunch is delivered from the central kitchen and brought into the classroom in buckets. Again, with the help of the daily monitors, the children march outside and wash their hands at the pump. By the time they return, a bowl of soybeans, vegetables, and shredded pork, a steamed bun, and a cup of water that has been boiled have been placed on each desk. Ms. Xiang reminds the children to eat in silence and not to waste any food: "Don't talk while you are eating. You must give full attention to your meal. Concentrate on your eating as much as you do on your studying. That's the correct way to eat."

While the children eat, the teachers walk up and down the aisles checking on comportment and progress. Ms. Wang stops at the desk of a girl who is not eating and whispers to her. The girl, without reply, picks up her bun and begins to eat. A boy stops Ms. Xiang to ask for seconds on buns. Ms. Xiang says to him: "If I give you another bun, will you eat the whole thing or will you eat only half, and waste the rest?" Chang nods affirmatively. "You're sure you can eat it all?" He nods again. "All right, then, here you are. Eat it all." As the children continue eating, the daily monitors join the teachers in encouraging them to finish all their food and let

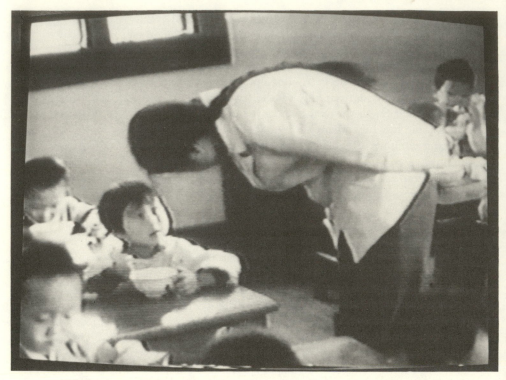

"Why aren't you eating?"

nothing go to waste. Standing impatiently beside the desk of a particularly slow eater, the girl monitor makes gestures as if to grab his bowl as she exhorts him in a whisper to hurry. The monitors collect the empty bowls and cups and place them in a bin to be returned to the kitchen. Other children wipe off the desk tops. Ms. Xiang then announces, "Naptime," and the children move to the dormitory room.

There are twenty-six beds in the dormitory room, each covered with a brightly colored, embroidered quilt. Next to the beds are shelves holding cups and washcloths. The children take their cups, scoop water from the bucket on a table, gargle loudly, spit into a spittoon on the floor, and wipe their faces with their washcloths. After putting away their towels and cups, the children place their shoes neatly under their beds, remove their pants and jackets and place them on a corner of the bed, and crawl under their quilts dressed in T-shirts and underpants. Naptime lasts from noon to 2:30, although most of the children do not sleep the whole time.

While the children rest, the teachers catch up on paperwork, eat, and relax in the classroom next door.

After nap, Ms. Chen once again takes the children to the bathroom and then to the pump where each child washes her hands and face and rinses her mouth. Next comes a snack of cookies and reconstituted powdered milk. Returning to their classroom, the children are taught to recite a patriotic story aloud in unison. Ms. Wang, holding up pictures of a little girl in a military uniform, recites the inspirational story line by line, and then the children echo her words:

> A long time ago . . .
> *A long time ago . . .*
> There lived a brave little girl . . .
> *There lived a brave little girl . . .*

After the story, the children move outside to the courtyard for some relay races. Ms. Xiang divides the children into four teams and says:

> Today we are going to play the "Traffic Rules Game." When I hold up this green card, you can run as fast as you can. Pretend you are bicycles flying down the street. When I hold up this red card, you must stop. Red means stop. If you don't stop, I will make you go back to the start and your team will fall behind. Do you understand? I wonder which team will win? Cheer for your teammates to help them do their best. Don't let your team down.

The game lasts for about twenty minutes, under the teachers' supervision. The children then play freely for another fifteen minutes or so.

At 5:00 P.M., following another group visit to the toilet, the children sit down at tables for supper. Before the meal is served, Ms. Xiang says "Let's do the Puppet Song." Following their teachers' stiff movements, the children imitate marionettes as they recite loudly in unison, "We are wooden puppets. We can neither speak nor move." As they finish the verse they freeze, holding their positions for ten seconds. After repeating the rhyme twice, the children are served their evening meal of a dish of meat cooked with vegetables and rice.

It is now 6:00 P.M. Outside in the courtyard children can be heard calling out to their parents, who have arrived to pick them up. Inside, the children of the boarding class listen to records. At 7:30 they move from the classroom to the dormitory room next door. They again rinse out their mouths, wipe off their faces, and struggle out of their clothes, some needing the assistance of a teacher. By 7:45 the children are all in bed under their warm quilts, and by 8:00 all are quiet and appear to be asleep.

Rehearsing for a concert

Doing Research in China

In the first chapter of this book we introduced our method of using visual ethnography to stimulate a series of narratives about the meaning of pre-schools in three cultures. As described in the last chapter, we held very closely to this research design in Japan, but this plan, which looked so manageable on paper and worked so well in Japan, ran into many problems in China. In the People's Republic we were forced to compromise our method in several ways for reasons ranging from a shortage of adequate electrical outlets to the necessity of securing permission from several levels of government officials to study and videotape preschools.

Perhaps the most imposing hurdle we faced in China was our hosts' very definite ideas about what we should see and tape in their schools. Unlike the United States and Japan, China has a well-organized national policy for dealing with foreign researchers and other guests, administered by carefully selected and trained interpreters and guides.

Children in costume at an Inner Mongolian preschool

Since China opened her doors to foreigners in the late 1970s, preschools in Beijing, Canton, and Shanghai have become favorite stops for visiting laymen as well as scholars. To make a good impression on foreign guests, frequently visited kindergartens in China's larger cities spend considerable time and energy preparing shows of children's songs and dances. It is thus not surprising that visitors come home with very similar stories about the poise, talent, and self-control of Chinese children (see, for example, Sidel, 1972; Kessen, 1975; Gentry, 1981).

For much of the time we spent in China on this project, it was this way for us as well. Even though we (David and Wei-lan Wu) were born and raised in Chinese culture (in Taiwan), we were in China as official "foreign guests," and as such we were provided with guides and interpreters and greeted in the preschools we visited with tea, an official presentation about the school, and a show. Children and teachers in frequently visited model schools, like Broadway troupers, can put on a show at a moment's notice. And like Broadway troupers, some of these performers at times are a bit cynical. One day we entered a university kindergarten without making prearrangements with the authorities (we were guests in the next-door university's dormitory). We encountered a little boy in the corridor who greeted us by saying, without malice, in obvious imitation of his teachers, "What a nuisance. It's foreign visitors [*wai bin*] again. How upsetting!"

Although there is something to be learned about a culture's preschools even from a prerehearsed show, one Chinese kindergarten show is very much like the next, and so, after seeing a dozen or more performances at preschools as invited guests and having made nuisances of ourselves with surprise, uninvited visits to other schools, we tried to persuade our guide, Ms. Li, to plead our case to officials in southwest China to let us see and tape a typical day in a kindergarten. Ms. Li, a very intelligent, sophisticated woman, works as a hospital administrator when she is not guiding foreigners around China and is a ranking member of the Communist party's foreign affairs committee. She was assigned to us by the Ministry of Public Health in deference to our affiliation with the University of Hawaii's medical school.

By the time we reached southwest China Ms. Li had seen our tapes of Komatsudani and St. Timothy's so often in screenings in other cities that she had come to understand our method and thus was able to convince the directors of Dong-feng that they had nothing to fear from letting us observe and tape freely. Ms. Li told us that she had reassured them that even without presenting us with an orchestrated performance their school would certainly come across in our tapes as much more organized and ordered and far less wild and chaotic than Komatsudani. At one point in our day of taping at Dong-feng Principal Hua, who was nervously looking in on the class to see how things were going, grew visibly more nervous when a child began to cry. Ms. Li reassured her by saying, "It won't do any harm if the tape shows a child crying. I've seen their tapes of schools in Japan and the United States, and there's a lot of crying and fighting and wildness. Don't worry." Thus, with the help of Ms. Li, we were able to videotape a typical day at Dong-feng.

Audiences of Japanese and American preschool parents, teachers, and administrators asked us many questions when we showed them the Dong-feng tape, and when we returned to China, we posed these same questions (and a few others) to parents and staff associated with Dong-feng and other Chinese preschools. Why the morning health checks? Don't the Chinese think separating young children from their parents for several days at a time is harsh? Aren't separation problems (like Aimei's) rampant among boarding children and their parents? Why are the bathrooms so devoid of privacy, and why must all the children go at once? Why the rigid approach to block play? Do all Chinese preschools look as institutional and drab as Dong-feng? Why so much emphasis on deportment, on the children's keeping quiet and being orderly? Don't the Chinese realize that this kind of overcontrol of young children is detrimental to their intellectual and emotional development?

The Single-Child Family and the Dangers of Spoiling

Wu: Why are there nurses here? Are they here every day?

Principal Hua: We do have a health-care worker assigned to our staff who is here every day to care for children who are ill. However, the nurses you saw this morning in front of the school are only here on Monday mornings. They are city nurses. Over the weekends the children are all home with their parents and grandparents who spoil them terribly with sweets and special foods. Often children come back to school on Mondays with stomachaches and other ailments.

The staff of Dong-feng pays a great deal of attention to health, hygiene, and safety. This concern is a reflection of traditional Chinese values and also of the energetic interventionism characteristic of China's revolutionary ideology: the Chinese do not react to illness; they root it out, eradicate it, and then work to prevent its return through education and prophylaxis. As the Kessen group described in 1975, Chinese medical care is highly decentralized and personal. The health of preschoolers is not left in the hands of pediatricians working out of offices and hospitals but is dealt with in the schools by school nurses, "barefoot doctors," and other paramedical personnel (Korbin, 1981).

The attention to children's health noted by the Kessen group in 1975 has grown even stronger in contemporary China. Much of this attention to and concern with health, including the Monday morning checkups, can be related directly or indirectly to China's single-child family policy. The nation's population, already over 500 million in 1949, had swelled to 1,000 million by 1979. Population control became a national concern in the 1960s, a national priority in the 1970s, and a national imperative in the 1980s. Chinese population control efforts are summarized in the slogan *"wan, xi, shao"* (later, longer, fewer), which means marry late, have longer intervals between children, and have fewer children. The meaning of *shao* (fewer) changed from "not many" in the 1960s, to two children in the 1970s, to one child in the 1980s (Engle, 1982).

Exceptions to the single-child policy are made for minority groups, and cooperation has been difficult to obtain in the more culturally traditional agricultural regions of the country. But in cities a system of economic sanctions and perquisites linked to family size, coupled with vigilant workplace and neighborhood birth-control monitoring, education, and counseling, has been largely successful: by 1985 over 90 percent of the children entering preschool in Nanjing and Beijing were single children (Tao and Chiu, 1985).

In China the single-child policy is widely viewed as a great achievement, but one that has its costs. Chinese parents, teachers, administrators, and child-development experts fear that children in single-child families are spoiled by their parents and grandparents and that this leads to many undesirable outcomes (Wu, 1983, 1985, 1988). Chinese say that a child indulged by as many as six doting adults is likely to come to think of himself as "a little sun." This problem is also called the "4-2-1 syndrome": four grandparents and two parents pouring their attention onto one spoiled child.

Chinese concerns about spoiling go far beyond sweets and upset stomachs. A few spoiled children are a nuisance; a whole generation of spoiled children could threaten China's modernization movement, reverse the gains of the past thirty years, and undermine the values of a society based on the principles of collectivity, selflessness, and comradeship. Chinese laymen and authorities alike worry about how a generation of single children can be taught to be socially responsible. Won't single children inevitably be spoiled, and won't spoiled children inevitably grow up to be counter-revolutionaries instead of good socialists? How can children growing up without siblings learn to cooperate, share, and treat their fellow citizens as brothers and sisters? What will happen to a social system in which one's nonrelated elders are called uncle and aunt in the years to come, when real uncles and aunts will be only a memory?

Although these worries are widespread in today's China, more positive perspectives on the single-child family also are heard. Some Chinese we spoke with see in the single-child family the possibility for a higher quality of parenting, with more care and less neglect, as a greater portion of China's limited resources go to a smaller group of healthier, better educated children. In the words of a slogan used to promote birth control: "One born. One well nurtured. One well educated." This slogan is an accurate description of reality in a society where sanctions and incentives heavily favor single children. For example, a study of preschool children in Nanjing shows that 80 percent of the single children drink milk at home for breakfast compared with only 12 percent of children with siblings (Tao and Chiu, 1985).

Like Principal Hua, Ms. Li also used China's single-child family policy to explain the presence at Dong-feng of nurses on Monday mornings, but her explanation, unlike Principal Hua's, had nothing to do with spoiling:

We are asking today's parents to have only one child. In generations past Chinese parents had more than one child. In the future, we hope that parents will again be able to have more than one. We are acutely aware that we are asking parents of this generation to make a sacrifice for the greater public good. Since we are asking parents to make a sacrifice, we feel a great responsibility to provide the best health and educational services possible to their single children. In a sense we make a covenant with these parents: "Have only one child for the sake of the country and modernization and we in turn will make sure your child is healthy and well provided for." One reason parents in the past wanted more than one child was to guarantee that even if something happened to one son, they would still have an heir, someone to care for them in old age and to carry on the family line. When parents see the nurses at school every Monday morning, it symbolizes to them China's commitment to make sure their child will grow to be a healthy adult.

In our discussions with Chinese preschool staff, parents, and government officials, the single-child family and spoiling repeatedly came up as issues of great concern. Many aspects of Dong-feng's program that seemed unusual or strange to Americans were explained by Dong-feng's staff as a direct or indirect result of China's single-child policy. Conversely, many of the features of Komatsudani and St. Timothy's that Chinese viewers found least attractive, including Hiroki's fighting and an American child's stubbornness, they attributed to the problem of spoiling.

For example, when we asked Ms. Xiang to comment on the scene in our tape of Dong-feng that shows Aimei struggling to part from her father, Ms. Xiang had no trouble identifying the problem:

This kind of separation difficulty is relatively rare, especially for children who have reached the age of four or five and have been in school for two years or more. When we see problems of this sort, we can be sure the fault lies with the parents who spoil them. If children cry when they are brought to school, it is because their parents have made them willful, weak, and bad-tempered by coddling them too much. I blame the parents. When children have trouble separating from their parents, it is usually because their parents have trouble releasing their children.

When we showed the Dong-feng tape to students and staff of the Department of Early Child Education of a university in northern China, a teacher commented:

Was that girl in your tape who wouldn't separate properly from her father almost five years old? That's not right. Of course at the beginning of the year, some very young children may have a hard time adjusting, but a four- or five-year-old child should no longer be acting so spoiled and clingy. We get spoiled children here too, but we work very hard with them to correct this kind of problem before they get to be so old.

Chinese preschool administrators and teachers who viewed our Komatsudani tape were outraged by what they regarded as Hiroki's spoiled behavior and by the failure of his teacher to correct him. Fully a third of our Chinese informants listed Hiroki's fighting as the worst thing they saw in our tapes. For example, a teacher in Shanghai wrote on her response sheet: "What a selfish little boy! What a bully! He is obviously used to completely getting his own way at home, to having everything he wants, to being a little king. He is so spoiled he has no consideration for others. He thinks the whole world revolves around him." And an administrator from Nanjing wrote: "He behaves like the worst kind of spoiled single child. I would bet he has no siblings. Do most Japanese families these days have only one child?"

Kerry, a little boy who can be seen in our St. Timothy's tape stubbornly refusing to put away the toys he played with, was also roundly criticized by our Chinese informants:

Is this kind of selfishness common in American children? There are so many toys in the classroom that children must get spoiled. When they have so much, children don't appreciate what they have. This kind of willfulness and obstinacy is common in children whose parents are too weak or indulgent to discipline them properly. Without discipline, a child will become obstinate and demanding, making his mother a slave. This little spoiled boy in your movie must be used to having his mother pick up after him at home, so he expects the same thing at school.

Another teacher added:

Indulgent parents make teachers' jobs harder. The other day that little girl [pointing at a girl in her class] tore up a bunch of sheets of the colored paper we use for paper-folding [*zhezhi,* or in Japanese, origami]. When I asked her to stop, she said to me, "My parents told me I can tear apart anything I wish. They've got money and they will buy me new ones." Once the other children hear this kind of talk it becomes very difficult to teach them proper conduct.

For the Chinese, the concept of "spoiled" covers a cluster of related negative behavior characteristics. Spoiling and the problem of raising single children are matters of concern not only to parents, teachers, and laymen but to government leaders and psychiatric and social science researchers as well. Child-development experts worry that children growing up without siblings will be lonely, self-centered, and unsociable as adults. In a study of "Psychological Ramifications of the One-Child Family Policy" (1985) Tao and Chiu of the Nanjing Neuropsychiatric Institute found the most common undesirable traits of single children to be: "marked food preferences, short attention span, obstinacy, demands for immediate gratification of their wishes, disrespect for elders, bossiness, lack of initiative, and outbursts of temper" (p. 158). In Dr. Yu Lian's 1985 study of mental health problems of young children, she lists "partiality for a kind of food," "overdependence on parents and adults," "sluggishness in daily life," and "nail sucking and biting" as the most common negative behaviors. Sociologist Wang Nianchen of Zhungshan University in Guangzhou writes: "Only children are usually viewed as selfish, spoiled, unsociable, maladjusted, narrow-minded, self-centered, conceited, fragile, and cowardly." Wang's studies (1984) led her to conclude that the number of single children displaying these spoiled behaviors in contemporary China may have been somewhat overestimated. She suggests that, depending on the quality of parenting and of kindergarten education, single children can turn out either spoiled or well adjusted. She provides case vignettes of typical spoiled and unspoiled single children:

————: male, five years old, healthy, very stubborn and aggressive, striking others for toys and picture-books and not accepting the teacher's advice. Father: worker, primary school graduate. Mother: worker, less than five years' education. Family income: about 120 yuan. He was spoiled by mother and orders her about. His father used to spoil him, too, but became very strict with him after he reached age three. His father began to beat him for the slightest fault. So the boy has a sense of inferiority and rebellion and refers to himself as a "bad boy."

————: male, six years old, strong, energetic, and brave, never submissive to the elder and stronger, never bullies the weaker, so he is becoming the hero of the class. Father: teacher, university education. Mother: athlete, graduated from senior middle school. Both parents are broad-minded and cheerful, attentive to the education of their only child, but not overprotective, always encouraging him to do things for himself from an early age. (p. 11)

Wang's case studies are clearly meant to be cautionary and prescriptive as well as paradigmatic. In addition to revealing contemporary Chinese attitudes toward higher education and broad-mindedness, they give voice to the depth of Chinese concerns about spoiling in this era of single-child parenting.

In discussions of spoiling the word *jiao* (tenderness) can often be heard. Many preschool administrators and teachers complained that children in China have become *tai jiao*—too delicate, too dependent, too fussy, too bourgeois. The character *jiao* contains the radical for "horse" and thus etymologically the phrase *tai jiao* carries with it a connotation close to the English *headstrong* or *unreined*. Tai jiao is caused by parents' foolishly giving their children free rein, and it is corrected by teachers' wisely tightening the reins. For example, Principal Hua told us:

> Some spoiled children are very stubborn, wild, and aggressive, like the Japanese boy in your tape. These children need to be treated with a firm hand and brought under control before it is too late. But more commonly, spoiled children are weak, soft, fussy, delicate. They don't play with enthusiasm. They don't eat with a hearty appetite, but instead leave food on their plates. They say, "It doesn't taste like the way my mother cooks it." They whine, "The beds at school are too hard. The teachers are too mean. They scold me." They are angry when other children won't yield to their demands.

Concern about spoiling in China did not originate with the single-child family, however. Long before the 1949 revolution Chinese child-rearing texts warned of the dangers of *ni-ai,* of "drowning a [child] in love" (Solomon, 1971, p. 65; Wu, 1981, p. 154). The American Delegation on Early Childhood Development in the People's Republic of China found widespread concern about spoiling, especially spoiling by grandparents, during the two-child-per-family era of the Cultural Revolution (Kessen, 1975). Spoiling is a long-standing Chinese concern; what is new in the contemporary Chinese discourse on child rearing is the linking of concern about spoiling with what is commonly believed to be the widespread tendency of parents and grandparents of single children to overindulge them. Tao and Chiu (1985) put the blame for spoiling squarely on the shoulders of parents:

> Many parents look upon their only child as their great treasure and place all their hope on him or her. They try their best to provide the best nutrition so that the child will be healthy. They do their best to grant the child's various demands (including unreasonable ones) in order to make him or her happy. They try to protect the

child from difficulty or danger. They have all sorts of fears and are overly anxious about whatever concerns their child. Thus, they spoil and indulge the child for fear of losing their only treasure. The child senses this and takes advantage of it and will threaten parents in order to fulfill unreasonable demands. For example, a little girl was very fussy about her food and refused to eat. Her parents urged her, "Oh come, eat your food. Tomorrow we'll make something delicious for you." She still refused to eat. Her parents tried to persuade her: "You will starve to death if you don't eat!" The little girl answered: "If I starve to death, you will have no daughter!" (p. 162).

Chinese fear that parents of single children all too often favor the short-term demands of their too-precious offspring over the greater long-term societal need for children to learn to be disciplined and selfless. As Zhou Nan of Beijing Normal University explained:

Most parents and grandparents disapprove of spoiling when they see it in other families, and they agree in theory with warnings from government leaders and educators that they must not spoil their children. But when it is their own child or grandchild, they often lose sight of the larger concern. It is understandable that parents should feel and behave this way, but that doesn't mean it's right. Clearly it is bad both for the children and for the future of our country.

Correcting Spoiling

Viewing spoiling as the most serious problem presented by the single-child family policy, Chinese look to preschools as a solution. Preschools provide single children with the chance to interact with other children and with teachers trained to correct the errors of single-child parents. Some Chinese education and mental health experts are quite explicit about the link between the need for preschools and the growing numbers of single children. Wang Nianchen (1984) writes: "Since the inception of the new population policy, the number [of Chinese preschools] has been greatly increased with the aim of raising the quality of the population while controlling the quantity" (pp. 3–4).

The Child Development Center of China, established with UNICEF funds in 1981, has a mandate to raise the quality of Chinese parenting and preschool education by coaching teachers and parents in nutrition, education, and "how not to spoil their single children" (Press, 1987). Chinese see the primary function of preschool, then, as giving children a good start academically while socializing them away from being spoiled and toward good citizenship (Press, 1987). The keys to achieving these goals are order and regimentation.

Regimentation

Most of the Americans and Japanese who viewed our China tape objected strongly to what they perceived to be Dong-feng's rigidity, severity, and overregimentation. These respondents gave Dong-feng negative ratings on the items "teachers directed children's play too much," "teachers set limits and controlled children's behavior too much," "the overall mood was too controlled," "children played independently too little," and "children's activity level was too passive, subdued, docile." For example, a Japanese preschool administrator said of Dong-feng:

> The children look so restricted. Nothing seems spontaneous. The feeling of the school is so cold, so joyless. The children are expected to be so, well, unchildlike. All that emphasis on sitting straight, on being perfectly quiet, on standing in straight lines. It reminds me of Japanese schools in the old days. I hope the Chinese didn't get this from us!

An American preschool teacher in Honolulu reacted similarly:

> There is so much regimentation. It looks more like the army than a preschool. I guess what bothers me most is that there is such an overemphasis on order and on behaving properly at the cost of stamping out the children's creativity. This is such an important age in children's cognitive and emotional development. What gets me in this film is the way the Chinese children are made to use blocks in a certain way instead of allowed to play in a natural, imaginative way. They are made to follow directions like workers on an assembly line, which negates the whole point of block play. Also the way the Chinese make all the kids go to the bathroom at once. I wonder, is this because of communism or is it something in Chinese culture, or a combination of both?

Although the kind of regimentation seen in our tape of Dong-feng is anathema to most Japanese and Americans, for many of our Chinese informants regimentation, order, and control are essential elements of preschool pedagogy and child socialization. Many (but, as we shall see, by no means all) of our Chinese informants were proud of the order and regimentation that came across in the tape. When they host foreign visitors, Chinese administrators and teachers therefore take pains to have their school appear even more regimented and controlled than usual. For example, when we visited Dong-feng, a teacher told us that the principal had instructed her to conduct a structured learning activity after naptime in place of the usually more relaxed afternoon schedule of free play. The shows Chinese preschools put on for visitors are another example. The irony here, of course, is that the harder the Chinese work to present an impressively ordered, regimented appearance, the more put off many of their foreign visitors are.

Most of our Chinese informants told us unapologetically that they see the role of the preschool as teaching children to behave properly and instilling in them an appreciation for the values of self-control, discipline, social harmony, and responsibility. By our third visit some of the teachers and administrators who had come to know and trust us confided that the children in their schools are noisier when visitors are not present. But even at their wildest, Chinese preschools surely are not as uninhibited as preschools in the United States or Japan.

Guan

The word used most frequently in China to refer to teachers' control and regimentation of children is *guan*—literally, "to govern." When Ms. Xiang told the children to eat their lunch in silence and finish every bite, that was guan. When Ms. Wang got all twenty-six children to squat at once in the bathroom, that was guan. When Ms. Wang criticized one child for squirming and smiling while praising another for sitting straight with her hands behind her back and a serious expression on her face, that, too, was guan.

Guan has a very positive connotation in China. It can mean "to care for" or even "to love" as well as "to govern." Chinese mothers often deal with their children's disobedience by saying to them, *"Wo bu guan ni!"* ("I am not going to interfere with your life"—meaning "I don't love you, I'm not going to care for you any more").

To govern children well is hard work. Chinese believe that preschool children are well behaved not because they are born that way but because teachers work long and hard to bring them under firm control. One secret of governing children well is to monitor and correct their behavior and deportment continuously. Instead of waiting to act until minor indiscretions grow into large ones or until slight lapses in attention deteriorate into chaos, a good Chinese preschool teacher intervenes aggressively at the beginning. As Ms. Xiang explained to us:

> When I see a child squirming in his seat or whispering to a seatmate
> during a lesson or not concentrating on eating his lunch but instead

playing absentmindedly with his food, I first let him know I see what
he is doing. I do this by walking over to him and staring at him until
I get his attention. If that is not enough, I call out his name, and
that generally does the trick. We aren't allowed to punish children
as the American teacher does in your film. In China we can't spank
children or put them in jail. [Ms. Xiang was referring here to the
short time-out she saw in our St. Timothy's tape.] Since we can't use
punishments, we can't afford to let children get out of control. We
control them by stopping them from misbehaving before they even
know they are about to misbehave.

In addition to surveillance and early prophylactic interventions, Chinese preschool teachers told us that they govern their classes by "taking
charge," by "being in control," and by using the technique of "compare
and appraise." Principal Hua of Dong-feng shared with us her secret of
good classroom management:

Teachers must take charge in the classroom. Teachers must provide
structure and order. That's their responsibility. That's what they
are there for. One way to take charge is to carefully plan lessons
ahead of time for the whole day and to anticipate children's moods
and needs. A teacher can take charge quietly, without raising her
voice, by preparing good instructional materials, materials which
will occupy children's minds and energy to the fullest. If things are
well planned and prepared in advance, then there will not be chaos,
and the teacher will find it easy to keep firm control.

A preschool administrator in Nanjing emphasized to us the importance
of structure and organization:

A preschool teacher should never waste time. Unstructured time
leads to trouble. We do not have much of the kind of "free time"
in our school that we saw in your tapes of schools in Japan and
the United States because we believe it is important for teachers to
organize their students' time, to govern [guan] the class so children
do not have a chance to become wild or aimless.

Zhou Nan emphasized to us that the key to governing children well is
consistent concern:

To maintain proper control and order in the classroom teachers must
be consistent and even-tempered. Many parents are inconsistent in
their parenting. One minute they overindulge their child, then the
next minute they realize they are spoiling him, so they overcompen-
sate by becoming suddenly too harsh and yelling at him. This kind of

inconsistency is confusing for children. Kindergarten teachers must be consistent and firm. They should always make it perfectly clear to children what is expected of them and what they will not be allowed to do. Control and order should not feel to the children like something foreign, something dropping suddenly out of the sky on top of them. Instead, control and order should come to be familiar to children, as expected, as much a part of their world, as the air they breathe or the ground they walk on.

In direct contrast to the approach taken by the staff of Komatsudani Hoikuen in Japan, most Chinese believe that it is important for teachers to intervene immediately in children's disputes. A Beijing teacher said of our tape of Komatsudani:

I think it's terrible that the teacher just stood there while the children fought. If you let a child behave that way in preschool, he will think that it is acceptable to be that way, and he will develop a bad character that may last his whole life. When children misbehave, teachers must correct their misbehavior immediately and make it clear to the children that their behavior is not acceptable.

Tao and Chiu (1985) suggest that intervention should be firm but gentle:

Only-children have the desire to improve just as other children do. Adults should respect them and cherish this desire. When we criticize their weak points, we should encourage their strong points and make stronger demands on them. Comparing and appraising each other's behavior is one way to encourage their desire to improve. (p. 163)

"Compare and appraise" is an example of the faith Chinese put in words to affect and control children's behavior. As Richard Solomon points out, "the Chinese phrase for obedience, *t'ing-hua,* [means] to 'listen to talk'" (1971, p. 52). In a class for five-year-olds at Dong-feng we observed a teacher getting her students ready for supper: "Now let's see. Who is sitting properly? How about Chen Ling—is he sitting properly? Who knows what is wrong with the way he is sitting? Should he be fiddling with his hands? Look at Lin Ping. Is she sitting nicely? See how straight her back is. See how she has her hands behind her back." In Heilungjiang in rural northern Manchuria we saw a teacher use a similar approach to get rows of children to compete for praise and avoid criticism: "I can see that the first row of little friends [*xiao-pengyou*] is sitting very nicely, but the third row is not sitting properly. Let's see which row of little friends can be the model row for the whole class."

Chinese preschool teachers, then, see their fundamental task as controlling children's behavior calmly, consistently, and without anger. The emphasis is less on punishing misdeeds than on explaining, modeling, and commending desirable behaviors. According to Chinese theories of child development, children are not born knowing how to behave correctly, and they are unlikely to come to know correct behavior through unsupervised play with peers (as many Japanese teachers believe) or through a process of self-discovery and self-actualization (as many American teachers believe). Both Confucius and Mao emphasize that since character is shaped by experience, teachers bear the responsibility of teaching students self-restraint and correct behavior. The regimentation and control Chinese preschool teachers typically exert over their classes are perceived by the teachers, the wider society, and perhaps by the children not as cold or harsh treatment but as an expression of care and concern.

Parents and Preschools

Many parents agree that they are guilty of spoiling their single children. A parent in Kunmin told us: "With only one child it is hard to resist spoiling him. We waited a long time to have our child. We know he is the only one we will ever have. So we treasure him. We want to give him everything. The teachers are right when they say it is parents who spoil kids. It's only natural." A majority of parents we interviewed in China told us that they deal with their children's misbehavior, demands, and tantrums not with discipline but with supplication (*hong*). When pressed for examples of hong, they mentioned pampering, soothing, placating, and even bribing their children to behave.

Parents of single children find themselves in a bind: they hesitate to deny or discipline their child, both because he is their "precious little treasure" and also because, with only one child to look after them in old age, they want to make sure that he does not develop feelings of resentment that might weaken the bonds of love and filial gratitude they are banking on for their future. But they can ill afford to have their child be spoiled, for a spoiled child is unlikely to turn out to be either economically successful enough or emotionally predisposed to care for an aging parent. Especially in urban areas, parents have high expectations for their children's success. They would like to see this success begin in preschool, to see their child get off to a good start academically on his way to higher education and a good job, with good housing, salary, and perks.

The emphasis on music and dance in the Chinese preschool curriculum and on music lessons in urban Chinese households can be understood, in part, as a product of this parental concern. A young child's ability to sing

有感孩子們的畫

趙之在五月八日的《科技日報》上，介紹北京清華中學初一（二）班學生張彥作的一幅畫，我和奶奶比童年（見圖）。

作者說，這是一幅孩子的畫，卻足以震撼天下父母心。

它是畫給孩子的，歌以當哭，淋漓地抒寫了孩子的煩惱。同時也是畫給奶奶們的，你們和我們在不同的歷史條件下度過童年，可是我們的童心為什麼也必須承受相似的摧殘？

每一個老師、教育工作者和一切關心孩子的人，也都會從孩子的畫裏感受到它的藝術力量，生發出自己的聯想。

它的藝術力量，來自小畫家對藝術形象的苦心經營。包括畫中的每一個細節。

墊起孩子屁股的，從前是磚頭，現在是大部頭的書籍。奶奶的小手，是生硬的，孫女的手腕是多麼柔軟。奶奶的頸都快壓折了，而孫女卻在眉宇間飽含着一種不應有的憂傷——那也是小畫家的憂傷。所以連窗外窺人的月亮，也蘊含着歷史的辛酸。

但是，愛——這種人間至美至善的情感，也需要反思，需要學習。

Child labor at the loom, before the Revolution, and at the piano today. A seventh-grade student drew the cartoon, on which the article was based. (Beijing People's Daily, overseas edition, June 1, 1987)

and dance well is seen as an indication of intelligence and potential in other cognitive domains. The current shortage of pianos in China thus is a reflection not only of the country's growing consumer prosperity (pianos sell for the equivalent of two years of a teacher's salary) but also of the single-child policy that leads parents to drive their children to cultivate their talents. Urban Chinese parents are also investing heavily in ballet, painting, and calligraphy equipment and after-school lessons for their children.

Several of the older, more experienced teachers told us that today's single-child parents are more likely than parents of previous eras to push preschool teachers to emphasize academic achievement. With three or four children, parents in earlier eras could assume that at least one would probably do well enough in school to get a good job and care for them in their old age. With just one child, educational and economic success is less likely to be left to chance (Xu, 1985).

Most Chinese parents want their children to be pushed academically and disciplined when necessary, but they would rather not be the ones doing the pushing and disciplining. Preschools offer an institutional solution to this problem. Many parents are relieved to let the teacher play the role of the heavy while they remain positive figures to their children. They feel less guilty and worried about the implications of indulging their children at home on weekends knowing that they can count on the preschool to correct the ill effects of this spoiling.

Parents also tend to favor the relatively harsh and demanding expectations of their children's preschools because parents perceive the teaching of order, control, and social-mindedness to be in the best interest of their country. Chinese parents are citizens as well as parents, concerned about the greater social good as well as about the good of their offspring. Although they may perceive aspects of social policy as in some way conflicting with the present or future well-being of their family, most Chinese parents believe that what is good for China is good for them. Parents of single children as parents may tend to spoil their children, but as citizens they share (or at least claim to share) the wider society's concern about the threat to the greater social good presented by spoiling.

In the United States, parents look for consistency between their approach to discipline and the preschool's; in China, parents expect their children's experience at school to be complementary and even corrective rather than consistent with life at home. American parents send their children to preschool because of the demands of their work and because they want the children to have fun, to make friends, and to learn. They generally do not send their children to preschool because they believe teachers are better qualified than they are to care for them. In contrast, many Chinese parents acknowledge that teachers as trained professionals without a dangerous emotional stake in the children are better suited than they are to socialize their offspring. Chinese parents send their children to preschool not only because they think, along with Japanese and American parents, that preschool offers a more stimulating and challenging environment than the home but also because they look to the teachers to compensate for the overzealous attention and misguided but well-meant indulgence children receive at home.

Boarding Preschools

Another aspect of Chinese preschool education that Americans and Japanese find disturbing is China's "whole-care," or boarding program. When

Waiting for breakfast

the lights came back on after our screenings of the Dong-feng tape, our audiences in Japan and the United States invariably asked us, "How can the Chinese do this to their children?" "Are Chinese parents forced to send their children away by the government?" and "Aren't the Chinese aware of how harmful this sort of round-the-clock institutional care can be to small children, who need the daily love and support of their parents?"* Our answers are the answers Chinese parents, teachers, administrators, and child-development specialists gave us when we asked them similar questions.

About 5 percent of Chinese preschoolers are boarding students. Boarding programs are much more common in cities than in rural areas. Some

---

*For an example of these concerns, see Sander Breiner's paper "Early Child Development in China" (1980).

programs keep the children at school from Monday morning to Saturday afternoon; in others the children go home for Wednesday as well as Saturday and Sunday nights. There are both boarding kindergartens, which accept children four years of age and older, and (somewhat rarer) boarding nurseries, which serve infants and toddlers.

Why boarding programs for young children? First and foremost, these programs are made available because they are needed by working parents who have no other child-care alternatives. Most Chinese preschool boarding programs were opened during the years of the Cultural Revolution to serve children of party leaders, of soldiers in the People's Liberation Army, and of urban parents assigned to work and reeducation in the countryside. Boarding programs continue to serve children of soldiers and party cadres and also children of parents who work at night or on schedules that preclude caring regularly for their children in the evening.

But no matter how inconvenient Chinese parents' schedules and how critical their work, for Americans and Japanese the question remains, how can Chinese let their young children be taken away for such long periods of time? Chinese informants told us that parents who must work at night and who find the idea of boarding school for their young children repugnant usually manage to make other arrangements, such as hiring retired neighbors or girls from the country to care for their children after school, or, most commonly, they solicit the help of relatives. But the usual response we heard to these questions was the counterquestion, "What's so terrible about boarding schools?" Principal Hua, for example, responded to our questions by saying:

> Most parents are quite happy to send their children to our whole-care program. Why shouldn't they be? It's not as if the children are being mistreated or neglected in any way. Just the opposite. Parents know that if they put their children into our whole-care program the children will receive the best possible food, health care, and education.

Indeed, instead of viewing boarding programs as a kind of punishment to be avoided, many Chinese parents "go through the backdoor" (using connections or bribes) to get their children admitted to a boarding preschool. Some young urban parents, viewing boarding programs as a way of guaranteeing that their children will receive first-rate care and a fast academic start, complain that slots in boarding programs are parceled out to a privileged few.

Signs and slogans posted in boarding schools support the notion that teachers can be as good as, if not better than, parents. At Dong-feng we heard three-year-old boarding children sing, "The kindergarten is my home. My teachers are like my mother." In Nanjing, we saw a slogan on the wall of a preschool: "Our love for children is as great as a mother's love." A flyer encouraging parents to have but one child and to put that child in kindergarten went a step further: "Teachers are better than real mothers."

In a paper presented in 1984 at the East-West Center in Honolulu the sociologist Wang Nianchen addressed herself directly to Western critics of China's boarding programs, arguing that boarding not only is not harmful but is beneficial for only children:

> Some Western psychologists may ask: Separated from their parents, will the children, particularly those trusted to the care of their pre-schools for a week at a time, be lacking love or may they even be terri-fied? Are they perhaps forced by their teacher's strict control to obey outwardly while they resist inwardly? After observing a boarding school program over a period of two months we drew the conclusion that though parents sometimes hit their children, teachers never do. Children in preschool learn how to behave through interaction with their peers and by imitating those children who are most praised. Children in whole-care programs, by having the chance to partici-pate in attractive activities and games, learn to accept regulations as something natural. Chinese collectivism stresses the harmony of the individual with society and with others. It is natural to be part of a collective, anxiety-provoking to be apart. The collective life to be enjoyed in kindergartens enables the only child to become aware not only of the existence of self but also of the existence of the collective. The praise they receive from teachers gives them a sense of deep sat-isfaction and acceptance. Such a positive self-concept will lead them to have a zest for life in the future. A child entering preschool will find intimate feelings growing between himself and his teacher and his peers. He may cling to his parents when they come to pick him up for a weekend at home, but after two days in the house he will feel lonely or dull. This suggests that the egalitarian, friendly, intimate interpersonal relationships to be found in kindergartens are beneficial to only children for the development of a properly prosocial attitude.

Chinese explanations of the benefits of boarding programs for young children are consistent with their views on the need for order and regimen-tation (guan) and more generally with the Chinese belief that preschools, whether day care or whole care, are institutions mandated to correct the failings of the single-child family. Like Wang Nianchen, most Chinese view their whole-care preschools less as problems than as solutions. View-ing preschools as healthy environments for children and believing that

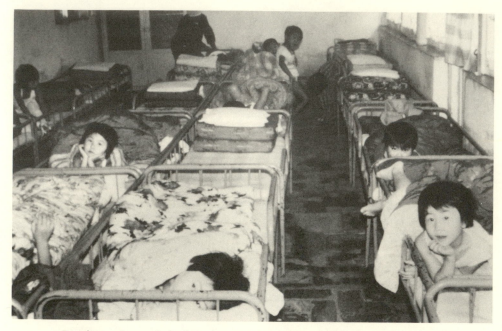

Boarding students ready for sleep

teachers are at least as qualified as parents to socialize children, Chinese find little that needs explaining or justifying about their boarding programs.

The horror Americans and Japanese feel when confronted with Chinese whole-care programs for young children, like the milder distaste they hold for Dong-feng's regimentation and shared trips to the bathroom, in the end have more to tell us about America and Japan than about China. Most Chinese view their boarding programs neutrally or positively, much as liberal-minded Americans and Japanese view their own systems of day care. Thus our Chinese informants tended to react to our questions about their boarding programs much as Americans with children in day care might react to being asked by a self-righteous accuser, "How can you do this to your child?" Our Chinese informants were surprised by our asking them to justify their boarding programs, and more irritated than defensive. A kindergarten administrator in Nanjing said to us: "Do they have whole-care programs for young children in the United States? No? Then how can they take good care of all of their children? In America how can mothers and fathers who must work at night be productive workers when they have to worry about having adequate child care?"

China is a poor, populous country struggling to find solutions to prob-

lems both old and new. Chinese parents, teachers, and preschool administrators have seen many changes in their lifetimes, changes they perceive
as far more profound and unsettling than the rise of boarding programs.
Having lived through major political, social, and economic transforma-
tions and having adapted to the necessity of having only one child per
family, Chinese find boarding programs for children of parents with difficult work and commuting schedules a relatively benign and easy change to
accept. A new society requires new customs and social institutions. The
few complaints we heard in China about boarding preschools had to do not
with the concept of separating young children from their parents but with
faults of particular programs.

Perhaps China's boarding programs shock and frighten Americans in
part because we project onto them our own ambivalence about the trade-
off we fear is necessary between women's careers and the good of children
(for example, see Sylvia Hewlett's 1986 *A Lesser Life*). These American
concerns are grounded in American culture, values, sexual politics, and
notions of family and society. None of the Chinese we spoke with referred
to a trade-off between their work and the well-being of their children.
In China working full time is a necessity for all women, not a matter
of choice. Therefore, there are no institutions equivalent to the Japanese
yōchien or the American nursery school, no half-day programs for children
of nonemployed or part-time working mothers. Chinese parents who work
days send their children to full-day preschools. Parents who work at night,
or who work far from their homes, get help from relatives or place their
children in boarding programs.

The notion held by many conservative Americans that children belong
exclusively to their parents, that they belong in nuclear-family homes, and
that there is something unwise, unnatural, or unhealthy about preschools
(boarding or otherwise) are other ideas by and large not found in China.
Americans and Japanese are horrified by the idea of boarding programs for
young children because we believe that children can be scarred for life by
traumatic events in childhood and that no event is more traumatic than
the premature severing of the mother-child bond (Goldman, 1977). These
are culturally constituted beliefs that for the most part are not held by
Chinese (and that, until relatively recently, were not common in the West
either). In Taiwan, Hong Kong, and overseas Chinese communities that
are ideologically and economically unlike the People's Republic, it is very
common for parents to send their young children to live temporarily with
relatives or with the families of household servants (Wu, 1981), with little
if any worry about possible long-range traumatization and little concern
about damaging the intensity of the mother-child bond.

Chinese parents admittedly often feel sad about the need to send their children to boarding school, but, as one parent told us, the sadness is felt more for themselves than for their children:

> It was hard for us when our daughter started preschool. I cried every Monday morning when I dropped her off at school for the first year. But she likes it, and we are very pleased with her development. It is a very sad thing for parents not to be able to spend more time with their children. But people must work, so this is a sadness we must bear. And the sadness goes away each weekend when we have time to be with our daughter. Other parents in our building have their children in day programs, but by the time they pick their children up and shop for dinner, it is almost time for the children to go to bed. For us a day program would not be all that different [from a boarding program]. I think children do fine in both, as long as the teachers are good.

These boarding programs can be viewed as an institutional version of an approach to child care found throughout traditional Chinese culture. In the People's Republic boarding care has been routinized, regulated, and, for the first time, provided with an ideological justification. An official of the Ministry of Public Health gave us the Marxist historical-materialist perspective on both boarding preschools and the single-child policy:

> We need to bring a broader historical and economic kind of thought to these issues. It is not the case that in the past Chinese mothers took care of their own children. Only rich women could afford not to work and most of them hired poor women to nurse their children. We must not romanticize where we have come from. In previous eras many children died of hunger and disease and many other children were neglected and mistreated. The old days were not good days for everyone. We should not view boarding schools as an instance of children being taken from their parents. That is a totally wrong understanding. Parents are concerned for their children, but they are not the only ones who are concerned. Children do not belong to their parents alone. Boarding schools are consistent with the highest ideals of socialism; they make possible the reality of a socially shared concern for the children of our society.

The Collective Good

As this statement makes clear, in China the social, the collective, and the group are valued over the personal, the familial, and the individual.

Ideally, the individual and the collective are not in conflict—what is good for society is good for the individual, and vice versa. But where private needs and desires are inconsistent with the greater social good, the individual must be ready to adjust and even sacrifice.

The promotion of selflessness and collectivism lies at the core of the Chinese preschool's mission. These values are far more easily taught in preschools than at home, as a manual for teachers makes clear:

> In the kindergarten we use the classroom as a big family to teach single children that they are members of a collective. We teach children to develop the habit of treating others equally, to be friendly, considerate, concerned, to mutually give in (*qian rang*) to others, and to obey the rules of the group. We nourish their concept of collectivism through numerous daily activities. For instance, in kindergartens children are organized to play games like "doing a good deed for the collective" and to role-play important occupations like policeman, store sales personnel, liberation army uncle, nurse, and doctor. The kindergarten is the ideal place to teach children the concept of collectivity.

In our Dong-feng videotape, the group bathroom scene, which many American and Japanese respondents found so disturbing, was seen as an unremarkable example of collectivity by most of our Chinese informants.

> Wu: Why do you make all the children go to the bathroom together?

> Chang: Why not? Why have small children go to the bathroom separately? It is much easier to have everyone go at the same time. Of course, if a child cannot wait, he is allowed to go to the bathroom when he needs to. But, as a matter of routine, it's good for children to learn to regulate their bodies and attune their rhythms to those of their classmates.

The Kessen group described Chinese preschool education in 1973 as highly ideological, with great emphasis given to moral education across the curriculum (Kessen, 1975). Ruth Sidel's impressions of Chinese preschools in 1976 were very similar. In the somewhat less radical and ideological era of the mid-1980s, when we did our fieldwork, we found that moral education remains a central feature of the Chinese preschool's mission (Sidel, 1982). Attending a lecture at a college of education in Beijing, we heard a professor describe the moral-education curriculum for kindergarten:

> The guiding principle for moral teaching in the preschool is to emphasize the unity of the group and to cultivate a love for friendship. First-year students [three-year-olds] must be taught to play with

other children in a friendly, loving manner; not to monopolize or fight over toys; and not to hit or curse other children. For second-year students [four-year-olds] the first rule of moral teaching is to teach children to be able to interact in a friendly way and to render help to other children. This is what teachers and parents wish children to learn. This is not just an official line or slogan—it is what you will be teaching children when you begin to work in kindergartens.

This emphasis on group harmony explains our Chinese informants' overwhelmingly negative reactions to Hiroki's fighting and Fukui-sensei's (non)response. Watching our Komatsudani tape, Chinese parents, teachers, and administrators were outraged by Fukui's failure to intervene and stop if not discipline Hiroki: they saw his aggression not just as evidence of spoiling but also as a dangerous display of individual will directed against the social order.

To individually oriented Westerners, both China and Japan are group-oriented societies. Yet our research clearly shows that Chinese and Japanese approaches to group identity, to classroom management, and to individual transgressions such as Hiroki's are strikingly different. Thus, the technique of nonintervention in children's disputes that Japanese educators employ to promote the development of social control and group solidarity was viewed by our Chinese informants as destructive to group formation.

> Principal Hua: Why didn't the Japanese teacher do anything to stop that fight? Didn't she see what was happening?

> Wu: She saw it. She told us she doesn't intervene in children's fights unless it is absolutely necessary, and she allows the children to play freely without adult supervision to give them a chance to learn on their own how to function as members of a group.

> Hua: But the big boy is using his greater strength to bully the weaker boy. If the teacher doesn't stop this behavior, the other children may imitate it. Children fighting and running wild in a classroom are not a group—they are a mob. In an atmosphere of bullying and chaos they cannot learn social responsibility and the self-control necessary for being a member of a group.

Chinese notions of the group are inextricably linked to the concept of order (Wilson, 1970, 1974). A disorderly collection of children is not a group. To the Japanese, in contrast, groups can be chaotic as well as orderly, spontaneous as well as structured, anarchic as well as prosocial. Children doing morning exercises are a group, but so are children playing wildly in the courtyard after lunch; quality-control circles in a factory are groups, but so are five or six workers going out together to a bar after work. Thus the tasks facing preschool teachers in Japan and China are different. To prepare children to be good members of a group, Japanese teachers emphasize camaraderie and place children in situations where they can interact freely, without adult interference. Chinese teachers emphasize order and common purpose and place children in situations where they can share the experience of discipline and control under the direction of a common leader. Group structure in the Chinese preschool tends to be more vertical and teacher-directed than in most Japanese preschools, where group-oriented means peer-group-oriented, and the less involved the teacher is perceived to be, the stronger the horizontal ties that form to bind the group together.

These differences in defining and promoting collectivity lead to differing approaches to the issue of competition.* We saw many more examples of individual competition among students at Dong-feng than at Komatsudani, and the staff of Dong-feng seemed far more comfortable than their counterparts in Kyoto speaking of individual differences in ability and temperament among children. In Japanese preschools, where groupism is closely associated with egalitarianism, talk of individual differences in children's ability is virtually taboo. In Chinese preschools, where groupism is associated with a shared acceptance of order and responsibility, individual differences in aptitude and performance are less threatening.

The Kessen group observed in 1973 that as strict Marxist environmentalists, Chinese educators were hesitant to acknowledge inborn differences in temperament or ability. We also found the Chinese to be highly egalitarian, but the preschool teachers and child-development experts we talked to seemed to be much less reluctant to discuss individual differences in children than the Kessen group had found twelve years earlier in the midst of the Cultural Revolution. Billie Press (1987) describes a contemporary Chinese study of "supernormal" (gifted) children (Zha, 1986) which would never have been approved during the era of the Cultural Revolution. Stevenson, Lee, and Stigler, in their 1981 summary of the state of Chinese studies in child development, point out that research on individual differences started to reappear in Chinese academic journals in 1980 and that aptitude testing of children, tabooed during the Cultural Revolution era, was coming into vogue.

Although in contemporary China, chaotic, selfish displays of individu-

---

*For a discussion of differences between Chinese and Japanese forms of collectivity, see Francis Hsu's *Iemoto, the Heart of Japan* (1975), and Michio Nagai and John Bennett's "A Summary and Analysis of 'The Family Structure of Japanese Society' by Takayoshi Kawashima" (1953).

alism (like Hiroki's fighting or the American child's refusal to pick up his toys) are abhorred, displays of individual talent or achievement that follow a clearly defined structure and stay within socially defined boundaries are considered pro- rather than antisocial. For example, children with musical talent are routinely presented as featured performers in Chinese preschool productions. Young children with special potential for success in academics, the arts, or sports are enrolled in "children's palaces" to cultivate their gifts. The Chinese understanding of groupism does not preclude such displays of competition or such open acknowledgment of differential ability as long as individual strivings follow socially approved channels and are clearly directed to serve the greater public good. It is selfishness, not competition or the acknowledgment of differential abilities, that poses a threat to the collective. As Kessen describes, it is fine for talented children to perform solo songs and dances for a visiting group as long as the soloists know, and show by their demeanor that they know, that they have been "selected for the performance to do a service to their school, not to bring attention to themselves. The children who had leads were also asked to undertake self-criticism to make sure that they were not taking the performance as an occasion for admiration of self" (Kessen, 1975, p. 91).

When the staff of Dong-feng speak of the importance of the group, the collective, and the social, they have in mind not only teaching children to play well with their classmates but also teaching them to feel a connection to something much larger—their nation. Chinese preschool teachers hope to instill in children less an identity with their class or school (as in Japan) than an identity as citizens, as cadres of the People's Republic. Thus in survey responses to our question, "What are the most important reasons for a society to have preschools?" twice as many Japanese respondents as Chinese (91 versus 44 percent) answered, "to give children experience being a member of a group," whereas far more Chinese than Japanese (30 versus 18 percent) answered "to start children on the road toward being good citizens." As Principal Hua explained:

> The work we do here is very important, more important than just caring for children while their parents work. We are not baby-sitters —we are educators. The most important lessons we teach children, in addition to numbers and reading and writing, are moral lessons. We teach children how to treat others, how to be friends, how to be citizens, concerned for others, rather than selfish. Our job here is to produce the next generation of Chinese citizens and leaders. Children are our precious seedlings and we have been entrusted with the important responsibility of making sure they grow and flower. We stress to the children a love of China, a love of socialism, and a feeling of patriotism to prepare them to fulfill their responsibilities to our country when they become adults.

This is the official Chinese party line on civic and moral education in the preschool, a point of view publicly endorsed by most Chinese. Unofficial, private beliefs are, of course, much more difficult to ascertain. But we have no reason to doubt that far more Chinese than Japanese or Americans believe wholeheartedly in the importance of teaching children to be patriotic, civic-minded, and group-oriented.

How Typical Is Dong-feng?

Clearly, parents, teachers, and administrators of China's more than 170,000 preschools do not share one common understanding of how best to educate and socialize young children. In contrast to the American system, however, where there is great variation in preschool rules and regulations from state to state, in China (as in Japan) there are national preschool standards and practices and a national curriculum, published each year in the handbook *Yoer Dagang* (*Guidelines for Kindergarten*). This means, in theory, that school hours, activities, and pedagogy are consistent across China. We did find great similarity in the model preschools we were shown from Inner Mongolia in the extreme north through Shanghai, the most cosmopolitan city of central China, to Guilin, a tourist town in the southwest. Nevertheless, the pedagogical and curricular directives put out each year for preschools by the government in Beijing have failed to eliminate significant regional, economic, and ethnic variations in quality and approach.

In China, as in Japan and the United States, there are private as well as official points of view, rural as well as urban perspectives, traditional as well as progressive schools of thought. Having described one Chinese preschool, we must now ask, in what ways is it typical and atypical? Having presented straightforward explanations of Chinese preschool pedagogy, we must now do some unexplaining. Having offered a chorus of teachers, administrators, parents, and government officials describing and supporting Dong-feng's approach to preschool education, it is time to introduce some discordant voices.

Kindergartens and Nurseries

In China, as in Japan, the distinction between nurseries (*tuo-er-so*) and kindergartens (*yo-er-yuan*) is very clear. Nurseries, which admit children from two months to three years of age, operate under the authority of the Ministry of Public Health with the official mission of "protecting [*bao*] and teaching [*jiao*] young children and laying the foundation for a generation of physically healthy and strong, morally good and intellectually sound citizens." Kindergartens, which serve children from three to six years old, are educational institutions intended to prepare children academically and socially for primary school. Unlike the Japanese yōchien and hoikuen and the American nursery school and day-care center, the Chinese kindergarten and nursery, at least in theory, are not in competition: their missions are distinct and they sequentially serve children of different ages. Their staffing patterns also differ: nurseries are staffed chiefly by *bao-mu* (nurses), whereas kindergartens employ *jiao-yang-yuan* (head teachers) and *bao-yu-yuan* (child-care workers).

In reality, however, the functions of these two institutions overlap. Many small kindergartens, especially in rural areas, serve less as educational institutions than as baby-sitting services. And kindergartens that, like Dong-feng, have boarding programs function as educational institutions during the day but as nurseries at night. In both urban and rural areas there are boarding kindergartens and nurseries as well as day programs and programs that, like Dong-feng, are mixed. There are preschools run by factories, communes, districts, municipalities, universities, political groups, and, increasingly, by individual entrepreneurs (Press, 1987).

Further complicating the picture are preschools that are neither kindergarten nor nursery but instead *bao-yu-yuan* (protection and child-raising institutions; the characters used are the same as those of the Japanese *hoikuen*). Bao-yu-yuan like "The Fourth Bao-yu-yuan of the Third People's Military Division" or "The Bao-yu-yuan of the Guangzhou Provincial Government" were created during the revolutionary period as child-care institutions to serve the families of soldiers. Many of them remain in operation thirty-five years later, providing day boarding programs for children of government workers and military dependents.

Although, as we shall see, Dong-feng in some important respects is very unlike model preschools in Beijing, Shanghai, and other sophisticated urban centers, the schedule on the day we videotaped there is very close to the one recommended in the government handbook:

6:30	Wake-up for boarders
7:00	Morning exercise for boarders
7:45	Breakfast for boarders and day students who arrive early
8:15	(Tuesday-Thursday): Group exercise for day students
	Monday: health check
8:30	Morning greetings in classrooms
8:45	First classroom sessions. For the upper grades (five- and six-year-olds) there will be two forty-minute instructional sessions each day; for the middle grades (four- and five-year-olds) there will be two twenty-five-minute instructional sessions; for lower grades (three-year-olds) there will be one fifteen-minute instructional session each day.
10:00	Break (bathroom)
10:30	Outdoor games and play
11:45	Lunch
12:15	Nap
3:00	Snack
3:30	Group games, singing, and dancing
4:15	Play
5:30	Dinner
6–6:30	Day students go home
6:30	Boarders watch television or movies or play freely
8:00	Bedtime for boarders

On the day we taped at Dong-feng extra structured learning sessions were added in the morning and afternoon to impress the foreign visitors.

Teachers: Trained and Untrained

Quality among China's 170,000 preschools varies greatly. Differences in staff educational level and years of training provide the clearest objective measure of these variations. In a university-run preschool we visited in Beijing, which had a very progressive curriculum, all the teachers had at least two years of training in preschool education beyond high school. In a provincial capital in the southwest, we visited schools run by a steel company for ten thousand children of employees. This chain of schools provided little more than centralized baby-sitting. Of the sixteen hundred staff members, only two hundred had education beyond intermediate school. In a village in the countryside we visited a preschool that was just a dirt-floored shed, where thirty children were being cared for by two illiterate older women. China is a huge country: it is a long way, economically and culturally as well as geographically, from Beijing to capital cities in the countryside and from rural capitals to hamlets and villages (Parish and Whyte, 1978).

A comparison of statistics for urban and rural districts of the greater Beijing area is instructive. In 1983, 77.4 percent of preschool-aged children in urban Beijing attended preschool as contrasted with only 34.2 percent of the children in Beijing's rural districts. There was an average of 22.7 students per class in urban preschools, whereas rural schools averaged 35.2 children per class. In the rural districts there were twice as many preschools as there were preschool administrators, suggesting that many such schools are run by a single teacher who is not qualified to use the official title of "director" (*yuan-zhang*). Among qualified directors of rural preschools, only 2.5 percent had a college degree in preschool education; 12.4 percent were graduates of normal high schools with a major in preschool education; others had no more than a junior high school education.

National statistics reveal a similar pattern of large differences among city, town, and rural preschools in student/teacher ratios and years of teacher training (see table 3.1). In 1985, preschools in cities averaged 22 students per teacher, as compared to 24/1 in county seats and country towns and 30/1 in rural areas. When other staff (administrators, nurses, teacher aides, custodial workers) are included, the differences are even greater, with ratios of 9.6 children to each staff member in cities, 17/1 in towns, and 29/1 in hamlets (SEC, 1986).

There is a severe shortage of teacher-training programs in China. Ideally, preschool teachers receive their training in normal high schools,

Table 3.1   Student/Teacher and Student/Staff Ratios by Locality for Chinese Preschools (1985)

Children Enrolled in Preschools (in millions)				Students per Teacher			Students per Total Staff		
TOTAL	URBAN	TOWN	RURAL	URBAN	TOWN	RURAL	URBAN	TOWN	RURAL
14.7	3.3	2.2	9.2	22.1	23.5	30.2	9.6	17.1	28.5

where they take courses in child psychology, children's hygiene, curriculum, and pedagogy. But there are not nearly enough normal high schools offering training in preschool education to fill the need for teachers (Press, 1987). As of 1982, only thirty-three normal high schools in the whole country specialized in preschool education. The rate of growth of these secondary school programs is slowed by a shortage of university programs offering training for prospective teachers of preschool education. To compensate for the shortage, some normal colleges offer correspondence, evening, and radio courses and run teacher-training workshops. But these efforts make only a small dent in such a large problem.

To explain China's deficiencies in preschool teacher training, we need to look back to the educational policies of the 1950s, when China emphasized primary school education for everyone over secondary education for the few (Hawkins, 1983). This helps explain why most older teachers, especially in the countryside, have only a junior high school education. But to fully appreciate the staffing problems of preschools in today's China we need to look to later Chinese history, especially to the Cultural Revolution, with its legacy of radical antiintellectualism. Many older administrators and teachers (including Principal Hua and Ms. Xiang of Dong-feng) are inadequately trained, poorly educated antiintellectuals who rose professionally during the era of revolutionary fervor. Young teachers (like Ms. Wang of Dong-feng) are often well-trained graduates of preschool training programs run by liberal-minded professors who regained their university positions in the post–Cultural Revolution period.

The Chinese Preschool in Historical Context

To understand the battle currently being waged in China between inward-looking, hard-line proletarian socialists and outward-looking progressive revisionists over preschool pedagogy and other social issues, we need to place contemporary preschool politics and ideology in a historical context. An ongoing opposition between old and new, between extremists and moderates, between learning from others and purifying from within is commonplace in the history of Chinese preschools. But what is defined as old or new, pure or impure, extreme or moderate, shifts with the flow of time.

Many different histories can be told of Chinese preschool. The history we present is more or less consistent with the point of view currently in official favor. According to this view, before 1949 the very few preschools in China were private and expensive and thus served only the very rich. Children attended kindergarten with their nannies. They spent only half-days in school, singing, dancing, and playing games.

The Communist Revolution in 1949 brought many changes to China, including (in theory) women's equality. As women joined their male comrades in the task of constructing a socialist society, the need for institutional child care became clear. Kindergartens and nurseries were established to meet the needs of this first generation of working parents.

The postrevolutionary period (1949–1957) is often viewed in China as a golden era of socialist transformation of important institutions, including preschools. The early 1950s saw the rise of the first generation of socialist preschool educators who combined "proper ideology with impressive educational qualifications." This cohort established a firm foundation for the future of Chinese preschool education by publishing in 1952 the first set of official kindergarten guidelines and by beginning a tradition of government-sponsored workshops for preschool training in 1954.

At the 1954 workshop, preschool teachers and nurses from Beijing and Tienjing came together to exchange ideas and experiences. Soon similar meetings were held in other cities. These "meetings to share experiences" established a tradition for preschool teacher training that has lasted to the present day. In 1956 the Ministry of Public Welfare ordered principals of model kindergartens to serve as volunteer leaders, who would train others to be good preschool teachers. In the same year the ministry brought "theoretical workers" (professors) and "practical workers" (preschool teachers and principals) together to draft *The Guidebook of Kindergarten Education*, which was distributed to schools across China. This golden period for preschool education reached its zenith in 1957 with the publication of *Rules for Kindergarten Curriculum* and the inaugural issue of the journal *Xue Qian Jiao Yu* (*Preschool Education*) under the editorial direction of the Ministry of Public Health, Beijing Normal University's education research group, and the Chinese Youth and Children's Publisher.

This first generation of postrevolutionary Chinese preschool experts was composed of self-consciously radical individuals, committed to transforming the social institutions, including preschools, that predated the revolution. As progressives, they believed in the importance of "furthering the revolution by learning from advanced countries"—which in the 1950s meant learning from the Soviet Union.

Soviet influence in Chinese society was profound during this period. Russian engineers came first, and technical advisers followed, some of whom helped the Chinese transform their higher education system along Soviet lines, with universities specializing in one or two specific vocational areas. The colleges and universities of education and nursing which would train the first cohort of preschool staff were established under Soviet influence. In this era, Chinese preschool pedagogy also became heavily influenced by Pavlovian behaviorism, with its environmentalist bias and emphasis on conditioning children's behavior.

From 1958 to 1960 there was a thirtyfold increase in the number of kindergartens. This explosive growth of preschools mirrored the rapid development of the rural economy during "the great leap forward." Chinese social historians now believe that the great leap was a result of "blind development" which failed to reflect true economic and social conditions. In the early 1960s the great leap forward collapsed in a heap of economic and agriculture failure. With the collapse of the rural economy, newly established rural preschools closed as fast as they had opened, and by 1962 the number of kindergartens had fallen to 1957 levels.

From 1966 to 1976, during the Cultural Revolution, preschool education was on the defensive. Ideological purism and proletarian antiintellectualism swept the country, putting an end to teacher training, relocating university professors to rural work, and proclaiming kindergartens and other schools to be bourgeois, revisionist institutions. During this era preschools were believed to be elitist because they nurtured children instead of toughening them and because they prepared children for further education rather than for productive labor. Radicals supported their accusation that preschools were breeding grounds for the bourgeoisie run by decadent revisionists by citing such passages from the 1956 kindergarten guidelines as "Children should be given a comfortable environment, good food, and ample time for playing and sleeping."

During the period of the Cultural Revolution the kindergartens and nurseries that remained opened were renamed Dong Fang Hong (The East Is Red) or Dong-feng (East Wind). The old administrators were replaced with ideologically correct party members, who usually lacked formal training in preschool education and child development. Teachers who were not simply dismissed or sent to labor in the countryside were demoted to *bao-yu-yuan,* which in this case meant janitor/nurse/teacher's aide. Many toys, books, and teacher-training manuals were destroyed.

Not all city dwellers were sent to the country, however. Many teachers and white-collar workers simply stayed home during much of the Cultural Revolution. Lacking the correct ideology, they were deemed unfit for work and were expected to attend meetings and shout slogans until they reha-bilitated themselves. Since they were at home much of the day, they no longer needed child care. In 1976 the Cultural Revolution came to an end, but it took several more years before most preschools reopened. In 1979 the Ministry of Education called together education officials from Beijing, Shanghai, and Tienjing to draft "New Regulations for Urban Kinder-gartens." This document suggested that "kindergartens should adopt the revolutionary style of the old liberated areas and put revolution above all other needs and priorities." The phrase "old liberated areas" refers to pockets of the country controlled by communist cadres before the revo-lution of 1949. The import of this message was to urge municipalities to begin in earnest the task of reestablishing the preschools closed during the Cultural Revolution. But this time, in contrast to the antiintellectual radical aims of the Cultural Revolution, the goal was to return to the more authentically revolutionary tradition of 1949, which viewed education as well as work as an important tool of proletarian struggle.

At the 1979 national meeting in Beijing officials from the ministries of Education and Public Health, the National Bureau of Labor, the National Labor Union, and the National Women's Association gathered to answer the call of the Four Modernizations Movement and to "address the need of government cadres as well as the masses to promote the quality and quan-tity of nurseries and kindergartens." Significantly, Deputy Premier Gang Yi addressed the delegates, calling for efforts to "elevate the political posi-tion of nurses and teachers." His presence along with his statement meant that the previously denounced and harshly treated preschool professionals were now once again to be accepted as respected members of society.

Thus, by the early 1980s the intensely inward-looking quest for ideo-logical purity of the Cultural Revolution had given way once more to an era of searching for new ideas from more advanced countries. But the Soviet Union was no longer considered an appropriate model. By the beginning of the 1980s the phrase "advanced countries" had come to mean the United States and Japan. Many academicians who had been discredited and relo-cated to the countryside during the Cultural Revolution returned to their positions in universities and began the work of rebuilding training pro-grams for preschool teachers and an apparatus for scholarly research in child development and early child education. Journals were reestablished and academic meetings held for the first time in over fifteen years (Steven-son et al., 1981). Scholars traveled abroad to Japan and especially the United States in an attempt to catch up with educational developments and make up for the lost years. Kindergartens were reopened, but staffing remains a problem to this day. A decade's worth of trained preschool teachers and teacher trainers was lost.

Many of the untrained, uncredentialed teachers and administrators who gained their positions on the basis of their political correctness and connections during the Cultural Revolution still hold those jobs today. Ten years after the end of the Cultural Revolution, many Chinese provinces are just getting back to the numbers of preschools they had twenty years ago. Some areas of the country still have no preschools, large cities have severe shortages of preschool slots, and even in Beijing demand outstrips supply and individual entrepreneurs are being asked to open preschool programs to fill the gap (Press, 1987). If many Chinese preschools (including Dong-feng) look backward to child-development experts in Tokyo, Chicago, and Beijing, it is partly because the effects of the Cultural Revolution on Chinese preschool theory and practice are still being felt keenly, especially in the countryside.

Revolutionaries and Intellectuals

From year to year different Chinese factions gain control of the political and ideological high ground. Changing political, social, and economic realities powerfully affect Chinese preschool pedagogy as well as the kinds of statements Chinese parents, teachers, administrators, government leaders, and other citizens are willing to make publicly about their preschools. What Chinese feel is wise or proper to say to foreign guests changes with the prevailing political mood. Fortunately, the political mood at the time of our study permitted the expression of a variety of points of view.

Some Chinese who watched our Dong-feng tape were highly critical of what they perceived to be an antiquated, joyless, unimaginative approach to preschool education. These informants used the words *old* and *dead* to refer to Dong-feng—old in the sense of old-fashioned, an unfortunate carryover from an era better forgotten, dead in the sense of petrified, rigid, inflexible, nonvital, like wood from a tree chopped down long ago.

Our informants from Beijing, Shanghai, and Guangzhou on the average were better educated and more sophisticated than those from southwest China. Several of them had traveled overseas, where they had visited preschools. Even those who had not had the chance to go abroad enjoyed opportunities to "learn from advanced countries." For example, the preschool teachers and administrators we spoke with in Shanghai frequently host visiting Americans and talk with them about preschool pedagogy. Our informants in Beijing have many opportunities to attend talks by researchers returning from abroad. In general, in large urban areas, and especially in cosmopolitan centers such as Beijing, Shanghai, and Guangzhou, there is much more penetration of Western ideas and more "progressive" thinking about preschools and other social issues than there is in rural areas or cities in more remote regions of the country.

Many of those from Beijing, Shanghai, and Guangzhou took issue with our choice of Dong-feng as a representative Chinese preschool. Having been exposed to foreign perspectives, they tended to see Dong-feng through critical foreign eyes:

> Why did you choose to film in such a remote, old-fashioned area? You should have filmed here in Beijing if you wanted to show Americans an example of a good Chinese kindergarten. The countryside is very backward. Even provincial capitals are way behind the times. You're going to show people in Japan and the United States this tape, right? Your foreign audiences will think we are very primitive. Whose idea was it for you to film in such a remote spot?

Many of our Chinese respondents were embarrassed by what they felt to be the inadequacy of Dong-feng's equipment in contrast to the much more lavishly equipped St. Timothy's and Komatsudani. Although they praised Dong-feng for its spacious grounds and large classrooms, college professors of preschool education were critical of Dong-feng's primitive toilet and washing facilities and also of the school's lack of toys, art supplies, and educational materials.[*]

Most of our Chinese informants were envious of Komatsudani's and St. Timothy's wealth of toys, books, and learning aids. They worried that shortages of these materials in their preschools put Chinese children at a competitive disadvantage in cognitive development: "How can we hope to catch up with advanced countries when our schools are so poorly equipped? Children in America have a big advantage in learning with all the educational games and art supplies and other educational materials they have in their schools."

On the other hand, a few were concerned about the cost of so many material goods and the possibility that such an abundance might spoil children. A kindergarten administrator in Beijing told us: "We are a socialist society. Perhaps American children need lots of material things in their kindergartens because they are preparing for life in a bourgeois society. Perhaps Chinese children need fewer things because they are preparing to live in a society where material possessions are less important."

Those Chinese education professionals who were most critical of Dong-feng felt that there was too much emphasis on regimentation and control,

---

[*]For a description of Chinese preschool physical plants and materials, see Kessen (1975, pp. 74–82).

resulting in a loss of liveliness in the children. A professor of preschool education, recently returned from a trip to the United States, said of Dong-feng: "The control is deadly rigid [*guan de tai si*]. The children in your tape of the American kindergarten are so much more lively. They have so many free activities [*ziyou huodong*] compared to Chinese children." Chinese parents who watched our tapes tended to be most critical of the Dong-feng teachers' lack of warmth. One mother commented: "I think teachers should give children more loving care. The younger teacher, the assistant, looked okay, but the older teacher didn't look to me as though she likes children enough. She seemed too disinterested, as if she just considers what she is doing a job."

The most progressive (in Japanese and Western terms) of our informants questioned the wisdom of emphasizing guan in kindergarten. One administrator called regimentation in preschool "a legacy of China's feudal past." Discussions of guan have begun to appear in Chinese magazines and education journals, suggesting that a shift in official views on preschool discipline and order has started. In an article in the *People's Daily* a director of a model kindergarten in Guangtong suggests:

> Children should be given more freedom. Guan must be done in a reasonable way. It must be orderly but flexible, governing but not rigid, lively but not chaotic. . . . For example, when a child wants to go to the toilet or to have a drink, he or she should be allowed to go at any time, provided the child obtains the teacher's permission first. At night a child should be allowed to visit freely with a friend and to play before going to bed. . . . With regard to allowing children to talk during mealtimes, of course this has never been allowed in the past, but in our kindergarten we will try in the future to loosen things up a bit, allowing children to whisper a bit during meals. Loosening things up a bit is good for teachers as well as children. In the past, our teachers had their mouths and hands going nonstop [trying to control children's behavior]. Teachers have become more relaxed, the children are happier, and there appears to be less tension and conflict between students and teachers.

In a 1985 issue of the journal *Yoer Jiaoyu* (*Preschool Education*), a Mr. Zhang writes:

> Teachers should not try to produce little adults who are stiff and non-creative. . . . In the kindergarten, we too often see children "pinned" in their room and forced to sit and listen in silence. Even during recess, one feels the deadly atmosphere. I don't think this is a sign that a kindergarten is well governed. On the contrary, I would call this abnormal.

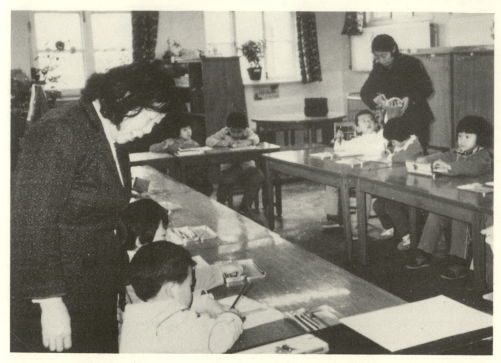

A preschool in Beijing

The fact that Principal Wang and Mr. Zhang felt the need in 1985 to write their reform-minded articles testifies to the conservatism that remains the norm in most Chinese preschools more than a decade after the end of the Cultural Revolution. Most of the Chinese who objected to our choice of Dong-feng as a representative Chinese preschool were unhappy not because Dong-feng is atypical but because it is all too typical, in their minds, of the kind of plodding mediocrity they are trying to leave behind in preschool education. A university professor in Beijing complained to us that Dong-feng is old-fashioned in making children sit at desks: "In most Chinese preschools the seating arrangements are much better. Children sit around large tables, facilitating group discussion, just like your Japanese and American classrooms." But one of her colleagues disagreed with this generalization: "You have not been to enough preschools in the countryside or you would not say that. The Dong-feng type of program, which treats preschool children like primary school pupils, is very common. To my knowledge, this school is much better than most you would find in provincial cities." A third professor added, "We have much work to do in liberalizing our preschool education to make up for the years we lost."

We saw several types of preschool classroom arrangements in China. Even in Beijing we visited preschools where children are required to sit several times each day in the traditional Chinese student posture, at attention with their arms behind their backs. Some preschool administrators in urban as well as rural China with little formal training in early child education are proud that their programs appear so regimented and schoollike. But educators in large cities who have been exposed to Western ideas see their preschools through Western eyes and thus are critical. In general, old-fashioned hard-liners praised Dong-feng for its "seriousness in tending to children," for its order, and for its promotion of the spirit of collectivity. Reform-minded liberals criticized Dong-feng for overemphasizing these values at the expense of creativity and individuality.

Whatever their view of the proper balance of freedom and order, virtually all our informants, urban and rural, young and old, parents and teachers, revisionists and reactionaries, found the levels of freedom at St. Timothy's and especially at Komatsudani extreme. Although praising the students' energy, they were disturbed by the chaos they saw in our tapes of both foreign schools.

Many Chinese would like their preschools to be livelier than Dong-feng, the teachers more imaginative, mealtimes less somber, the children more spontaneous in their play. But even the most ardently Western-oriented would-be preschool reformers were concerned about spoiling and agreed that it is appropriate and important for preschools to correct the errors of parental overindulgence of single children. Many of those who campaign enthusiastically for more flexibility and less regimentation in Chinese preschools are less interested in freedom for its own sake than in promoting more effective preschool pedagogy. That is, they are not seeking an alternative to collectivism, order, or socialism but see in the freedom and creativity of Japanese and American classrooms the possibility for a more active, child-centered, effective mode of teaching. In the words of Zhou Li Jun, a preschool education professor:

> There are many wonderful things we can learn from Japan and the United States about preschools. The long lost years [of the Cultural Revolution] left us far behind these advanced countries. We must make many changes, many improvements. But China is a very different kind of society than the United States and Japan. And China is a different culture. We can learn much from Japan and the United States about preschools and our schools need to change and will

change, but they will not, they should not, become just like Japanese and American schools. That would not be right for us. That would not be good.

Culture or Ideology?

When we showed our videotape of Dong-feng to audiences in Japan and the United States and when the three of us analyzed our China data, this question inevitably arose: are the distinctive features of Chinese preschools shown in our tapes—the focus on order and control, the academic emphasis, the earnestness and perseverance of teachers and students, the patriotic content of the curriculum, the attention given to health and hygiene, and the group ethos—a reflection of five thousand years of Chinese culture or thirty-five years of Chinese communism? The answer, of course, is both. Just as the writings of Chairman Mao are quintessentially both Marxist and Chinese (Solomon, 1971), so are China's preschools the product of a fusion of political ideology and cultural tradition.

One way to begin disentangling the influence of Chinese culture from the influence of Chinese communist ideology would be to compare preschools in mainland China to preschools in Taiwan, Hong Kong, and other Chinese communities (Tseng and Wu, 1985). A preliminary comparison suggests that for better or worse neither the Chinese Revolution of 1949 nor the Cultural Revolution succeeded in totally purging the socialist People's Republic of China of cultural traditions for rearing and educating children characteristic of nonsocialist Chinese societies.

Preschools in Taiwan, which was colonized by the Japanese for over fifty years and which now, like Japan, is a capitalist, technological society, look like a cross between mainland Chinese and Japanese preschools. The knickered uniforms with Peter Pan collars and straw hats worn by private school students, the perky school buses, the cheery piped-in music and announcements, the Froebel-influenced music/movement/crafts/play curriculum—these are all features that preschools in Taiwan and Japan share. In Taipei, as in Tokyo, upscale nursery schools offer English conversation, ballet, and swimming to children of parents willing to pay a premium to get their offspring off on the right foot. But other features of the Taiwanese preschool are distinctly non-Japanese and very like mainland Chinese preschools, suggesting the resilience of Chinese culture in adapting to dramatically changing economic, political, and social environments.

Dong-feng is very like many Taiwanese preschools we have visited in its emphasis on maintaining order and correcting the spoiling caused by parental overindulgence. These paired concerns can be found in Chinese culture going back well before the birth of the People's Republic (Wu, 1966, 1981). Chinese child-raising manuals from the prewar era and earlier emphasize the dangers of tai jiao, of spoiling and pampering. In his 1918 critique of the Confucian tradition, Lu Xun, a writer and social critic still greatly esteemed in China, warned that Chinese parents tend to err by being either too soft or too hard. "They overemphasize either *ren* (indulgence), or *jin* (prohibition), nearly always failing to strike a balance in between" (Lu, 1956).

A comparison of preschools on the Chinese mainland and in Taiwan suggests that the regimentation we saw at Dong-feng does not necessarily represent an example of the workings of communist authoritarianism. Although some Chinese see an emphasis on order and regimentation as old-fashioned and harmful to children, many in Taiwan as well as on the mainland believe that order and regimentation are essential to healthy child development. Chinese preschools such as Dong-feng are regimented both because regimentation is consistent with Maoist ideology and also because fifty years after Lu Xun warned against the Chinese cultural propensity to be too strict with their children, most Chinese continue to subscribe to the Confucian belief in the value of regimentation and restraint (*zhi*) for children (Wu, 1966, 1985, 1988; King and Bond, 1985; Ho, 1986).

The Chinese preschool's emphasis on academic achievement, like the emphasis on order, is also both communist and Chinese (Tseng and Wu, 1985). During the Cultural Revolution Confucian traditions of academic achievement clashed dramatically with the Maoist revolt against academic elitism and intellectual social irresponsibility. This revolt was as much a reaction against a Soviet-style credentialized elitism as against an American-style capitalism. In the mid-1980s Chinese preschool teachers and teacher trainers are working to reassemble a preschool curriculum and pedagogy that combine the traditional Chinese interest in academic achievement with a socialist concern for equality and a communist respect for productive labor. The challenge is to open up avenues of academic achievement once available only to the wealthy and the privileged to the widest segments of society and thereby facilitate China's modernization without excessively restratifying society.

Perseverance (*rennai*) is another feature of the Chinese preschool that is equal parts Chinese culture and communist ideology. The emphasis Chinese place on perseverance is apparent in the typical length of a Chinese preschool learning activity. In American preschools children are rarely expected or encouraged to stick to one task for longer than twenty minutes. In China, in contrast, preschoolers are taught to sit still and concentrate on one task for forty minutes or more. Dong-feng's approach to block play —of building exactly to specifications and then rebuilding—is another example of encouraging perseverance.

The value of perseverance in Chinese culture is dramatized for children in the ancient tale *Yugong Yishan* (The Foolish Old Man Who Moved a Mountain). Chinese children today, as 50 years ago and perhaps 250 years ago, all know the story of the old man who, despite his neighbors' ridicule, each day with his sons dug away at a mountain separating his village from the nearby town. In response to his jeerers the old man would say, "I will dig until I die and then my sons and grandsons and their sons and grandsons will carry on. The mountain can grow no higher, and with every shovelful we make it that much lower." This story, though at heart Confucian, was often quoted by Chairman Mao in his speeches and writings to illustrate his belief in the power of persistence and the ability of ordinary people working collectively to overcome any obstacle and transform their environment. The only change teachers have had to make in this old parable in order to instruct a new generation of preschoolers is to add female progeny to the list of mountain movers.

The great attention to children eating well (finishing all the food they are served) and properly (not talking while they eat) that we saw at Dong-feng reflects a combination of the communist belief that property, including one's food, is not something private that an individual is free to waste and the traditional Chinese concern (some would say obsession) with eating (Solomon, 1971, pp. 44–48).

Spoiling, a traditional Chinese concern, has taken on a special salience in the People's Republic during the era of the single-child family (Wu, 1983, 1985). There is no good scientific evidence that single children are in fact more spoiled than children with siblings (Clausen and Clausen, 1973; Thompson, 1974; Poston and Yu, 1984), but in China as in many other cultures this is widely believed to be the case (Arnold and Fawcett, 1975, p. 153). An increase in spoiling is viewed by most Chinese as an unfortunate but inevitable side effect of population control. China's long-range struggle to correct the indulgence and authoritarianism that Lu Xun identified as characteristic weaknesses of Chinese parenting has had to take a back seat to confronting the more immediate threat of overpopulation.

The single-child policy has also complicated Chinese society's attempts to eradicate the traditional parental preference for boys over girls (Wolf and Witke, 1975; Smedley, 1976). Sons are seen as economic assets; daughters, as liabilities ("Raising a daughter is like fattening a duck for another man's table"). Sons also are preferred as a source of security in old age and as the key to keeping the family name and lineage alive (M. Freedman, 1970; Pasternak, 1985; Wolf, 1985). The gains Chinese society has made since the revolution in reducing the power of patriarchy, raising the status of women, and stamping out female infanticide are threatened by the single-child policy (Korbin, 1981). Educating people to treat their daughters as well as their sons is one thing. Getting people to accept the fact that there is a 50 percent chance they will never have a son is quite another.

The ongoing battle against a powerful cultural tradition of misogyny and patrilineality is being fought on several fronts, including in preschools, where children are taught that "girls are treasures" and "girls are just as good as boys." The fact that this still must be said is an indication of the tenacity of the problem. Significant strides have been made in urban China, but in rural areas the desire to have at least one son has proven to be very difficult to dislodge.

Chinese culture and communist ideology complement each other in promoting an ethos of collectivity and group harmony in the preschool classroom. The collective behaviors that bothered many American viewers of our tape of Dong-feng* are the result of a union of traditional Chinese groupism with the communist ideology of collectivism. As one of our interpreters said to us, "We're better than the Soviets at being good communists. We've had thousands of years of practice! Doing things collectively comes naturally to us."

Naturally or not, it is in preschools that most Chinese children first learn to integrate traditional Chinese culture with an ever-evolving communist ideology. This is an experiment that is still in progress. For this first cohort of single children, for their parents and teachers, and for the society as a whole, it is indeed an exciting and brave new world.

*Pseudonyms have been used in this chapter for the names of teachers and schools.

Chapter Four

St. Timothy's:
An American Preschool

St. Timothy's Child Center operates a set of programs including full-day and half-day care for children two through five years old, a kindergarten for five- and six-year-olds, and after-school care for elementary school children. The center, a nonprofit institution affiliated with St. Timothy's Episcopal Church of Honolulu, is located on the church grounds in a neighborhood of mixed single-family homes, condominiums, and shopping centers. The preschool program, which serves ninety-five children, is housed in five large classrooms bordering a central playground.

A Day at St. Timothy's

On the day we are videotaping, Linda Rios and Pat McNair, two of St. Timothy's ten teachers, arrive a few minutes after 7:00 A.M. to open the school. Children begin to arrive soon after. At 7:30 a compact car pulls into the parking lot and a father and his three-year-old son get out and walk hand in hand through the gate of the school, across the playground, and into one of the classrooms. While Steve Cooper signs in on the attendance sheet, his son, Mark, puts his He-Man lunch box away in his cubby. Steve says to Mark, "What do you want to do first today? How about the sandbox? No? Well, let's go see what Pat is doing, then. Here you go, Mark; you can help Pat feed Pinky and clean his cage." Pat says, "Yeah, come on, Marky. We could use your help." Steve gives Mark a pat on the back and says, "Have a good day, Champ," but Mark spins around and grabs his father's arm:

126

Mark: You said you'd stay a little while.

Steve: I have stayed a little while already. I can't stay long today, Mark. I've got to get to work. I'll stay just a minute, and then I have to go.

Mark: How long's a minute? Stay millions of minutes.

Steve: I'm sorry. I've got to go.

Mark (grabbing his father's leg): No. Stay.

Steve (prying Mark's arms off his leg): I can only stay one minute more.

Pat (picking up Mark in her arms): Let's walk your father to the gate and say good-bye there. Come on, Mark. We'll stand at the gate and wave good-bye to your dad.

Steve: See you later, Buddy. Thanks, Pat.

Mark (beginning to cry): Don't go, Daddy.

Steve: You'll be okay, Mark. I've got to go. Don't cry.

Pat: Say good-bye to your daddy. Let's see how long we can see his car.

With a final wave, Steve gets into his car and drives off. As soon as the car is out of sight, Mark stops crying. Pat says, "Now will you help me feed Pinky? I've got some lettuce you can give him." Mark and Pat walk hand in hand over to Pinky's cage, Pat talking animatedly about how Pinky should be fed.

By 7:45, thirty children and four more teachers have arrived. Two teachers supervise the playground while the others prepare their classrooms for the day. Some mothers and fathers dropping off their children stop to chat with other parents or one of the teachers. A few parents stay as long as thirty minutes, chatting or playing with children in one of the classrooms or on the playground. By 8:30 all the staff and most of the children have arrived. At St. Timothy's, from arrival until 9:00 A.M. is a free-play period when children can play outside, in the sandbox, on the tricycles, or on the climbing apparatus, or inside, with blocks, paper, crayons, and scissors, or books and puzzles.

At 9:00 A.M. the school day formally begins. Cheryl Takashige calls the children in her class to come inside and sit in a circle on the rug in the middle of the room. Once the eighteen four-year-olds are seated, Cheryl and her assistant teacher, Linda Rios, join the group and say good morning to each of the children. Linda asks, "Does anyone know what day it is today?" Several children call out the right answer. "Does anyone know the date?" Again, several children call out "Monday." Linda says, "Monday is the day, not the date. The date is March 18, 1985."

Cheryl then asks if anyone has anything to "show and tell" to the class today. Three hands go up. Cheryl calls on Lance, who, with Cheryl's prompting, relates a weekend family trip to see an active volcano. Next Rose shows the class her newest Care Bear, describing the difficulty she had choosing it over a My Little Pony. Mike proudly exhibits a wooden boat he made with his father at home.

Cheryl then leads the class in an activity involving a felt board and cut-out flannel shapes. Each of the children is called on one at a time to come forward and select a white piece of flannel background. Cheryl explains, "This blue board is the sky and the white shapes are clouds. Put a cloud on the sky and tell us what the cloud looks like."

Lisa (in a whisper): A bird.

Cheryl: Speak louder, Lisa, so everyone can hear you.

Lisa: A bird.

Cheryl: The cloud looks like a bird? [To the class] What do you think? Do you think it looks like a bird? Yes, it does. Good. Thank you, Lisa.

Mike: This is a cloud.

Cheryl: Yes, it's a cloud. What does your cloud look like, Mike?

Mike: Like a cloud.

As Cheryl works her way through the group, Linda prepares a large tray with a book, a paintbrush, a block, a puzzle piece, a toy frying pan, and a small brass ring. While Cheryl puts away the felt and flannel, Linda leads the children in singing a song:

Three little monkeys jumping on the bed.
One fell off and hurt his head.

Mama called the doctor and the doctor said,
"NO MORE MONKEYS JUMPING ON THE BED!"

Two little monkeys jumping on the bed . . .

After finishing the other two verses of the song, Linda holds out the tray and says:

> Look. Here are the [learning] centers for this morning. [Holding up a paintbrush] Who would like to paint? Michelle. Mayumi. Nicole. Okay, you three get your smocks from your cubbies and you can paint. [Holding up a wooden block] Who wants to do this? Mike? Okay, that's one. Stu, that makes two. Billy is three. Mark, we will start with just three in the block corner. You know our rule. When one of the other boys is done, you may go into the block corner. Why don't you choose something else to start playing with? Here's a puzzle piece. You want to start on the puzzles? Okay? [Holding up the toy frying pan] Who wants to start in the house? Lisa, Rose, Derek. Go ahead to the housekeeping corner. Kerry, what do you want to do? The Legos? You're going to work on the radio, Carl? That's fine. Who is going to come over to the book corner to read this book? It's called *Stone Soup*. Okay, come on with me.

In the housekeeping corner, which includes a small table and chairs, a toy stove, sink, refrigerator, and shelves stocked with empty food boxes, plastic pots and pans, and miscellaneous dress-up clothes, Lisa decides that she will be the mother and Rose the auntie. Derek refuses to play the role Lisa assigns him as the baby, opting instead to be the family dog. Lisa and Rose dress up in adult shoes and fancy dresses. Derek crawls around the housekeeping corner on all fours, demanding to be fed. Lisa pretends to serve him dog food while Rose prepares dinner, noisily banging a toy frying pan around on top of the toy stove. In the block corner the boys argue about what to build with the hundred or more wooden blocks available. Mike wants to build a fort, Stu a road for the toy trucks. Billy is neutral. Eventually, Mike and Billy begin to build a fort while Stu makes a long road. Mike says to Billy, "Give me one of those real long blocks." Billy picks up a block from the carpet. Stu screams, "Hey, I'm using that for my road!" Billy hands the block to Mike. Stu yelps and grabs it out of Mike's hand. Mike kicks Stu's road and is about to hit Stu when Cheryl intervenes:

Cheryl: What's going on here?

Stu: Look what he did to my road and he told Billy, "Take my block."

Mike: It's not your stupid block.

Stu: I had it first.

Mike (grabbing for the block): I need it.

Cheryl (separating the boys with her arms): Let's not have any fighting. Mike, can you tell Stu with words what you want instead of grabbing?

Mike: I told him, "I want the block."

Cheryl: And what did he say? Did he tell you why he wouldn't give you the block?

Stu: 'Cuz I had it first. The other day when John was here first you said he was first so today I'm first.

Cheryl: Stu, when Mike took the block from you, how did you feel? Did you tell him that made you angry? Did it make you angry?

Stu: Mad.

Cheryl: Okay, mad. When you felt mad is there something you could have done instead of grabbing the block? Tell me in words. What could you have done?

Stu: I did ask him.

Mike: No, you didn't. You just grabbed it and hurt my . . .

Stu: I did not.

Cheryl: Just a second. One at a time or I can't understand what you're saying. Mike, did you hit Stu when he took the block? You should use words instead of fighting when you're angry. Besides, you're too good friends to be fighting like this. I want you to figure out a way to play together. Why don't you both say you're sorry? Then you can make a fort with a road around it, okay? Look, like this. See, you can put two of these shorter blocks together, Stu. Yeah. That's it.

In the story corner, sitting on a big stuffed pillow in an alcove surrounded by shelves filled with books, Linda reads to Kelly and Suzy, who are leaning against her. Across the room, Pete works at unscrewing parts from an old radio (donated to the school by a parent). Lisa is working intently with some brass rings. Three girls are painting, standing at easels on the porch adjoining the classroom. Richie brings his finished puzzle over to Cheryl in the block corner and holds it out to her.

Cheryl: What did you do? Tell me.

Richie: I made this puzzle.

Cheryl: You made a puzzle with zoo animals. You did very nice work.

Walking toward the center of the room, Cheryl finds a pile of unattended Legos. She looks around the room and, spotting Kerry in a corner with a puzzle, calls in his direction:

Who was playing with these Legos and didn't put them away? Kerry, was it you? No? You didn't play with these Legos? I think you did. Please come here and put them away. Come on, Kerry, you know you are responsible for cleaning up toys you take out. Kerry! Come clean this up right now.

Kerry doesn't budge. He shakes his head and looks down, refusing to make eye contact with Cheryl. Cheryl walks over to him, bends down, and puts her face directly in front of Kerry's:

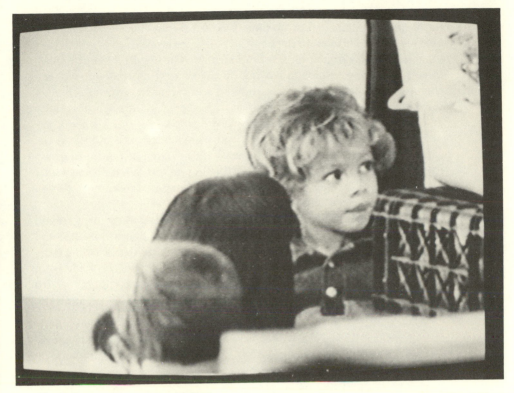

Cheryl tries to make eye contact with Kerry

Kerry, listen to me. Look at me while I'm talking to you. I want you to go over there and clean up the Legos you dumped out before someone steps on them and gets hurt. No? [Holding Kerry's chin in her hand and turning his head toward her] Look at me. Tell me about those Legos. You have nothing to say? Then you can sit over there on the time-out chair and think about it until you are ready to clean up.

Kerry, head down, walks over to the chair and sits with his head in his hands. After a minute or so, Cheryl calls to him, "Are you ready to clean up now? Good. You can get up now and clean up the Legos."

During this forty-five-minute learning-center period, the children shift from activity to activity according to their interests. Cheryl and Linda are busy tieing and untieing smocks, helping children into and out of dress-up clothes, putting new pieces of paper on easels, reading stories, and arbitrating disputes. At 10:15 the period draws to a close with Cheryl flicking the lights to announce clean-up time. Once all the toys have been put away, Linda leads the children to the boys' and girls' bathrooms, after which they run onto the playground for free outdoor play. The children join the two-, three-, and five-year-olds in playing on the swings, on the large wooden climbing apparatus, and in the sandbox, and riding the tricycles. Five of the school's ten teachers and the director, Barbara Culler, monitor activity on the playground while the other teachers prepare for snack time. Children line up for a cup of grape juice and a graham cracker and sit on the grass to eat. The last child to be served stands in front of Linda, who says to her: "Do you want juice, Rhonda? Milk? A cracker? What do you want? Don't just keep shaking your head. How am I supposed to know what you want if you don't tell me?"

Snacks finished, the children return to their classrooms for a second round of learning centers. In addition to the blocks, books, puzzles, and housekeeping corner, this time there are four new activities: washing baby dolls in a small basin, playing with Play-Doh (an ersatz clay made from flour, oil, water, and food coloring), stringing beads, and cooking. With the children sitting in a circle, Cheryl explains about making potato soup:

> What's this? A potato, right? What color is it? Brown. What color is it inside? Right, it's white. Is it hard or soft? Very hard. If you tasted it, would it be crunchy? Yes, but after we cooked it, it would be soft. But now it would be crunchy. Today we are going to use this potato and this onion and these carrots to make potato soup. Everybody can have a turn to help. We have to cut up the potato and the carrots and pour in the milk and stir and stir so it won't burn. We have to be very careful because we will be cutting and using fire.

Working with dull plastic knives under Cheryl's supervision, the children, in shifts of six, laboriously cut up the potatoes and carrots. Cheryl adds the vegetables to a pot and each child takes a turn stirring. Children not cooking work with Play-Doh, wash the "babies," look at books, draw with crayons, or play in the housekeeping or block corners. After about forty-five minutes Cheryl flicks the lights to signal clean-up time, and the children put away their toys and then come to sit in their assigned places in a circle in the middle of the room. Cheryl sits on the floor beside Kerry and puts her arm around his shoulders. Linda leads them in a song:

> One gray elephant went out to play
> He went out on a sunny day
> He had such enormous fun
> He called another elephant: COME!

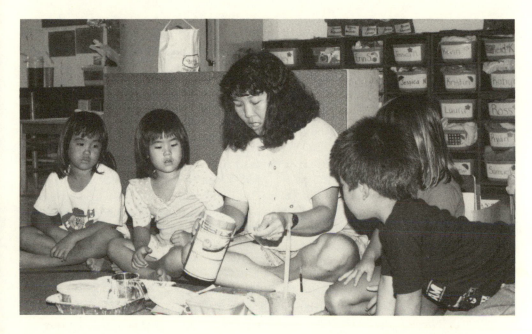

On the word "Come" a child standing in the center of the circle reaches
out for the hand of a child sitting down and pulls him into the middle.
The song continues until all the children are standing and singing. Sitting
down again, the children are served the soup they helped make. As they
eat, Cheryl reminds them of how the soup was made and explains what
makes it nutritious. When the children finish their soup, they throw away
their Styrofoam cups and spoons, grab their lunch boxes (decorated with
cartoon and television characters), and go outside to sit around the low
table to eat lunch. The children talk animatedly while eating. Cheryl and
Linda sit with the children, helping them unscrew thermos bottles and tear
open plastic bags. Cheryl says to Stu, "What's that in your bag? Chips?"
Stu says, "No, not chips, Doritos." Cheryl replies, "Please ask your mother
not to send you to school with that kind of food, okay, Stu? Remind her
about how we feel about junk food, okay? Will you do that for me?"

When the children finish eating they close their lunch boxes and return
them to their cubbies. Mothers arrive to pick up the half-day children,
who go home at 12:30. Mike hands his mother his lunch box. She opens
it and says to Cheryl, "Look at that. He hardly touched his sandwich. He
doesn't eat a thing at school." Mike explains, "I'm saving my sandwich to
eat on the way home."

As Mike and two more children leave with their mothers, the other children play in the playground or feed the rabbits. At 12:45 the teachers announce that it is naptime. The children go to the bathroom to brush their teeth and then return to the classroom, where they unroll the mats they keep in their cubbies and find a spot to stretch out. Cheryl and Linda walk quietly around the room occasionally whispering to children to keep quiet or rubbing the backs of those having trouble falling asleep. By 1:15 all the children are asleep, and the teachers have about an hour to relax and prepare for afternoon activities.

Naptime ends at 2:30. The afternoon schedule is less structured than the morning. Following a snack of fruit and juice, the children play outside with balls, listen to the record player, look at picture books, and draw and cut and paste. From 4:00 on children begin to be picked up by their mothers or fathers. Many of the parents stop to chat with Cheryl, Linda, or Barbara, the school's director, who supervises the playground in the late afternoon.

By 5:20 only three children and two teachers (whose day it is to stay late and close up) are still at St. Timothy's. Cheryl is one of the two teachers, and four-year-old Nicole from her class is one of the three children. At 5:25 Nicole's mother, Sandy, finally arrives. Cheryl calls out, "Nicole, your mom's here," and Nicole runs over to give her mother a hug. After sending Nicole inside to get her lunch box, Sandy engages Cheryl in conversation:

Sandy: Sorry, Cheryl. Am I very late? What time is it, anyway?

Cheryl: No, that's okay, you made it.

Sandy: How'd Nicole do today?

Cheryl: Fine, I think.

Sandy: Did she have any more trouble with Mayumi and Michelle?

Cheryl: I think it's getting a little better. Nicole's playing more with Jessica.

Sandy: Last night she told me that Michelle told her she wouldn't be her friend anymore because she has stupid hair.

Cheryl: You know, what we were discussing the other day, it might really be for the best if Nicole gets out of that Three Musketeers thing for a while and plays more with Jessica and some of the others. I'll keep my eye on it.

Explaining St. Timothy's

We filmed "A Day at St. Timothy's" in March of 1985. In June we returned to show St. Timothy's parents, children, and staff twenty-minute versions of our tapes of their school, Japan's Komatsudani, and China's Dong-feng. Thirty-five parents attended an evening screening. Our impression was that they came in part to see our tapes of preschools in China and Japan but mostly to get a glimpse of what their children's school looks like between drop-off and pick-up times.

We also showed our tapes in separate screenings to the children of St. Timothy's, to the teachers, and to the director, and to audiences of parents, preschool staff, and students in colleges of education in State College, Pennsylvania; Nashville, Tennessee; and Claremont, California.

In the discussions that followed these screenings it became clear Americans hold some truths about preschools to be self-evident, and some rights of preschool children, parents, and teachers to be inalienable. Preschools should promote life, liberty, and the pursuit of happiness. They should teach children to exercise their right of free speech (but not their right to remain silent). Of the self-evident truths mentioned in the preamble to the U.S. Constitution, we found only equality to be conspicuously absent from the American discourse on preschools.

The truths and rights Americans hold dear lie at the core of St. Timothy's philosophy of preschool education, as summarized in the first paragraph of the orientation packet sent out to parents of entering children:

> St. Timothy's Child Center views the child as an individual, a learner with potential for growth who needs a supportive, nurturing and optimally stimulating environment. Because STCC takes a holistic view of the child (that is, we view the child as a physical, social, emotional, intellectual and spiritual whole), it is both philosophy and policy that the school will provide an environment for the child that is safe, challenging, developmentally appropriate, supportive, stimulating, nurturing, and respectful of the child and his/her family.

For an explication of this philosophy, we turn to the parents and staff.

Liberty

On the open-ended items in our questionnaire that asked "What were the best and worst aspects of the school you've just seen in our tapes?"

American respondents praised St. Timothy's for its "freedom of choice," "free play," "wide variety of learning experiences," and "encouragement of creativity and individuality," and for the "self-direction," "autonomy," and "independence" of its children. They criticized Komatsudani for being "too group-oriented" and for not offering children "enough individual attention." Dong-feng was criticized for being "rigid," "totalitarian," "too group-oriented," and "restrictive," for offering "too little free time" and "too little free choice," for "insisting on conformity," for having a "one-size-fits-all approach to education," and for making children "drab," "colorless," and "robot-like."

At the core of Americans' positive reactions to St. Timothy's and negative reactions to Komatsudani and Dong-feng is a belief in the value of liberty and the related notions of self-reliance, independence, individuality, and free choice.

Self-Reliance and Independence

Our American respondents' top answer to the question, "What is the most important reason for a society to have preschools?" was "to make young children more independent and self-reliant." A St. Timothy's parent gave us an example of self-reliance and its opposite, overdependence:

> We're very pleased with the progress Derek has made this year in school. He isn't nearly so clingy any more. Last fall when he started here we had a terrible time getting him to let us go each morning. He would cry, have a tantrum, whatever he thought might work to keep us from dropping him off at school. But now he's pretty happy going to school most mornings.

Another parent told us:

> Sherry has become so independent since she's been in school. She used to always be whining, "Mommy, do it for me. I can't do it," "Find it for me, I can't find it." Since she's been in school she's come around 180 degrees. Her big expression now is, "I can do it myself." She won't even let me button her outfits that button in the back. The turning point for her was she saw that her friends at school could do more for themselves and she wanted to be just like them, and they would tease her sometimes for being kind of babyish, so she just determined to grow up.

Commenting on the scene in our tape where four-year-old Mark has trouble separating from his father, Linda explained:

At the beginning of each year that kind of problem is pretty common, but as the year goes on it gets kind of rarer. I guess Marky was having a bad day the day you filmed. The longer they're in school, the more self-confidence they get. You'd be surprised how much these kids have changed just since you filmed here. Marky has become real independent.

Americans view self-reliance, autonomy, and independence as important dimensions of freedom and liberty. But Americans are not unique in this respect; our Japanese and Chinese respondents also listed "to make children more self-reliant and independent" as one of their three top answers to the question, "What is the most important reason for a society to have preschools?" Teachers in all three cultures told us that they work to foster children's self-reliance in leave-taking from parents and in dressing, eating, toileting, and putting away toys and learning materials—partly to make their jobs easier and also to meet the responsibility they share with parents and other caretakers for helping children develop and mature.

Americans tend to view independence as a characteristically Western trait and dependence as characteristically Asian. Yet our interviews and questionnaries suggest that Chinese view the most important mission of the preschool as making spoiled, overdependent single children less spoiled, more self-reliant, and less dependent on their parents. And we have seen that Japanese children, in classrooms with ratios of thirty students to one teacher, are by both necessity and design more independent of adult supervision than are their peers in American preschool classrooms with much smaller student/teacher ratios. The promotion of self-reliance and independence in young children is therefore not uniquely American. The emphasis on variety and choice we found at St. Timothy's, however, does seem to be far more characteristic of American than Chinese or Japanese preschools.

Freedom of Choice and Variety of Experience

Many of the Americans who viewed our tapes criticized Dong-feng for offering a limited range of activities. For example, a preschool administrator in Chicago said:

What is most glaringly wrong with the Chinese school from my point of view is the lack of variety in the curriculum. It's not only that there is so much emphasis on academic work. From what I can see there is a total lack of balance between academics and other kinds of development. It just seems to lack color and variety. It doesn't seem stimulating enough. . . . This school looks like elementary schools looked in America a hundred years ago. All the emphasis is on control. No realization that kids learn best when the environment is stimulating and varied and when they are made to be active rather than passive learners.

Americans also criticized Komatsudani for not offering children enough opportunity to exercise free choice. Eighty percent of the Americans who viewed our tapes rated Komatsudani's materials as "just right," but many faulted the school for not giving children the chance to use these materials freely. For example, Colleen Momohara, one of the teachers of St. Timothy's five-year-olds, said of Komatsudani:

They have some very nice materials. The activities with the cray-pas and the origami and the workbooks looked good. The only thing missing is children don't seem to have much chance to choose how to play. Here, we're more likely to let children choose to draw or do paper folding and cutting or to work on their letters or numbers. We don't usually tell them to do the same thing at the same time. When we do art projects we encourage them to make whatever they want. In the Chinese school all the children had to build the same thing with the blocks. That's totally opposite to our approach. If you leave children alone, they make things we could never think of to tell them to make.

At the heart of St. Timothy's commitment to providing children with variety and choice are the three forty-five-minute learning-center periods held each day. The school's orientation packet for parents includes a discussion of learning centers:

In the classrooms there are specific activities and/or curriculum learning centers. We believe a balance of activities best meets the needs of young children. We plan experiences and opportunities in all areas so that your children can develop a wide variety of skills. Since the *children* choose activities that interest them, they are meeting their own needs. Consequently, children develop feelings of confidence, responsibility, and creativity.

We asked St. Timothy's staff if they attempt to influence children's choices of what to do during learning-center periods:

Takashige: Well, the whole idea of learning centers, of course, is to let children choose. But we do sometimes get involved in these choices. Like on the day you filmed, . . . right at the beginning of the first learning-center period more than three children want to play in the block corner. And so Linda encourages the fourth boy to choose another center to start with because we have found that if we don't limit the number of children in that particular center we run into problems.

Davidson: What do you do if a child always chooses the same center activities and, say, is always playing in the block corner or with trucks?

Takashige: A few of the boys do have a tendency to stay holed up in the block corner with the trucks. I chase them out of there occasionally and suggest they do something else. But usually the problem takes care of itself, because if they keep doing the same thing they get bored, so then they naturally gravitate to something else. Sometimes they come up to me and say, "What should I do? I don't know what to do. I'm bored." Or sometimes what happens is they get bored and then an argument breaks out, so then I come over and suggest that one or more of the boys choose another activity.

In addition to learning centers, lunchtime, outdoor play, and show-and-tell periods offer further opportunities for children at St. Timothy's to learn to exercise free choice. At lunchtime children choose whom to sit with. At naptime they sleep wherever they choose to sleep. During outdoor play twice a day they are free to choose from a variety of large-motor activities. Once a week, each child gets a chance to bring something from home to show to the class or to tell about something the child has done or seen.

Freedom and Constraint

Although the children of St. Timothy's are free to make many choices, these choices are by no means unconstrained. Children are not free to choose to eat junk food or refuse to take a nap or to play war games on the playground. They can freely choose what toys to play with, but they are not free to choose not to clean up. The teachers at St. Timothy's believe that whenever possible children should be given the opportunity to make choices. But they see their job as carefully structuring the range of available choices and setting clear limits on acceptable behavior. Colleen Momohara explained to us the importance of rules and structure.

Momohara: Children at this age need to have very clear boundaries laid out for them. They must learn that there are some behaviors which are just plain unacceptable. At the beginning of the year it's a little tough for some of them. But they get used to the rules pretty quickly. They actually like rules because it gives them a kind of security knowing there are limits.

Davidson: What are some of the rules you have?

Momohara: Oh, there are many. No fighting. No bringing toys from home to school except for show and tell. There are a lot of rules about what can be brought for lunch. I'll show you the list of food rules. There are rules about no war toys or toy guns, but of course that rule is hard to enforce since children can pick up a block or a banana and go "bang bang." A teacher must go with you when you go to the bathroom. Each teacher has her own rules for her classroom. Like, only three children at once in the block corner. Rules like that.

The staff and parents of St. Timothy's perceive their school as being moderately structured, more free than schools they classify as too conservative and restrictive, but not so free as to fall into the category of "alternative" or "free" schools. As Barbara Culler explained:

I would say we are maybe a little toward the free end but pretty much in the middle. We're not quite as far out as some of the alternative programs, but we're more like them than we are like these real gung-ho learn-to-read-by-the-time-you're-three programs. We're much looser and more easygoing than most programs, but we have a fair amount of structure.

We ran into a similar "Goldilocks" effect in our American respondents' comparisons of St. Timothy's with Komatsudani and Dong-feng. Americans who viewed our three tapes generally found the Chinese preschool "too controlled," the Japanese preschool "too uncontrolled," and the American preschool "just right." On the items "teachers set limits and controlled children's behavior" and "teachers directed children's activities and play," our American respondents rated Dong-feng as directing and controlling "too much," Komatsudani "too little," and St. Timothy's "just right." On the items asking about the children's mood and activity level, Chinese children were rated as "too controlled," "passive," and "subdued," Japanese children as "too wild and chaotic," and the American children at St. Timothy's as "just right."

Most of the American preschool parents we spoke with told us that what they look for in a preschool for their child is a balance between freedom and order, free play and structured activities, indulgence and discipline. Parents want their children to be high-spirited, independent, curious, and imaginative, but also well mannered, well socialized, and cooperative. Most St. Timothy's parents appreciate their preschool's balanced approach

to discipline, as one parent told us: "I'm glad my daughter is finally learning how to behave this year. She was a terror until recently. I'm glad they are firm with her here. That's just what she needs. This experience she's getting now will give her an advantage when she gets to kindergarten and first grade."

The importance the staff of St. Timothy's gives to setting clear limits for behavior and keeping children under control also can be seen clearly in Barbara Culler's and Cheryl Takashige's reactions to Komatsudani's management (or apparent lack of management) of Hiroki, the "bad boy" of our Japan tape. Most of our American respondents were very critical of Fukui's failure to stop Hiroki from fighting and in other ways disrupting the class. Cheryl's reaction was typical:

I think it was a mistake for Hiroki's teacher to let him get that far out of control. Children always are testing the limits of what they can get away with. A kid like that is testing you all the time, looking for a consistent response. His teacher looks like she's just ignoring him. It is hard to bring a child like that back under control once he has been allowed to get so out of control. The key is not to let things get so far out of control in the first place.

A preschool parent in Chicago commented:

> The way that boy is allowed to behave is bad for the whole class. One child should not be allowed to infringe on the other children's rights. Children should be able to go to school without having to worry about being constantly pounded on by other children. They have a right to a calm, secure atmosphere in the classroom.

The parents and staff of St. Timothy's believe that it is important for children to be free and independent. But they believe that to nurture freedom and independence in young children they must provide an environment that, although varied, is also clearly structured and, although offering many choices, also presents clearly defined limits. Americans perceive programs like Dong-feng's as providing too little variety, too little choice, and too little opportunity for self-expression; programs such as Komatsudani appear to most Americans to be too chaotic and unstructured to allow for the exercise of responsible choice and the development of an appropriate sense of freedom.

Individualism

An emphasis on the rights and priority of the individual is apparent throughout St. Timothy's discourse, beginning with the orientation manual for parents:

> St. Timothy's Child Center views the child as an individual, a learner with a potential for growth. . . . Teachers know and care about each child and show this concern through their interactions with individuals. . . . [You can] help your child to become a socially competent and responsible individual by treating him or her as a valued member of your family with input and opinions that count.

It is in their commitment to treating children as individuals that the staff of St. Timothy's differ most significantly from their counterparts in China and Japan. Our interviews suggest that Americans hold a profound belief in the essential un-alikeness of same-age children in temperament, interests, rate of development, attention span, and intelligence. And with this belief comes an equally strong belief in the right of every child to a preschool curriculum appropriate to his or her unique abilities and needs.

Many American viewers deplored both Dong-feng's regimented approach as well as Komatsudani's "treat them all the same" style of teaching. For example, a parent at St. Timothy's, referring to Komatsudani's policy of not intervening in children's fights, said "That approach of staying out of disputes and leaving children to handle things on their own might work out well for the strongest kids. But what about the kid who gets the short end of the fight? What about kids who just sort of get lost in the woodwork and get no attention?" A graduate student in early child education wrote of Dong-feng: "All the children are expected to behave in a particular way. It's like a boot camp, where you grind down individuality to make everyone the same so you can control them more easily."

Many Americans were especially critical of Dong-feng's policy of having all the children use the bathroom together at the same time, a practice they suggested was a particularly disturbing example of China's disregard for the rights and needs of individuals. One American parent wrote on his response sheet, "This is communism taken to its logical extreme: big brother is watching—and even telling you when and where to go!"

Japanese preschool teachers are very reluctant to discuss individual differences in ability among the children in their care and believe that it is their responsibility to see that all children are treated equally. In contrast, teachers at St. Timothy's speak without hesitation of individual differences among the children and stress the importance of tailoring the curriculum to each child's unique temperament, needs, interests, and abilities. Cheryl told us:

> As a teacher my job is to work with each child in my class wherever he is at. If a child is ready to read, then my job with that child is to be a reading teacher. Many of our children aren't quite ready to read. So my job with these kids is to work with them wherever they are on the skills they need. Some children like Kerry need a lot of work on their problem-solving skills and self-control. I have to give Kerry a lot more individual attention and work more with him than I do with some of the other children right now. Kerry is a little younger than most of the others and he has a little more trouble with his self-control. But he's getting there.

Barbara Culler stressed to us that what makes St. Timothy's special is its commitment to giving every child a chance to grow at his or her own pace:

> We are a developmentally based program. Many schools are hurrying children these days, shoving reading and math down their throats, ready or not. They say to parents, "We'll have your kid reading by the time he's four." We don't have these kinds of expectations for our

children. We focus on helping children feel good about themselves. Children at this age have such wide differences in abilities that it doesn't make any sense to demand or expect them all to learn the same things at the same rate. Our program tries to be sensitive to their individual needs. . . . We have five or six children each year out of our total enrollment of ninety or so who need some form of special help. Usually we have one or two with some form of physical handicaps and a few others with learning disabilities, dyslexia, attention-deficit disorders. On the other end of the continuum we have some kids who are extremely quick and bright who also have special needs.

Liberty, Equality, Fraternity

The staff of St. Timothy's strive to promote self-reliance, independence, free choice, and individuality in children. But this does not preclude a concern for helping children develop skills in interpersonal relations and the ability to function as members of a group. Predictably, our American respondents listed "to make young children more self-reliant and independent" (23 percent) and "to give children a good start academically" (22 percent) as their first- and second-choice answers to the question "Why should a society have preschools?" But, surprisingly, "to teach children to be a member of a group" was a close third (20 percent). For Americans as for Chinese and Japanese, independence and the ability to function as a member of a group are not seen as incompatible. Children need to have made at least some initial strides toward self-reliance and independence from their parents before they can make friends and participate in the preschool group. At the same time, friendships and group camaraderie enjoyed at preschool help children further separate and individuate. Most of the American teachers, administrators, and parents we spoke with had mixed feelings about how much group emphasis there should be in preschools. This ambivalence can be seen in their very different reactions to Dong-feng and Komatsudani.

Most of the Americans deplored what they felt to be the oppressive authoritarianism and antiindividualism of the Chinese preschool while they were generally impressed by what they perceived to be Komatsudani's more relaxed, upbeat group spirit: 62 percent rated Dong-feng as having "too much" emphasis on group feeling, but 59 percent rated Komatsudani's group emphasis as "just right." One St. Timothy's parent said to us after watching our tapes: "I really like the energy the Japanese bring to their groups—the group exercises, the singing, the closeness the Japanese children enjoy with each other. I feel a lot of positive energy there. I think we could do with a little more of that." Other Americans, although interested in Japan's groupism, felt it would be difficult to import to the United States. A preschool teacher in Honolulu told us:

> Group exercise works for the Japanese because it fits with their culture. But for us, I just don't think it would ever feel right. I can't quite picture us doing the morning calisthenic bit at our school. It seems a little too much like the military, I guess. I mean, lining up in the morning to go through calisthenics just doesn't seem to Americans to be something you do with four-year-olds. It seems more like something the army does with new recruits.

In the eyes of Americans, individualism can be compatible with being a member of a group, but rationalizing individualism with equality is more problematic. In contrast to Japan, where egalitarian sentiment dominated the discourse on preschool education, we heard very little from our American informants about the importance of preschools providing an equal experience to all children. The emphasis Americans give to the importance of individualism, freedom, and self-actualization displaces discussion of equality. Egalitarian concerns emerged clearly only in discussions of admission policies, not with regard to the treatment of children in preschool. For example, Barbara Culler contrasted St. Timothy's admissions policy with the more elitist, less egalitarian selection and admission procedures of many other preschools in Hawaii.

> We are strictly a first-come, first-serve operation here. We have a waiting list, and we go by our waiting list to decide who will be admitted for the coming year. We don't use any sort of tests or interviews for selection purposes, like some other preschools. With this policy, I like to think we get about the best mix of kids of any program in Hawaii. We have the kids of military officers, secretaries, doctors, nurses, house-painters, teachers, all in the same class.

In our discussions with Americans we heard much about the importance of recognizing that no two children are alike, little about all children being created equal. We heard much about the importance of treating children differently according to their differing abilities, temperament, and needs, little about the importance of treating children equally. We heard much about helping children become uniquely themselves, fully individuated, and self-actualized, little about helping children feel identified with each other, aware of their basic sameness, equality, and shared destiny. Perhaps a cost of the American emphasis on individualized preschool education is an inevitable silencing of egalitarian concerns, whereas the cost of the Japanese and Chinese emphasis on equality in preschool education is less emphasis on the needs of children as individuals.*

Yet our sense is that American, Japanese, and Chinese preschools' approaches to balancing groupism with individualism and equality differ more in theory than in practice. In all three societies, preschool children spend most of their day as members of groups. In addition to the explicitly group-oriented "small-group" and "large-group" activities scheduled each day at St. Timothy's, the children spend much of the rest of the day in group activities that are not labeled or thought of as such. Consciously valuing individuality, staff members freight individual-oriented activities such as learning centers with heavy pedagogical import. More ambivalent about the value of groupism, they apply no special pedagogical significance to periods of the day, including naptime and lunch, that the children spend in group activities.

Words

Language and Cognitive Development

Children at St. Timothy's are continually encouraged to use words to describe, evaluate, and name objects in their world and to give verbal accounts of their work and play. For example, Cheryl insisted on Richie's *telling* her about his puzzle rather than only *showing* it to her. The felt-board exercise we taped provides another good example of how the staff of St. Timothy's approaches the teaching of language and cognition. As Cheryl explained, each child had a turn to enjoy the teacher's undivided attention while standing at the board performing a cognitive act demanding imagination, symbolism, and speech:

> The idea of this activity is to teach children the concept of simile. I gave the children an example of the pattern: "This cloud is like a da-da-da." Then they each had their chance. I was less concerned here with what they thought the cloud looked like than with making sure they had the concept of something being like another thing without *being* the other thing. It's a trickier concept for some kids than others.

*In *Human Conditions* (1986), Robert LeVine and Merry White, following Ralf Dahrendorf (1979), conceptualize this issue as a tradeoff between "options" and "ligatures."

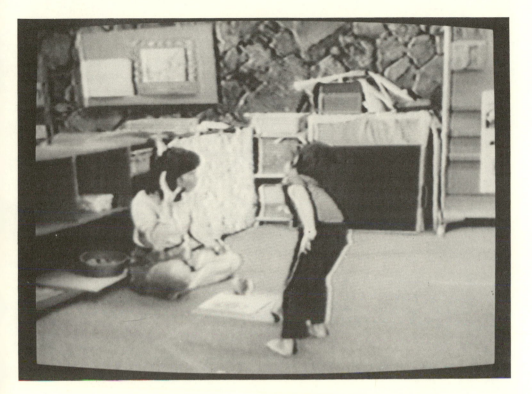

Show and tell is yet another component of the St. Timothy's curriculum deemed important for developing thought and language.* Colleen explained:

> The point of show and tell? Well, when children tell stories of what they did on the weekend they are developing a sense of linear story-telling which is a building block for reading. They are experimenting with sequencing, for instance. And the children listening are improving their comprehension abilities. Or when children choose to share a toy or something else they bring in from home, they get a chance to develop their ability to use words to describe things, to paint word pictures.

Colleen told us that it is especially important in Hawaii to stress the development of language skills in preschool.

*For a discussion of "sharing" and, more generally, of language in the American preschool, see Courtney Cazden's 1988 *Classroom Discourse*.

It's crucial we stress verbal skills because the test scores are showing
we're lagging behind most of the other states on the [verbal section
of the] SAT and other standardized tests they're using in elementary
school. I don't know how much of it is pidgin [Hawaiian Creole En-
glish] and how much is cultural factors—you know, Hawaii having
so many people who come from Asian cultures that aren't as verbal
as Haoles [Caucasians]. Whatever the reason, it's really important
that children get off to a good start in their language ability before
they get to kindergarten.

In American preschools, teachers put a great deal of energy and effort
into modeling, correcting, and prompting children's informal speech. In
Chinese preschools there is relatively little spontaneous child-to-child conversation to monitor or correct: Chinese teachers are vigilant in their
supervision of children, but their efforts are usually directed more at limiting than at facilitating children's spontaneous use of language. Japanese
preschool classrooms, in marked contrast to classrooms in China, are ex-

tremely noisy, full of the voices of shouting, freely conversing children. But unlike American teachers, Japanese teachers do very little monitoring or correcting of children's speech during these periods of unconstrained child-to-child discourse, which make up much of the preschool day.

As at Komatsudani, children at St. Timothy's spend much of the day talking freely. But the teachers vigilantly monitor children's conversation and intervene to arbitrate verbal disputes, to interpret unclear communication, to discourage asocial discourse, and to model effective modes of speech (Cazden, 1988; Newkirk, 1989). For example, in the following sequence Cheryl models pronunciation, improves word choice, introduces grammatical forms, and suggests possibilities for producing more complex sentences likely to be clearer and of more interest to listeners.

Lance: The other day, the other day my Mom and me and my Dad and, we went to the Big Island the other day.

Cheryl: You went to the Big Island on the weekend. What a lucky boy! How did you get there?

Lance: Airplane.

Cheryl: You went to the Big Island on an airplane. What was the most interesting thing you saw there?

Lance: Where?

Cheryl: On the Big Island. What was the most interesting thing you saw on the Big Island, Lance?

Lance: The bolcano.

Cheryl: The volcano. Kileaua? You saw Kileaua volcano. How many of you have seen a volcano?

At St. Timothy's we heard many other examples of teachers monitoring and correcting children's speech—telling children to modulate the volume and tone of their voice ("Please use your indoor voice"), suggesting the inappropriateness of vulgar terms ("We don't like to hear those kinds of words"), and helping children be more exact in their word choice ("Monday is the day, not the date").

The Pedagogy of Self-Expression

At St. Timothy's, words are thought to be critical for social as well as cognitive development. Our interviews suggest that American preschool parents and staff believe that to be a friend, a group participant, a member of society, a citizen in a democracy, children need to be taught to express their wants, needs, and feelings.

In our taping at St. Timothy's we recorded many examples of children being encouraged to use words for what staff members call "problem solving." The approach Cheryl used to break up a fight in the block corner is a good example: "Mike, can you tell Stu with words what you want instead of grabbing? . . . Stu, when Mike took the block from you, how did you feel? Did you tell him that made you angry? Did it make you angry?" Cheryl explained her strategy to us when we watched the tape together: "What I'm trying to do there is get them to use words instead of their hands to express their feelings. With kids this age, as soon as they get angry or frustrated their first reaction is to hit someone. I try and get them to realize what they are feeling and to express it verbally."

When we watched this same fight scene with a group of preschool teachers in Kyoto, the young Japanese teachers were impressed but also tactfully critical.

Yagi: Wow, that's amazing! Talking so directly with such young children about their feelings.

Taniguchi: The teacher really gets right in there and deals with the problem.

Tanaka: Talking with children about disagreements like that . . . it seems a bit heavy, doesn't it? It reminds me of marriage counseling.

Most of our American respondents praised St. Timothy's for its verbal approach to conflict resolution and discipline. For example, several American teachers were impressed with Cheryl's management of Kerry, the boy who would not pick up his blocks:

I like the way she is firm with him, but doesn't yell or raise her voice. She makes him look her in the eye and talk over their disagreement. When he won't look her in the eye, well, when you can't engage a child, when you can't get him to look at you or talk to you, then you have no choice but to do like she did there and use a time-out to let him settle down and think about the implications of his behavior.

Teachers at St. Timothy's encourage children to use words to express their positive feelings as well as to resolve disputes. We frequently heard teachers at American preschools encouraging children to express their mood in words: "Are you having fun?" "How did you feel during the play when the witch came out? Excited? Scared? How about at the end when the witch was chased away?"

American preschool children also are encouraged to verbalize their wants and needs. Linda's interchange with Rhonda during snack time is a good example: "Do you want juice, Rhonda? Milk? A cracker? What do you want? If you just keep shaking your head, how am I supposed to know what you want if you don't tell me?"

Several of our American respondents criticized Dong-feng for not giving children a chance to express their feelings. A parent at St. Timothy's said to us after watching our tape of Dong-feng, "The atmosphere is so cold. It's like there's no room or time for feelings. I didn't see any touching or real communicating between teachers and students." A graduate student wrote on her questionnaire, "The mood in the Chinese school reminds me of our schools a hundred years ago, during the era when we believed that children 'should be seen and not heard.'" Another American teacher commented, "It's almost eerie to hear a room of little children being that quiet. You wonder what they've done to the kids to make them so silent."

Comparing St. Timothy's to preschools in Japan and China, the ideological dimension of American views of language becomes clear. Although speech in American preschools like St. Timothy's is more spontaneous than in Chinese preschools like Dong-feng, it is more carefully monitored and constrained by adults than at Komatsudani, where teachers avoid intervening in children's communication. American children enjoy great freedom to express their opinions and feelings, but conversely, they are much less free than children in China or Japan to remain silent and hide their feelings. Speech in American preschools, then, is constrained differently, not less, than in China and Japan (Newkirk, 1989). It could be argued that in a culture such as the United States, where children are encouraged and expected to verbalize their feelings, talk about feelings, and perhaps even feelings themselves, will inevitably be more conventional and socially constrained than in a culture such as China, where children are not exposed to public discourse about feelings, or in a culture such as Japan, where teachers stay largely outside the world of children's discourse.

Play and the Pursuit of Happiness

The great majority of the preschool children we saw and taped in all three countries seemed happy. But we found significant variations in the way our Chinese, Japanese, and American respondents discussed the importance of happiness and play in preschools. Most of the Chinese we spoke with made it clear that they view preschool as a place for serious learning; it is fine if children are happy in their learning, but happiness is not an important goal of school. In Japan many preschool teachers and administrators told us that they see the most important function of preschool as producing kodomo-rashii kodomo (literally, childlike children), children who are innocent, straightforward, and bright. To be childlike is to be happy but also, at times, to be angry, frustrated, and selfish. Japanese believe children can be most childlike in a loosely structured (albeit carefully planned) environment where energetic, friendly teachers facilitate, but stay on the fringes of, children's play. In the United States the pursuit of happiness is an explicit goal of many preschools, including St. Timothy's. At the core of St. Timothy's notion of pursuing happiness is the crucial function of play and the role of teachers in facilitating play. The St. Timothy's orientation manual states:

> Play is one of the most enjoyable and valuable aspects of childhood. Children learn through play. They learn about the social and physical world around them and about themselves. Play is their opportunity for inquiry, problem-solving, self-understanding, and social interactions. Play is a right of childhood.

Teachers at St. Timothy's do not believe that play and happiness are more important than work and learning. They believe, rather, that play *is* children's work and that learning should be a source of satisfaction and joy.

Most of the school's parents we spoke with agreed that play and happiness are of great importance. After watching our tape, several parents told us they were pleased to see how happy their children seemed at school. For example, Mike's father said:

> Hey, it really looks great. The school comes across looking great. The kids look real happy. Active. Geez, I never really realized there's so many different things for them to play here. My son looked like he was having a great old time, except of course for that little altercation in the block corner. How much [money] would it take to get you to edit that out? I don't want that fight to go on my kid's record. Naw, I'm only kidding. Kids will be kids. I'm glad to see him in there scrapping. That's how I was when I was a kid.

Other parents, like Nicole's mother, Sandy, worry more about their children's success in making friends at school. Cheryl, who shared Sandy's concern about Nicole, told us that she is careful to pay attention to friendship patterns in her class.

> It's a problem sometimes that children hurt each other's feelings when they're playing. When they make friends, they often leave other children out. They are just learning how to be real friends, what friendship really means. We hear a lot of "I'll be your friend if

you let me play with that toy." We tell children not to say "You're not my friend" or "I'll be your friend if . . ." We don't want them using friendship as something to buy and sell. If we notice a child in the class never playing with other children, we will work on it. If a couple of kids are excluding another, like what's happening to Nicole with Mayumi and Michelle, we try to do something to help them work it out.

In China and Japan as well as in the United States parents and teachers want children to be happy and to have friends at school. But St. Timothy's is unlike Dong-feng in the importance it attributes to these concerns and unlike Komatsudani in the active role teachers play in attempting to influence friendship patterns and structure children's free play.

Play and Things

American preschoolers have a wealth of materials to play with: toy trucks and kitchen equipment, dolls, games, and puzzles; paints, easels, crayons, scissors, paste, and clay; pencils and paper; books, records, and simple musical instruments; firemen's hats, stethoscopes, adult shoes, party dresses, neckties, and other props; climbing apparatus, swings, balls, a sandbox, and tricycles.

The decor of some American preschools exudes gaiety—a children's wonderland. Preschools with names like Teddy Bear Day Care, Merry-Go-Round Child Center, or Babes in Toyland are decorated with posters and paintings depicting traditionally popular juvenile themes (like nursery rhymes) or drawings done in an exaggeratedly childlike style by adults, including words scrawled in a childlike hand, full of reversed and upside-down letters. St. Timothy's decor is child-oriented in a different sense. Most of the drawings on the walls are the work of children in the class. Travel posters and large pictures of fish, birds, and wild animals cover big sections of the wall. There are no posters of nursery rhyme or Disney characters, no Raggedy Ann and Andy. Much of the wall space is filled with calendars and class projects—photos from a recent trip to the zoo, a display on flowers that can be used to make leis.

Throughout the day the range of materials available to the children changes. On the day we taped, during the first learning-center period the children could choose to draw or cut and paste, to read in the library, or to play in the housekeeping or block corners. During the second learning-center period the pegboard, painting equipment, and scissors and paste were replaced by a basin for washing baby dolls, Play-Doh, and beads for making necklaces. Each day the teachers select additional materials for the

learning centers from a central supply room. Some materials, such as egg and milk cartons, empty cans, and aluminum foil, are brought from home for special art projects.

Our American respondents generally were impressed with Komatsu-dani's materials and critical of Dong-feng's. American preschool teachers in particular admired Komatsudani's art supplies, wall decorations, and outdoor climbing apparatus. In contrast, 88 percent of our American respondents rated Dong-feng's materials as "poor." An American preschool teacher's comments were typical:

> That is a very poorly equipped school. Now, I'm not sure how much of this has to do with China being a poor country and how much with communism, you know antimaterialism and all. But it is pretty barren. As far as I'm concerned, it's not a good environment for young children. I'd have to say in this school the children get a good

chance to develop musically, since I saw a fair bit of dancing and singing and there was a lot of music playing in the background. But I saw no evidence of other arts. No artwork on the walls. No drawing materials out for the children to manipulate. No toys or books. No blocks for large-motor development.

A great majority of American (85 percent) and Chinese (80 percent) preschool parents, teachers, and administrators who viewed our tapes rated St. Timothy's materials as "just right." Japanese respondents were more critical: 44 percent faulted the school for having too many materials. For example, a teacher in a Kyoto preschool was ambivalent about St. Timothy's housekeeping corner.

> We don't have a make-believe corner, but children in our school play lots of imaginary games. They play house and store and fireman. You don't need costumes and plastic dishes to play house. You don't need a fireman's hat to pretend you're a fireman. I don't think that children need all of those special things to play. Don't teachers in American believe children have imagination?

Principal Yoshizawa of Komatsudani was critical of the use of space and material in both American and Japanese preschools:

> America is so rich! The children are fortunate to have such a wonderful place to play. Compared to the Chinese, they have so much space, and so many things for children to do. But that's not necessarily good for children, is it? We Japanese have grown rich, too, just like Americans. But children these days don't appreciate what they have. They lose their ability to play on their own without special things to play with, like in the old days. The more you have the more you waste and the less you appreciate it.

An American preschool administrator agreed:

> We are too wasteful with our materials. We use unlimited amounts of water and paper. We use paper cups and plates and napkins. We let children use as much paper as they want, start a drawing, then crumple it up. They are much less wasteful with their resources in the Chinese preschool, but the kids look happy enough.

Imagination and Creativity

Most of the American preschool parents, teachers, administrators, and child-development experts who saw "A Day at St. Timothy's" approved of the housekeeping corner as a good example of an activity that facilitates imaginative play. The staff view children as naturally creative and imaginative, and the role of the preschool as providing an environment where creativity and imagination can flourish. As Barbara Culler explained to us:

> Children are creative. You don't have to make them creative. Children can do amazingly creative things if you give them a chance. Much more creative than me, that's for sure. You should see some of the art projects they do. Children haven't yet learned what not to draw or what not to say. So they draw really amazing things. They're saying amazing things all the time, if you listen carefully.

In the eyes of American early child educators, creativity is not something that can be taught, but it can be channeled and encouraged. St. Timothy's teachers believe that through play activities like the housekeeping corner, children can be helped to use their natural creativity, imagination, and sense of fantasy to come to understand the social world, to work out complex feelings and emotions, and to rehearse adult roles. Colleen explained:

> When the children play house it's play but it's also important work. When they play imaginary family and pretend they're the mother and father and baby brother they imagine what it's like to be someone else. They imagine what it means to go off to work. When they play the part of the mother or father and discipline the naughty baby, they get a chance to work through some of their feelings about the way their parents discipline them, and maybe it gives them an understanding of why their parents do what they do. Sometimes we will have a child here whose parents are getting divorced, and some heavy things come out in the housekeeping corner. The housekeeping corner along with doll-play give kids the chance to deal with these big issues down on their level, on a level where they can cope with them.

Self-Actualization through Play

Play, according to many American child-development experts, offers children a way to discover who they are and who they can be (for example, see the 1980 book *Who Am I in the Lives of Children?* by Feeney et al., Bergen's 1988 book *Play as a Medium for Learning and Development* and Vivian Paley's 1986 *Boys and Girls: Superheroes in the Doll Corner*). Children given the chance to enjoy a variety of experiences of play—role-playing, make-believe play, social play with peers, individual creative and artistic play, dyadic play with an adult—not only develop cognitively and socially but

also become self-actualized. As an instructor of preschool education in Chicago told us:

> Inside each child there is a child struggling to break out. This child inside the child is the child's potential, the person he can become. Our job, working with young children, is to help this process happen. If children don't get a chance to explore all the richness inside of them while they are young, then this child inside may never get out. In too many preschools children get this spirit inside of them crushed.

At St. Timothy's children are seen as most themselves when playing. There is a Rousseauian assumption that children are born knowing how to play. Society, teachers, schools, and parents too often destroy this natural understanding of play, destroy the child's innate sense of how to be in the world. At St. Timothy's as at Komatsudani, it is believed that the teacher's most important role is to provide a world where children can be children, can play and discover friendship and the joy of learning. For children who have already lost their knowledge of how to play, for those whose natural process of self-actualization has been stymied, teachers at St. Timothy's feel a responsibility to intervene, to actively help the child get back on course, back in touch with his innate creativity and direction.

Life

In the United States today the health and safety of children are believed to be in jeopardy. Preschools like St. Timothy's are mandated by parents and the larger community not only to educate, socialize, and nurture but also to protect children from dangers ranging in severity from dental problems and sugar-induced hyperactivity to abduction and abuse.

Nutrition

In their orientation packets parents of children entering St. Timothy's receive three pages on the school's lunch policy. St. Timothy's provides children with mid-morning and mid-afternoon snacks, but lunch must be brought each day from home. The contents of home lunch are a subject of concern and occasionally conflict among parents, children, and staff. Soda and other sugary drinks, candy, and gum are prohibited; cakes, cookies, and nonnutritious starches (chips) are strongly discouraged. Strongly encouraged are lunches offering a balance of protein, fruits and vegetables, and starch. Even for birthday treats, there are clear restrictions: "Please. No birthday cakes, frosting, or ice cream." In addition to prohibiting some foods, St. Timothy's orientation booklet offers lunch suggestions and ideas: "Send cheese, peanut butter sandwiches on whole wheat bread, hard-boiled eggs, yogurt, raisins, dinner leftovers such as spaghetti."

At St. Timothy's, when a child comes to school with chips or other contraband food items, the staff hold his parents responsible. Cheryl explained to us: "When parents come to pick up their kids I'll say something to them about lunches if it's been a problem. I'll ask them not to send sweets or junk food in the lunch box. In this case, I asked Stu to tell his mother not to send chips in his lunch anymore."

American adults offered several rationales for monitoring the contents of children's lunch. Barbara Culler suggested to us that it is the responsibility of preschools to educate parents as well as children about the importance of nutrition:

One area we'd like to get even more into is family life education. . . .
For instance, I think we have a role to play in helping parents raise
their awareness of nutrition. We believe strongly in the importance
of a good diet. Do you know Francis Moore Lappé's *Diet for a Small
Planet*? Without preaching too much we try to introduce children
and parents to these kinds of ideas. We've got to reach both children
and parents to have a lasting impact.

Colleen told us that restricting sweets and junk foods is important
for classroom management: "When the kids load up on sweets they can
get really hyper. It can get really hard to settle them back down." St.
Timothy's written materials on nutrition echo Colleen's concerns:

> Young children's ability to learn and their behavior are very closely
> linked to what they put in their mouths. We notice immediate be-
> havioral changes in children who eat high-sugar foods like candy,
> doughnuts, and soda. Especially bad are chocolate and cola drinks.
> These foods contain high levels of sugar and caffeine (notice the
> effects of a few cups of coffee and a piece of pie on yourself), and the
> effects are amplified because they take place in a small body.

Cheryl argued that junk foods should be kept out of preschools for reasons beyond their nutritional worthlessness and the side effect of physio-
logical overstimulation:

> If you don't have rules limiting sweets and other junk foods you are
> just asking for trouble. If kids are allowed to bring highly desirable
> items like Ho-Hos and Doritos [to school], it drives the other kids
> nuts. You get fights over food, or the kids make trades, like they
> trade their whole sandwich for three Cheetos. It's a whole lot easier
> on everyone involved, especially the teacher, when you have clear
> rules about what kids can and can't bring in their lunch boxes.

Merry White points out that in Japan junk food is believed to produce lethargy, whereas in the United States (and in China, where sweets
are associated with spoiling and willfulness) the effect is assumed to be
just the opposite. In nutrition, as in other domains, the staff of American (and Chinese) preschools worry about children getting out of control;
the Japanese are more concerned about children being insufficiently energetic. "The Japanese fear disengagement and apathy; we [Americans] fear
uncontrollable, wild behavior" (M. White, 1987, pp. 136–137).

Hygiene

The teaching of good hygiene, like the teaching of nutritional awareness, is part of St. Timothy's curriculum. Hand washing precedes lunch and snacks; toothbrushing and face washing follow each meal. Children are free to use the child-sized toilets in the separate boys' and girls' bathrooms whenever they feel the need. Teachers also remind children three or four times a day to use the bathrooms between activities.

American teachers see themselves as paying attention to health and hygiene, but these issues are not given highest priority. In response to our questionnaire item, "What are the most important things for children to learn in preschool?" only 7 percent of our American respondents listed "good health, hygiene, and grooming habits" among their top three answers as compared with 49 percent of Japanese and 60 percent of Chinese. Although our Chinese respondents saw themselves as very vigilant about hygiene, 57 percent of the Americans who viewed "A Day at Dong-feng" found the Chinese preschool insufficiently safe and healthy. The group bathroom scenes shown in our tape of Dong-feng contributed most heavily to this harsh judgment. For example, a preschool teacher in Honolulu wrote: "The bathroom seems so primitive, like a barn. Those trenches, in terms of being modern—I mean, they're just awful."

At St. Timothy's, learning good hygiene means learning to be independent, clean, and discreet in toileting and remembering to wash one's hands after using the toilet and before eating. At Dong-feng, the toilets are communal and the bathroom schedule fixed, yet the goals in the teaching of hygiene are similar. Differences we observed among the three programs' approaches to hygiene were mostly matters of emphasis. Japanese preschools emphasize hand washing and wearing appropriate footwear inside and out. Chinese preschools are very concerned with germs and emphasize precautions for limiting the spread of disease. American preschools emphasize teaching children to develop the habit of taking personal responsibility for toileting, hand washing, and toothbrushing.

Abuse

Among the three countries in our study, child abduction and abuse are uniquely American concerns. Many of our Chinese and Japanese informants, finding the concept foreign, had difficulty understanding our questions about child abuse. Our descriptions of the scope of the problem in the United States generally were met with a mixture of incredulity and horror. "No," Higashino-sensei of Komatsudani told us, "we've never had a case of abuse of the kind you describe in our school." Principal Hua of

Dong-feng told us similarly, "Such things occurred before the revolution, but not in today's China."

Our American informants, in contrast, were acutely aware of the problem of child abuse, and most saw themselves as having an important role to play in its detection and prevention. Children arriving at St. Timothy's each morning are signed in by their parents on a sheet posted in each classroom. At the end of the day parents sign their children out. Children are allowed to go home only with their parents or with other caretakers who have been authorized in writing to pick them up from school. Whenever children are outside the classrooms on the playground a teacher is assigned to watch the gate, to make sure no one comes in or goes out. At many American preschools children are not allowed to enter the bathrooms unless accompanied by a teacher. Honolulu, like other American cities, has recently had a highly publicized case of a child's being abducted from preschool and sexually abused. In the aftermath of such cases preschool directors and teachers are very much aware both of the need to take precautions and of the need to be perceived to be taking precautions.

In addition to using sign-in sheets and fencing and monitoring play areas, St. Timothy's deals with the danger of abuse and abduction by teaching children to protect themselves. During the spring we were taping at St. Timothy's a social worker was brought in to provide workshops for parents and children on child abuse. The children, in their workshop, were taught to consider their bodies their own and to be fierce about fending off uncomfortable, unwanted touching of any kind from anybody, "including people in your family." This message was reinforced in the days and weeks following the workshop by readings of stories that make it clear that children should be wary of the attention of strangers, not get into strangers' cars, and refuse gifts from people they do not know.

Concern about child abuse and abduction is communicated to children in other ways as well. Milk and juice cartons carry pictures of missing children. Fingerprinting of children is offered in shopping malls. Children's television shows are punctuated with public service messages that suggest ways children can protect themselves.

A day-care center director described for us the care and delicacy preschools must bring to dealing with these issues: "Parents are very concerned these days in a way they weren't even just a couple of years ago about how we will protect their children while they are at school. We have to make children realize the need to be careful without terrorizing them. It's tough, but do-able."

The threat of child abuse comes from inside as well as from outside the preschool, and especially from within families. Teachers at St. Timothy's are instructed to report to the Department of Health or to the police incidents of children who come to school with stories or physical or emotional signs of having been abused at home. Preschool teachers and administrators are not above suspicion: in Honolulu as in other American cities legislation has been introduced calling for fingerprinting and criminal-records checks for all preschool staff.

In a society as litigious as the contemporary United States an inevitable sequel of child abuse is rapidly rising liability-insurance rates. As a preschool director explained:

> Down the road, actually it's unfortunately already started, but down the road it'll be much worse. We've been told we are facing huge insurance costs. Our long-range plan calls for raising staff salaries and offering more scholarships and making some capital improvements, but all of these plans are jeopardized by this liability-insurance thing. Some people are wondering if small programs will even be able to stay in business if the rates go much higher.

Child abuse and abduction are perceived by some Americans as posing a significant threat not only to the lives of the children abducted and abused but also to the freedom, happiness, and emotional well-being of a whole generation of American children. An American preschool parent, who is also an elementary school teacher, raised some of these concerns in an evening meeting we attended on child abuse:

> I want my daughter to believe the world is a good place. I want her to feel good about people. I worry that with our constant warnings and talking so much about our fears . . . there is something about adults suddenly talking so much about child abuse that worries me somehow. I'm worried a little that we are doing to our children with child abuse and abduction stories what our parents or grandparents did to us with stories of the boogie man.

Truth, Justice, and the American Way

No one we spoke with at St. Timothy's explicitly mentioned the importance of teaching children the principles of democracy or instilling an understanding and appreciation of the American system of justice. Only 14 percent of our American respondents, as compared to 30 percent of our respondents in China, listed "to start children on the road toward being good citizens" as one of their top three reasons for a society to have preschools. Yet there is much in the everyday curriculum and practice of American preschools that both echoes and anticipates the system of law (and lawyers) and voting (and politicians) by which the United States is run.

Voting

St. Timothy's has no elected class officers, but there are often elections and referenda in which children get the chance to vote. Laughing, Cheryl explained to us her simple rules for preschool elections: "Let children vote on something only when the outcome doesn't matter or when you are sure before they vote of what the outcome will be."

We did not happen to visit St. Timothy's on a day when a vote took place, but we had a chance to witness an election at another Honolulu preschool where nine children voted on a new nickname for their group. The teacher started off by saying "Okay. Nominations? Ideas? Suggestions for a new name?" The children then responded:

—My Little Pony
—Golden Girls
—Gobots
—Rainbows
—Goldilocks
—Ghostbusters
—Spiders in Black

The teacher closed the nominations, saying "Okay, let's have a vote. Everyone can hold up their hand for just one name. Ready. How many for My Little Pony . . . ?" At the end of the first round of voting the totals were three for Ghostbusters, two for Golden Girls, two for My Little Pony, one for Goldilocks, and one for Spiders in Black. The teacher suggested a compromise: "The word 'gold' is in two of these names. What if we have a name with 'gold' in it? Why don't you all try to think of a name with 'gold' in it and we'll have another vote tomorrow." When we returned to the school the following week we asked about the outcome of the election. The teacher told us, "The name that won was Goldbusters. The boys wanted Ghostbusters and the girls wanted Golden Girls. One child suggested a combination—Goldbusters. So they voted and Goldbusters won."

The Rule of Law

In Cheryl's classroom at St. Timothy's only three children at a time are allowed in the block corner. Cheryl explained how this rule came about:

We used to have so many fights in the block corner—much worse than that disagreement you got on tape between Stu and Mike. Five or six boys would play in there at a time, and it was just too crowded and there weren't enough blocks to go around. So we had a class discussion, and we came up with the idea of allowing just three children at a time in there. There was some discussion about whether it should be two or three, but in the end everyone agreed on making the rule three and it seems to be working pretty well. The children always notice how many kids are in there. They count and keep track.

There are many rules at St. Timothy's, some created by the children, most by the staff. Colleen explained that for these rules to be most effective, their rationale should be explained to children:

Children like having rules. It gives them a sense of security. At this age they want to know where they stand, to have clear limits. Whenever we tell children about a rule we believe it is important to give them the reason behind the rule so they see how rules work to make things run smoothly. That's why we also encourage them to problem-solve and come up with their own rules when there are disputes.

Justice

Justice in American preschools is negotiated daily with children playing the roles of plaintiff, defendant, and attorney, and teachers playing the role of judge. As in the dispute we filmed in the block corner, teachers at St. Timothy's deal with conflict by leading children step by step through the processes of litigation and arbitration. As soon as Cheryl arrived in the block corner to break up the fight, the trial began. In this case, each of the parties chose to represent himself. Under Cheryl's direction, Stu and Mike each testified, offered evidence, referred to precedents, and objected to aspects of each other's testimony:

Cheryl: What's going on here?

Stu: Look what he did to my road and he told Billy, "Take my block."

Mike: I told him, "I want the block."

Cheryl: And what did he say? Did he tell you why he wouldn't give you the block?

Stu: 'Cuz I had it first. The other day when John was here first you said he was first so today I'm first.

Where do children at St. Timothy's and other American preschools learn these techniques of jurisprudence? Many children with siblings have experience pleading similar cases at home, with parents playing the part of judge and siblings the part of co-litigant. For children without siblings and for children growing up in homes that do not encourage this basically middle-class American approach to conflict resolution, the preschool is an important classroom for learning how to defend oneself from accusations and to seek redress when one feels wronged. Key lessons to be learned about justice in American preschools are that words and reason are preferable to fists in conflict resolution; that, with patience, justice can emerge out of adversarial positions; and that one is innocent (and thus unpunishable) until proven guilty.

The interaction between Cheryl and Kerry we taped was excruciating for both parties (as well as for viewers of the scene) because Cheryl, although firmly believing Kerry to be guilty of not picking up toys he had played with, would not punish him until she could extract at least a semblance of a confession. Similarly, Cheryl would not make a ruling in the dispute between Mike and Stu until she had given each of them a chance (and indeed, led him through the steps) of pleading his case.

St. Timothy's legalistic approach to resolving classroom disputes struck many of our Chinese and Japanese respondents as cumbersome and heavy-handed. A teacher in Beijing commented, "When children fight and misbehave teachers should tell them forcefully that that kind of behavior is unacceptable and just will not be tolerated." A preschool teacher from Tokyo wrote on her response sheet, "I was surprised by the way the American teacher got right in the middle of the children's disputes."

Issues of truth and justice are more negotiable at St. Timothy's than at Dong-feng, where disputes usually are settled quickly and definitively by a teacher's ruling. And teachers at St. Timothy's play a much more active role in arbitrating disputes than do teachers at Komatsudani, who believe that children should be left, as much as possible, to devise their own techniques for conflict resolution. At St. Timothy's fairness and justice are issues to be continuously negotiated, lobbied for, voted on, pleaded, litigated, and adjudicated, all under the modeling, encouraging, correcting, arbitrating influence of the teachers.

St. Timothy's in Context

Most of the Americans who viewed our videotapes found St. Timothy's unexceptional. A day-care teacher from Nashville described it as "a good, middle-of-the-road American preschool." A professor of preschool education in Honolulu told us, "There are a few little things that I don't like particularly they do. But all in all, I think you've chosen a pretty nice program. A lot of the things we stress to students in our classes are there in your video." A nursery school administrator from Pennsylvania wrote: "Except for the number of Asian kids and teachers, a very typical-looking American day-care program."

Some of our American informants, however, worried that our focus on St. Timothy's would mislead foreign audiences who viewed our tapes. The problem lies less in St. Timothy's atypicality than in the inability of any single American (or Chinese or Japanese) preschool to represent the preschools of the whole nation. American preschools vary across several important dimensions, including nursery school versus day-care hours and ethos; a curricular emphasis on play (social and emotional development) versus work (academic readiness); and private nonprofit versus public versus private for-profit organization and administration. To locate St. Timothy's within the range of American preschools, we need first to present a brief history of the American nursery school, day-care center, and kindergarten and then to discuss some of the political, economic, and cultural forces that affect preschool care in the contemporary United States. These forces include local, national, and even international political events; changes in labor and the economy; and changes in the ideology of motherhood, women's work, and the family.

Nursery Schools and Day-Care Centers

The first care programs for young children in the United States began in the mid-nineteenth century. These early programs included kindergartens (which were heavily influenced by the theories of Frederich Froebel) and settlement house nurseries (the most famous being Jane Addams's Hull House in Chicago), where immigrant children were fed, clothed, and acculturated (Addams, 1910). At first the boundaries between kindergartens, nursery schools, and day-care centers were indistinct: kindergartens, not yet part of the public school system, shared with settlement house nurseries a concern for socializing as well as feeding the next generation of American citizens. The words of the president of New York's first kindergarten association make this clear:

You cannot catch your citizens too early in order to make him a good citizen. The kindergarten age is your earliest opportunity to catch the little Russian, little Italian, the little Pole . . . and begin to make an American citizen out of him. . . . The children are brought into a new social order—along with a new respect for law and order. . . . The social uplift is felt—first, by the child; second, by the family; and third, by the neighborhood. . . . The training will naturally tend to good manners, good morals, and good citizenship in the years to come. (quoted in Osborn, 1980, p. 98)

Nineteenth-century feminists, social activists, and educational innovators, spurred by the goals of freeing poor women to work to support their families and freeing middle- and upper-class women from the oppressive tedium of full-time motherhood, led the crusade to create more kindergartens and nursery schools as well as settlement house day-care programs (Finkelstein, 1988). By the 1920s, in many states, kindergarten was well on its way to becoming the first year of public education. Settlement house nursery programs evolved into day-care centers—full-day programs for children of the very poor and children of blue-collar, lower-middle-class working mothers. Nursery schools—half-day programs set up to provide intellectual stimulation and promote social and emotional development in three-, four-, and five-year-olds—became increasingly popular among upper-middle- and upper-class families.

Over the past fifty years, enrollments in nursery schools and day-care centers have fluctuated. Day-care programs swelled in numbers during the depression, stimulated by the availability of public programs funded by the Federal Economic Recovery Act and the Works Project Administration. During World War II the number of day-care programs grew still larger in response to wartime labor shortages, which brought more mothers of young children into the full-time work force.

In the late 1940s, with the return of a large cohort of men from the war, public and government support for day care quickly evaporated. Many child-care programs were forced to close, and the number of children enrolled in full-time care dropped precipitously. In this conservative baby-boom era, the split between day care and nursery schools widened along class and economic lines, with nursery schools providing half-day care to middle- and upper-class children of nonworking mothers while day-care centers went back to serving mostly poor and working-class families.

The Rise of the Extended-Day Nursery School

The women's liberation movement of the 1960s and 1970s, a rising divorce rate, and changes in middle-class women's career paths have had a significant effect on American preschool education. During the past twenty years, with increasing numbers of middle- and upper-middle-class mothers working outside the home, demand for full-day day care has risen dramatically. Poor and working-class women had always needed day care, but in the 1970s a growing demand was heard from the wealthier and more influential middle and upper-middle classes for more and better full-day programs for their three-, four-, and five-year-olds. Rather than place their children in existing day-care programs, which continued to serve mostly children from lower-class families, middle-class parents looked for other child-care arrangements. A rising divorce rate leading to more working mothers also contributed to the demand for quality full-day child care. To serve this new generation of dual-career and single-parent families, some nursery schools in wealthier communities began to offer "extended-day" programs for a surcharge on regular nursery school tuition. At the same time community organizations, churches, a few progressive corporations, and some entrepreneurs opened full-day and flexible-hour child-care centers intended to meet families' changing needs. As a result, class distinctions that for years had separated nursery schools from day care began to break down: full-day, five-day-a-week programs became a respectable child-care choice for middle-class families who a generation before would have looked on day care with disdain.

St. Timothy's is an example of this fusion of the respectability of the nursery school with the utility of day care. St. Timothy's calls itself not a nursery school or a day-care center but rather a child center. It offers families a choice between half-day (8:00 A.M. to 1:00 P.M.), three-quarter-day (8:00 A.M. to 3:00 P.M.), and full-day (8:00 A.M. to 5:00 P.M.) care. The part-day and full-day children are mixed in the classrooms, so that in effect a traditional half-day nursery school program is embedded in a full-day day-care center. A vestige of the traditional nursery school schedule can be perceived in St. Timothy's daily routine: most pedagogically important activities are scheduled for the morning, when all the children are in attendance. In the afternoon the schedule is more relaxed and play is freer and more unsupervised as some children are picked up by their parents at noon and others as late as 6:00 P.M. In many American extended-day child-care centers, staffing patterns also reveal their nursery school origins, as the "regular" staff work from 8:00 A.M. to 3:00 P.M., with part-time teachers and aides filling in from mid-afternoon until closing.

St. Timothy's is typical of an evolving and increasingly popular form of American preschool: the child center, a hybrid of the extended-day nursery and the middle-class day-care center. Child centers like St. Timothy's are in important ways unlike both traditional day-care centers, which continue to serve mostly poor and working-class families, and traditional nursery schools, which continue to serve middle- and upper-class families with mothers who either do not work outside the home, work only part time, or work full time and arrange for home care for their children for part of the day.

There are regional variations across the United States in the availability and popularity of nursery schools, day-care centers, and child centers. In some areas of the country, half-day nursery schools are still plentiful and popular. In other areas, including Honolulu, where the cost of living is very high and two-job families are the great majority, old-fashioned half-day nursery school programs have virtually disappeared, having been transformed into child centers like St. Timothy's.

Work and Play

In 1964 the federal government, in the spirit of President Lyndon Johnson's War on Poverty, launched Head Start. By the summer of 1965 more than half a million preschoolers were enrolled. Head Start was intended to reach underprivileged children before they entered public school to give them the early cognitive stimulation they presumably were lacking at home and thereby break the cycle of educational underachievement and poverty (Zigler and Lamb, 1983).

Although Head Start's success in meeting these lofty goals has been ambiguous and its reputation among legislators and academic evaluators controversial,* many American middle- and upper-middle-class parents nevertheless have drawn unambiguous conclusions from this and other compensatory educational programs. If Head Start can help a child from a disadvantaged home catch up, why can't the same principles of early cognitive stimulation and two or more years of prekindergarten education help already advantaged children get further ahead?

In the past few years preschools in many urban, suburban, and university communities have begun offering special classes for children who score above average on intelligence tests as well as for those whom parents or teachers feel are "gifted" (Alvino, 1986). Modeled loosely on Head Start and informed by the American beliefs that children differ widely in ability and that every child has the right to realize his unique potential, these programs for the gifted and talented are special-education classes for the intellectually, culturally, and economically advantaged.

Unlike some other Honolulu preschools with excellent reputations, St. Timothy's has no testing, no tracking, and no special programs for gifted children. But the staff nevertheless feel pressure from middle-class parents to provide the children in their care with a head start toward educational success. Indirect pressure comes from enrollment concerns: middle-class preschool programs in Honolulu succeed or fail in part according to their record in placing their graduates in prestigious private elementary schools, which select students partly on the basis of their performance on entrance exams. Direct pressure comes from parents who expect to hear glowing reports from teachers of their children's academic progress. As Cheryl complained to us:

> At the parent conferences they [parents] ask about how their kids are doing in a way that makes it clear that they mean, "Have you taught my son to read yet?" It's this sort of look you can read in parents' expression that says to you, "Other children my son's age are reading already and they're going to get into Punahou [a prestigious private elementary school]. What's taking you so long to teach my child to read?" I always try to broaden the scope of these discussions to include social and emotional development of the whole child, to get

*Compare the 1969 Westinghouse Learning Corporation report with studies by Bronfenbrenner (1974), Lazar (1982), and Weikart (1982).

the parents away from this narrow focus on the ABCs and reading and being in such a hurry.

Jean Piaget complained that Americans nearly always asked him the same question about his work: "How can children be accelerated through your stages of cognitive development?" (Fitzgerald and Brackbill, 1976). Piaget called this, sarcastically, "the American question."

In their quest for answers to the American question, parents turn for help not only to preschools like St. Timothy's and teachers like Cheryl but also to a growing industry of how-to books for parents and educational materials designed to catalyze the development of children's intelligence and put them on the fast track in the education race. In the most extreme, mid-1980s version of this struggle, American infants look up from their cribs to see not pictures of clowns and birds but reproductions of works by Monet and Mondrian. Their lullabies are recordings of Beethoven concerti and Berlitz French conversation tapes. A sign with the words "Baby's Crib" printed in large block letters hangs over their beds in the hopes that literacy, knowledge, and intelligence will blossom in this hothouse cognitive atmosphere.

The above description is a caricature, but American child-development experts warn that the problem of the hurried child is all too real (Elkind, 1981; Suransky, 1982). It is also not new. Some observers date the origins of the current wave of education mania to the launching of the first Sputnik in 1959 and the fear that swept America that if our children were not quickly enrolled in accelerated curricula we soon would fall hopelessly and dangerously behind the Soviets. These days the perceived threat used to marshal support for early-educational achievement efforts is not Sputnik but rather "The Japanese Educational Challenge," the title of Merry White's 1987 book. We are losing the economic war with Japan, the current American reasoning goes, because we lag behind the Japanese in educational achievement and investment in children. Japanese educational superiority begins at least as early as preschool, so we must begin our compensatory efforts no later than preschool if we are to have any hope of competing.

One result of this pressure for early academic achievement is that many American preschools today offer a curriculum for four- and five-year-olds that is very schoollike. This tendency to want to speed up children's development, though responsive to economic and political events including Sputnik and the trade imbalance, surely also reflects something more fundamental in American society and character. In a socially mobile society, where the direct inheritance of wealth and social status is difficult and education the surest path to social and economic success, the temptation to try to hurry one's child along by investing early and heavily in his cognitive capital is an understandable parental strategy.

The staff of St. Timothy's is not diametrically opposed to parents' goals for accelerated cognitive development and early educational achievement for their children. Teachers find themselves resisting parental demands that reading and writing be taught in the preschool not because they are disinterested in achievement but because they believe too much academic pressure too soon can be counterproductive and even harmful to children's emotional, social, and cognitive growth. The philosophy that guides St. Timothy's pedagogy is that children have a natural thirst for knowledge that will lead them to learn quickly, thoroughly, and authentically when parents and teachers facilitate but do not interfere in this natural process. Thus the staff stress that in a preschool classroom that is carefully structured for emotional and social as well as cognitive development and supervised by a professional staff, children learn best through play.

We would place St. Timothy's approximately mid-range among American preschools along the play/work, process/content (Fein and Clarke-Stewart, 1973) continuum. The staff are highly critical of the academically oriented "workbook and cuisinaire rod" preschools, which they view as hurrying and thus harming children. But they also see themselves as more skilled in facilitating children's cognitive growth than are old-fashioned nursery school programs, which they view as offering only unstructured play and group baby-sitting.

There was some disagreement among our American informants about whether St. Timothy's is too work- or too play-oriented. Some faulted St. Timothy's for giving too little emphasis to academic readiness, whereas others felt the approach was too structured and rigid, inhibiting children's play. For example, a teacher from an alternative preschool commented about St. Timothy's: "Don't you think schools like this take themselves too seriously? There's something about their perfect little housekeeping corner and their perfect Piagetian learning activities for conservation and classification and all that. It's not quite as bad as Montessori but it's close."

But comments like these were in the clear minority. Most of our American informants felt that St. Timothy's appeared in our tape to give appropriate emphasis to academic readiness and to present children with a good balance between play and work, integrating cognitive with social and emotional development.

The Business of Preschool

In America, unlike China and Japan where preschools are heavily subsidized, cost is a critical factor for many families in their search for care for their preschool-aged children. In 1986 the full-day program at St. Timothy's cost three thousand dollars a year for a four-year-old child. Tuition can run much higher in New York and other large cities. Middle-class families with young children thus can expect to spend a sizable percentage of their income on child care, more for infant care, and much more if they must find care for more than one preschooler (Winget, 1982).

Middle-class and upper-class families get some help in meeting preschool expenses through child-care tax credits. Poor families receive some assistance with preschool tuition through Title XX funds. St. Timothy's, like many other nonprofit preschools, has a scholarship program, which makes it possible for less affluent families to enroll their children and thereby provide the school with what Barbara Culler calls "a really good mix of children." But scholarship funds are limited; 90 percent of St. Timothy's families pay the full tuition.

Although the tuition they charge parents is high, nearly all American preschools struggle financially. Preschool in America is a marginal enterprise in the nonprofit as well as in the for-profit and public sectors.

Approximately 25 percent of American preschoolers attend private for-profit programs. Many of these small-scale proprietary preschools are being forced out of business by rising labor, utility, and insurance costs. Larger operations manage to turn a profit only by keeping salaries low and student/teacher ratios high while benefiting from an economy of scale which saves on administrative costs and other overhead.

During the past fifteen years several national child-care corporations have emerged in the United States. By opening new centers and buying out old ones, they have created networks of child-care franchises sarcastically referred to as "McChildcare" and "Kentucky Fried Children" (Featherstone, 1970) by critics who point out that staff turnover (always high in preschools) runs over 50 percent a year in the private for-profit sector (Maynard, 1985). Generally, for-profit preschools have a poor record for quality except in those rare instances when an early-education expert has been allowed to play a major role in decisions about staff qualifications and salary, teacher/student ratios, and materials (Lake, 1974).

Approximately 10 percent of American preschoolers attend day-care programs run and supported by state, county, and city governments. The great majority of slots in public programs are earmarked for children from disadvantaged families. The federal government, though not directly in the business of running preschools, supports public and private non-profit preschool programs through Head Start funds and other grants. Many universities and junior colleges run preschool programs for the purposes of research and teacher training as well as to serve the needs of faculty, students, and staff seeking quality day care for their children. Some high schools run preschools as part of their vocational education program for careers in child-care, education, and home economics.

The majority of American preschools (60 percent) are, like St. Timothy's, private nonprofit organizations, and most of these (70 percent) are also housed in churches, which provide space gratis or for a modest rent. Without this sort of subsidy most nonprofit preschools would be unable to stay in operation. As it is, a program like St. Timothy's, which pays only a nominal rental fee to the Church of St. Timothy's for the use of its grounds and classrooms, must still struggle continuously to juggle salaries, tuition, and student/teacher ratios.

Even with high tuitions and rent subsidies, most nonprofit preschools in the United States need additional revenues to function effectively. Scholarships and capital improvements usually are funded not by tuition (which barely covers salaries) but by fund-raising efforts such as bake sales and charity auctions.

There is a great range in quality and approach among American private, nonprofit preschools. Many of these programs, in addition to being housed in churches, are church-run and offer a curriculum that includes light, moderate, or heavy doses of religious education. Other nonprofit programs are run by community organizations. Corporate-sponsored preschools currently are rare (in 1984 only two thousand out of six million U.S. businesses gave any support to employee child-care needs) but may become increasingly important in the future. Legislation has been proposed in Congress offering tax benefits to companies that make child care available to employees. Proponents of employer-provided child care point to studies suggesting that these programs promote worker loyalty, reduce absenteeism and job turnover, and lead to greater overall productivity (Kiplinger Report, 1987).

In all, these various forms of preschool add up to about one million available slots for some eight million preschool-aged children. The seven million children who do not go to preschool are cared for by relatives and paid sitters, by group-care home providers, and by siblings, by neighbors who look in sporadically, or by no one at all (Hinze, 1987).

All preschools in the United States are subject to state rules and regulations. But the United States, unlike Japan and China, lacks national statutes governing preschools, and no one national agency is directly responsible for licensing preschool teachers and directors, establishing curriculum requirements, or prescribing student/teacher ratios. Responsibility for assuring the quality of preschool programs therefore rests with each of the fifty states and the District of Columbia. State rules and regulations for preschools vary widely (Orton, 1980). In some states preschools are under the jurisdiction of the state department of education. In most states, however, preschools are under the control of the state department of health and human services. This distinction has important implications. Some Americans who would like to see free preschool child care made available to every American child believe that putting preschools under the control of state departments of education would be an important step in that direction.* Those who believe that American public school education is already in shambles and that preschoolers are already too hurried object to letting preschools fall into the hands of the education bureaucracy.

Although there is a shortage of preschool programs for three- to five-year-old children, the need for infant and toddler care and for weekend, evening, and sick care is even more acute. Most American preschools do not accept children under the age of three or children who are ill, and most are not open weekends, evenings, or holidays. Where programs for infants and toddlers are available they tend to be prohibitively expensive for poor and working-class families, who must turn instead to more affordable day-care homes. (Preschool tuitions are much higher for younger than for older children since infants and toddlers require much lower child/caregiver ratios than do older children.)

With little government regulation and minimal public financial support, the quality and availability of preschool care in America vary dramatically along class lines. Wealthy parents are able to choose from among several high-quality nonprofit nursery schools and child centers or to hire a full-time nanny to care for their child in their own home. Middle-class parents are more likely to have to scramble to find a program they can afford that has an open slot for their child. Fortunate middle-class families manage to place their children in good-quality programs, which, like St. Timothy's, are usually nonprofit and church-connected. Other middle-class families must settle for less good nonprofit and proprietary programs. Many middle-class families, finding no affordable and available programs open during the right hours to cover their work schedules, end up with group baby-sitting arrangements. Poor families not fortunate enough to place their children in federally or locally subsidized programs are left with low-quality private-sector preschools, with underfunded community programs, or with informal child-care arrangements.

*For a range of views on this issue, see Kagan and Zigler's *Early Schooling: The National Debate* (1988).

Teachers, Parents, and Children

The Breakdown of the American Family?

American preschools function in a milieu of crisis and conflict. The crisis is the perceived breakdown of the American family. The conflict lies in the perception that the needs of preschool children, parents, and teachers are competing and at times even irreconcilable.

According to one dominant thread in America's public discourse, there was a time before television, before recreational drugs, before Vietnam and Watergate, before women's liberation and nursing homes and AIDS and a 50-percent divorce rate, when the American family was vital: children grew up knowing their wise and kindly grandparents, respecting their hard-working father, secure in the attention of a full-time mother. Embedded in safe, stable, supportive communities where people trusted their neighbors, drew sustenance from their church, had faith in their schools and government leaders, and were guided by clearly defined sex roles, the middle-class American family had no need for preschools.

Social critics, politicians, and scholars from the right, left, and center of the American political spectrum decry the deterioration of the American family and the consequent crisis facing young children. Christopher Lasch, for example, in *Haven in a Heartless World* (1977) and *The Culture of Narcissism* (1979), argues that the welfare state has had an intrusive, destabilizing effect on the American family. Conservative politicians seek support for their domestic agenda with references to the need to strengthen family bonds. In arguing the decline of the family, critics cite the rising divorce rate, widespread acceptance of extramarital promiscuity, rampant child abuse and neglect, the loss of parental authority and respect for elders, growing materialism, and a selfish, "me-first" mentality in parents as well as children.

Preschools are viewed variously as part of the problem or part of the solution. According to the former version, preschools contribute to social instability by removing children from the bosom of the family and depriving them of essential maternal care (see, for example, Selma Fraiberg's *Every Child's Birthright: In Defense of Mothering*, 1977). Proponents of preschools see them as essentially ameliorative, supporting struggling families that could not stay intact without child-care assistance. Proponents as well as opponents of day care tend to share a commitment to the goals of life, liberty, and the pursuit of happiness. The conflict lies in the question of whose life, whose liberty, and whose happiness is to have priority.

Mothers versus Children

In the years since World War II, the number of working mothers in the United States with children under eighteen years of age has increased approximately sixfold (Breitbart, 1974). By 1984, 57 percent of preschool-aged children had mothers in the work force (U.S. Department of Labor, 1985; Children's Defense Fund, 1986).

Mothers of young children work for a variety of reasons. Approximately a quarter of these working mothers are never-married, divorced, or widowed single parents who are their families' sole wage earners. Roughly another quarter are married, lower-middle-class women who work less out of choice than out of necessity, pooling their earnings with their husbands' to keep their families above the poverty line. Many middle-class American women choose to work even while their children are small in order to supplement their husbands' income and help to buy a home or save for their children's college education. Other middle- and upper-class mothers work for personal fulfillment as well as for financial gain. Many Americans believe that it is just as natural, appropriate, and important for women as for men to have a career. As the mother of a four-year-old at St. Timothy's told us:

> I don't really feel guilty about working and putting Michael in school because I know myself well enough to know I wouldn't be doing him a favor if I gave up my career to stay home with him. I would be so frustrated if I was home all day, and then I'd take this frustration out on him without meaning to. If I had to be stuck at home all day I'd go nuts. Believe me. I tried it for a little while and it just didn't work.

Several working mothers told us that they are struggling to mix parenting with work because they are determined not to make the mistake their mothers made by organizing their lives around parenting:

> When I was born my mom quit school to take care of me. Her plan was always to go back to school and have a career. She was going to go back when my little brother started elementary school; then she put it off until he was in high school; then it was too late and she felt she was too old to have a career. Now she has no kids left at home and no job and she's only fifty-one and she has basically nothing to do. A lot of women of that generation—I've talked about this with lots of my friends—and a lot of women our mothers' age are in the same boat.

Another preschool parent told us:

I basically stopped working and became a full-time mother for almost three years after Brad was born. The plan was I was supposedly going to write my Ph.D. thesis during this stage while my husband supported us. I got a little bit of it done, but only a little. I finally decided I was never going to finish up without working on it full time. A thesis isn't the kind of thing you can pick up and work on a few minutes each day while your baby naps. So we put Brad in preschool when he turned three. I still feel that was the right decision even though it was hard on him. Ideally we would have liked to have been able to wait until he was a little older, but I felt like I was pushing my luck as it was. I could start to feel from my adviser, well, that he was beginning to write me off, to stop taking me seriously, you know, to put me in the category of full-time mother/amateur scholar, another one of those middle-aged women pursuing their Ph.D.s as a hobby. I just knew that it was now or never for getting back to full-time status with my studies if I were to have any chance of having an academic career.

A majority of American mothers of preschool-aged children, however, work less out of desire for personal fulfillment than out of economic need and even desperation (Hewlett, 1986). In 1985, 23 percent of American households were headed by single mothers. Nearly half of the children in America living below the poverty line live in female-headed households. Forty-five percent of unemployed single mothers say they would seek employment if they could find affordable child care (Children's Defense Fund, 1986). Federal Title XX regulations provide for child-care assistance to lower-income families, but there are not enough funds available to make a major impact and the situation is getting worse rather than better: as the number of families living in poverty has rise in the 1980s, Title XX grants have decreased significantly in after-inflation dollars (National Commission, 1985).

As the feminization of poverty spreads across the nation, the need for affordable child care for working women is becoming increasingly acute. Yet, the belief persists that placing children in full-time child care is unwise, selfish, and irresponsible. Instead of moving ahead as a nation to institute a comprehensive child-care system, Americans fight and refight, study and restudy the issue of whether various forms of paid, nonparental child care are harmful to children.

Arguments against working mothers and institutional child care come from an unusual concurrence in thought between academic child-development experts on the one hand and the conservative religious laity (the so-called Moral Majority) on the other.

Sigmund Freud's theories of child traumatization; Anna Freud's work on orphaned, group-reared Holocaust survivors (Freud and Dunn, 1951); René Spitz's writings on institutionalized children's failure to thrive (1965); the Robertsons' films (1967, 1968), which show children deteriorating rapidly after brief separations from their parents; Bruno Bettelheim's writings on infantile autism (1967); Margaret Mahler's assertion that the child must feel in control of the process of separation and individuation (Mahler et al., 1975); the Harlows' experiments with mother-deprived monkeys (1962); John Bowlby's books on attachment and loss (1980)—all these and other studies are cited as evidence in the case against institutional child care and against working mothers of young children. Child-development scholars including Selma Fraiberg (1977) and Burton White (1985a, 1985b) have written books for general audiences that warn of the dangers of precipitately separating children from their mothers. Recent works by Vivian Suransky (*The Erosion of Childhood*, 1982) and Sylvia Hewlett (*A Lesser Life*, 1986) have drawn on psychodynamic and economic studies to criticize the feminist movement for placing the needs of women over what is best for children.

Conservative nonacademic elements in American society echo these warnings of the dangers of child care outside the home. Phyllis Schafly, Jerry Falwell, and other conservative social activists share a belief in the sanctity of the mother-child bond and a horror of their premature separation. Many of these conservatives support the idea of preschool care only for the children of the poor, on the assumption that poor mothers are rarely capable of providing nurturant care or a cognitively enriched environment for their children.

The point is not that child-development specialists and conservative religious and political figures hold the same belief for the same reasons but rather that working mothers in America who place their children in child care are subject to criticism from several quarters, including the academy, the medical establishment, and the Moral Majority. To exacerbate the problem, working mothers receive unambivalent encouragement from feminists for their decision to work, but little support or understanding for their need for quality child care.

Hewlett (1986) and Suransky (1982), among others, have criticized the women's movement for failing to give priority to the need for quality child care and for being contemptuous of women who choose parenting over careers. To be sure, there are feminist voices (for example, Friedan, 1986) supporting child care just as there are academic voices arguing, against the prevailing wisdom, that preschool can have beneficial rather than harmful effects on children (see, for example, Clarke-Stewart, 1982; Fein et al., 1982; Belsky et al., 1984; Lazar, 1982; Weikart, 1982). But on the whole

American women with young children feel themselves in a double bind: frustrated and looked down upon if they choose to be full-time mothers and housekeepers, frustrated and guilty if they choose to work and find someone else to care for their children (Harper and Richards, 1979).

In the midst of this cacophony of discordant, often accusatory voices, American mothers cannot help but feel accused and confused. Even if a mother, after some difficulty, manages to locate a good preschool for her child, she inevitably feels a sense of guilt and dereliction of duty. Conversely, a woman who chooses to stay home with her child is subject to real or imagined criticism from feminists and other employed women. American fathers are not completely immune to these feelings, but in the United States today balancing parenting and work remains clearly a woman's problem.

Certainly in China and Japan as well as in the United States, combining the duties of parenting and working is difficult. But only in the United States did we hear widespread expression of ambivalence, angst, guilt, and confusion over the decision to place children in child care.

Parents versus Teachers

Preschool teachers and parents share a concern for children, but they often disagree about what is best for them. At times they also are separated by competing personal needs, as a preschool teacher told us when we spoke with him at the end of his long day of work:

> I was here late today and Mrs. Smith finally got here at about 6:01 which is after the absolute deadline for picking kids up. When she got here, Sean and I were both really happy to see his mother. But Mrs. Smith didn't just pick Sean up and go home. While Sean was getting his things from his cubby, she tried to get me into a big conversation. She says, "Look at him, he's so energetic. How long did he sleep today? He's going to be up all night." She goes on complaining, you know, telling me that if Sean has a two-hour nap he won't go to sleep before eleven. She tells me that she has exams coming up next week and is exhausted at night, and all that. She asked me, couldn't I start waking Sean up from his nap after thirty minutes or so and let him play quietly, and didn't I think that maybe he no longer needs a nap at all now that he's almost five. I've got to tell you, frankly, I didn't listen all that sympathetically to this. When I'm telling all this to you now, I suppose she comes across sounding kind of sympathetic, but at the time my only reaction was, "Hey, lady, he's your son. You had him, and now you drop him off

at 7 A.M. and pick him up at 6 P.M. and if he doesn't fall asleep in the car on the way home you're angry with us. What's your goal, not to see him at all from Monday morning to Friday night?"

Many American preschool parents, like Sean's mother, are clearly needy. Preschool teachers can sometimes but not always respond to these needs. Mrs. Smith's request that her son be allowed to skip his daily nap at school angered Sean's teacher both because he felt it in Sean's best interest to spend more waking time with his mother and because he and his fellow teachers count on children's naptime for a much-needed break. In this case the conflict between teacher and parent is unusually clear, as a preschool teacher and a mother battle over ninety minutes of a child's sleeping time, time they both feel they need and deserve (Sidel, 1986).

Preschool teachers are usually in the forefront of Americans concerned about the crisis in the contemporary family because they feel they have been asked, fairly or not, to bear a primary responsibility to minister to these ills. For example, Colleen and Cheryl pointed out that the high divorce rate of St. Timothy's families makes their job more difficult:

Davidson: Are many of the children here from divorced families?

Momohara: I don't know if I'd say many, but enough. Maybe a third or a fourth. It seems to go in cycles. I don't know. [To Cheryl] What would you say? Some years there's a lot; other years it seems like less.

Takashige: Definitely. Last year I had the four-year-olds, and we had a bunch of divorces and separations right at the beginning of the year. It was like an epidemic.

Momohara: Yeah. It's almost like some parents wait till they get their kids in preschool to announce they're getting divorced so we can pick up the pieces.

Takashige: That's no joke. That's exactly what one parent said to me. He actually told me he and his wife waited till their son was in school for a few months before telling him about the divorce because he wanted us to be there to help his kid with the troubles at home.

American preschool teachers are made to feel that parents as well as children are their clients. Many parents who need advice, counseling, or just someone to talk to about their children and themselves turn to preschool teachers. As a former teacher in Hawaii told us:

Some parents are just so needy. Some single mothers, for instance. You can just see it all over their faces—they need someone to talk

to, to spill their guts out to. Sometimes a parent will kind of stall
when she's picking up her kid, and you can tell immediately she's
waiting till no other parents are around so she can talk to you. And
then she'll start making small talk, trying to get up her nerve to talk
about something heavy. Finally she'll get around to it, so you stand
there for five or ten minutes, in the doorway, right at closing time,
rocking back and forth from one leg to the other. That's why I call
them "one-legged conferences."

In addition to these spontaneous before- and after-school exchanges,
formal parent-teacher conferences are scheduled at St. Timothy's twice a
year. At these fifteen-minute conferences the child's progress and adjustment are discussed, and parents and teachers have a chance to raise issues
of concern. Barbara Culler told us that the most difficult issue to resolve
arises when parents and teachers have very different approaches to dealing
with children:

Children this age need some consistency between home and school.
Everything doesn't have to be just like home. It can't be. But it's
important that children don't get totally mixed messages. Occasionally we've had situations where we have trouble controlling a child's
behavior and we call in the parents and learn they control him at
home by using corporal punishment. We counsel them and suggest
other ways to discipline. If that doesn't work, if they won't change,
we may have to tell parents that it looks like our approach to discipline is very different from theirs, so they might do better to transfer
their child to another preschool.

We heard about the need for consistency between home and school
much more frequently from parents, teachers, and administrators in the
United States than in China, where preschools are expected to correct
parents' mistakes, or in Japan, where preschools are expected to provide
experiences children cannot get at home.

American preschool staff, in addition to caring for children, provide
support, advice, referrals, and even counseling to needy parents (Provence
et al., 1979; Kagan et al., 1987). Some teachers welcome this role;
others resent it. Many preschool administrators would like to see their
programs evolve from preschools to family centers and to get their staffs
more involved in family-life education. But most teachers feel that though
parents look to them to provide a range of professional services, they are
paid and treated less like professionals than like untrained, service-sector
employees.

Most American preschool teachers, in terms of earnings, place near the bottom of the American work force. Fringe benefits, including sick leave, health insurance, and retirement plans, are often inadequate. Public respect for preschool teaching as a profession is low as measured not only by the low salaries but also by low standards in most states for the licensing of teachers and by the reluctance of young educated Americans, particularly men, to seek careers in early child education. Because the pay and prestige are so low, preschools have trouble attracting and retaining skilled staff (E. Cummings, 1980). At St. Timothy's the staff is unusually well trained: Barbara Culler and Colleen Momohara have master's degrees in early child education; Cheryl Takashige and the other head teachers all have four-year college degrees; Linda Rios and the other assistant teachers have two-year college degrees. Teachers in many American preschools lack any formal training, and many states have no educational requirements for preschool teaching or directing.

Some Americans suggest that the low status of preschool teaching reflects the lack of importance Americans in power positions give to the world of women and children. Feeney, Christensen, and Moravcik (1987) point out that the younger the children a teacher works with, the poorer the pay and the less likely the teacher will be male. Feminists suggest that in the United States women's concerns (including child care) and women's careers (including preschool teaching) belong to a separate sphere, ignored, denigrated, sneered at, unappreciated. Barbara Finkelstein, in her 1988 paper "The Revolt against Selfishness: Women and the Dilemmas of Professionalism in Early Childhood Education," suggests that the low status and pay of contemporary American preschool teachers are a result of an ambiguous historical legacy. She argues that preschool teaching is underpaid and unappreciated partly because its early champions, including Catharine Beecher and Jane Addams, unlike "equal rights" or "economic" feminists such as Susan B. Anthony and Elizabeth Cady Stanton, were unconcerned with the issue of remuneration for work they viewed more as a crusade than a job. Finkelstein concludes:

> Early childhood educators are the recipients of a problematic professional legacy—mired in an historical tradition of child-advocacy, economic unselfishness, political powerlessness . . . and narrow concepts of moral, cultural, political and economic possibility for women. . . . The template of professionalism in early childhood education is one which promotes knowledge of child development as an indispensable professional ingredient, but discourages efforts to raise the economic and occupational well-being of nursery school teachers, day care workers, mothers, and the variety of guardians who oversee the development of the young. (1988, p. 26)

Underpaid and underappreciated, preschool teachers suffer frequent burn-out, contributing to an annual job turnover rate of about 40 percent (National Commission, 1985). The year after we taped at St. Timothy's Cheryl Takashige left preschool teaching to begin a new career.* Barbara Culler explained:

> Cheryl had been thinking about quitting for the past few months. She'd been here seven years altogether. She just finally felt that she'd had it with teaching, at least for a while. It's a shame because she is such an excellent teacher, but I didn't really try to talk her out of her decision to quit, because I knew how she felt. She's taking a few months off now, then she's thinking about going back to school. With what we pay teachers and all the headaches that come along with the job, sooner or later just about everyone burns out. I do what I can to keep my teachers going. I encourage them to take their sick-days and all professional development time. They've got to get some break from the kids and the pressure. One of the teachers that quit last year told me, "I've been working with little kids so long I'm talking in monosyllables to my husband." The shame of it is the way things are now in preschool teaching, it's usually the best teachers that have the most going for them that quit teaching to do something else where they can get paid what they're worth.

Barbara Culler is acutely aware that her staff is overworked and under-paid, but she is limited in what she can do to redress the situation. Like other American preschool administrators, she must struggle to balance the needs of parents, children, and teachers (Ainslie, 1984). To raise teachers' salaries, St. Timothy's is faced with the choice of raising tuition and thus narrowing the range of families that can afford their program, or raising student/teacher ratios and thus compromising their commitment to indi-vidualized child care (Fein and Clarke-Stewart, 1973, p. 31). Teachers as well as administrators are well aware of the hard realities of this equation, as a day-care teacher in Honolulu explained to us:

> We want higher salaries, not to get rich, but a reasonable wage, what we deserve. But the way it always comes back to us from the board is that the only way they can raise our salaries substantially, which they admit we deserve, they would have to increase ratios or raise tuitions. Those are unacceptable alternatives to us. If tuition gets much higher than it is now, the only ones that will be able to afford us will be the

---

*After one year away, Cheryl returned to her old job at St. Timothy's in 1987. Barbara Culler left to work for military programs in child care.

total YUPs, you know, the BMW types: both the mother and father are attorneys or doctors. At that point I would begin to feel like I am just a servant for the rich, like a nanny in England or something. Raising ratios is no answer either. We already have ratios of around ten or eleven to one, which is more than is really good for kids this age. Six or seven to one would be better. Funding our salary increases with bigger ratios would just make our job harder and be bad for the kids. What it comes down to is the message we always get: that the only way they can offer a top-flight program is by teachers agreeing to work for too little pay. So basically, what you've got is a system where teachers are subsidizing preschools by working for so little.

Chapter Five

A Comparative Perspective

Until now we have discussed Japanese, Chinese, and American preschools on their own terms, privileging insiders' explanations and allowing parents and staff to speak directly about what preschools are meant to do and to be. In this chapter we change our approach, offering an outsider's explicitly comparative perspective on the most significant differences and similarities in Japanese, Chinese, and American views of the function of preschool. We take the discussion outside the walls of the preschool, as we explore the question of how institutional child care affects and reflects change in the structure of the family.

We use questionnaire results as a departure point for our discussion. In addition to showing preschool teachers, administrators, parents, and child-development specialists our videotapes of preschools, we also asked them to fill out questionnaires. Three hundred Japanese, 240 Chinese, and 210 Americans answered questions including "What are the three most important reasons for a society to have preschools?" "What are the most important things for children to learn in preschool?" and "What are the most important characteristics of a good preschool teacher?" We use responses to these questions not to test hypotheses or to demonstrate statistical correlations but to facilitate intercultural comparison of how three cultures prioritize the function of preschool.

Language

In China and Japan as well as in the United States, helping children develop language skills is believed to be central to the mission of the preschool. But although the three cultures share a concern for children's

language, they have very different notions of the power and purpose of words.

In China, the emphasis in language development is on enunciation, diction, memorization, and self-confidence in speaking and performing. Chinese children learn in preschool to recite stories and inspirational moral tales and to sing and dance both alone and in groups. American and Japanese visitors to Chinese preschools are invariably impressed by the self-possession and command of language of Chinese children who flawlessly deliver long, rehearsed speeches and belt out multiversed songs.

Language in Japan, both in and out of preschools, is divided into formal and informal systems of discourse. Children in preschools are allowed to speak freely, loudly, even vulgarly to each other during much of the day. But this unrestrained use of language alternates with periods of polite, formal, teacher-directed group recitation of expressions of greeting, thanks, blessing, and farewell. Language in Japan—at least the kind of language teachers teach children—is viewed less as a tool for self-expression than as a medium for expressing group solidarity and shared social purpose. Americans, in contrast, view words as the key to promoting individuality, autonomy, problem solving, friendship, and cognitive development in children. In American preschools children are taught the

Table 5.1   *"What are the most important things for children to learn in preschool?"*

	China		Japan		USA	
	FIRST CHOICE	TOP THREE	FIRST CHOICE	TOP THREE	FIRST CHOICE	TOP THREE
Perseverance	13%	20%	2%	16%	3%	5%
Cooperation and how to be a member of a group	37	58	30	67	32	68
Sympathy/empathy/ concern for others	4	20	31	80	5	39
Creativity	17	50	9	30	6	37
Beginning reading and math skills	6	23	0	1	1	22
Self-reliance/self-confidence	6	29	11	44	34	73
Art/music/dance	1	8	.3	4	1	3
Communication skills	4	27	1	5	8	38
Physical skills	1	3	.3	4	1	6
Good health, hygiene, and grooming habits	11	60	14	49	1	7
Gentleness	0	2	0	0	0	1

rules and conventions of self-expression and free speech (Cazden, 1988; Newkirk, 1989).

Our questionnaire results demonstrate these differences. Japanese respondents gave less emphasis than Americans and Chinese to the importance of children learning to express themselves verbally: 38 percent of Americans and 27 percent of Chinese made "communication skills" one of their top three priorities for children to learn in preschool, as compared to only 5 percent of Japanese (see table 5.1). In contrast, Japanese emphasize skills in listening over speaking: the top Japanese answer to the question, "What are the most important things for children to learn in preschool?" was "sympathy, empathy, concern for others." Thirty-one percent of Japanese respondents made this their first choice, compared to just 5 percent of Americans and 4 percent of Chinese. In China and the United States, where successful communication is believed to depend largely on the clarity of expression of the speaker, the emphasis is on teaching children to express themselves clearly, whereas in Japan, where successful communication is believed to depend largely on the empathic and intuitive abilities of the listener (Lebra, 1976), children are taught less to express themselves than to be sensitive to others' spoken and unspoken forms of self-expression.

Language teaching in Japan, as in China, is centered on encouraging children to express that which is socially shared rather than, as in the United States, on that which is individual and personal. Preschool teachers in China and Japan use the techniques of choral recitation and memorization of stories much more than in the United States, where teachers spend a larger proportion of their time working with children individually, coaching them in how to express their personal thoughts and beliefs. In Japan, where language is viewed as a poor medium for expressing feelings but a useful medium for expressing social cohesion, preschool teachers frequently lead formal group recitation but rarely take an active role in modeling, correcting, or soliciting children's informal speech. In Chinese preschools oral skills are approached as an academic subject: Chinese teachers frequently correct children's mispronunciations and misusage and encourage them to learn public speaking as well as reading, writing, and arithmetic.

Preschool as School

In the midst of a self-proclaimed crisis of low academic achievement, many Americans are turning for answers to Japan, a country of high academic achievement and enviable economic success. The answers provided by Japanese preschools, however, are not the ones Americans expect to hear. In most Japanese preschools there is surprisingly little emphasis on academic instruction. Only 2 percent of our Japanese respondents listed "to give children a good start academically" as one of their top three reasons for a society to have preschools. In contrast, over half of our American respondents chose this as one of their top choices (see table 5.2).

While Americans are beefing up preschool and kindergarten curricula in an attempt to close the educational and economic gap with Japan, the Japanese are spending little time reading, writing, and counting in their preschools. But the Japanese de-emphasis on narrowly defined academic subjects in preschool does not reflect a lack of interest in academic readiness; instead it is part of a long-range strategy for promoting children's educational success. In a society worried about kyōiku mamas driving their children to succeed academically, preschools are seen as havens from academic pressure and competition.

Japanese preschool teachers do not need to teach reading since the majority of children in their charge learn to read at home. The relative ease of reading the Japanese phonetic syllabary (kana) as compared to reading

Table 5.2   "Why should a society have preschools?"

	China		Japan		USA	
	FIRST CHOICE	TOP THREE	FIRST CHOICE	TOP THREE	FIRST CHOICE	TOP THREE
To give children a good start academically	37%	67%	.3%	2%	22%	51%
To reduce spoiling and make up for deficiencies of parents	3	12	.3	2	.5	2
To free parents for work and other pursuits	17	48	1	8	7	25
To give children a chance to play with other children	8	25	14	70	14	42
To start young children on the road toward being good citizens	12	30	5	18	4	14
To give children experience being a member of a group	12	44	61	91	20	62
To provide children with a fun place to go each day	1	7	3	24	4	18
To make young children more independent and self-reliant	11	67	14	80	23	66
To supplement, educate, and support parents	0	0	.3	5	6	20

English or Chinese ideographs makes learning to read relatively unproblematic in Japan (Stevenson et al., 1986). But this alone cannot account for the Japanese preschool's lack of emphasis on academic instruction, since arithmetic, which presumably is equally difficult to master in any language, is also given little attention in most Japanese preschools. To prepare children for successful careers in first grade and beyond, Japanese preschools teach not reading, writing, and mathematics but more fundamental preacademic skills, including perseverance, concentration, and the ability to function as a member of a group.

As compared to only 5 percent of our American respondents, 16 percent of the Japanese and 20 percent of the Chinese who filled out our questionnaires listed perseverance (*nintai* in Japanese, *rennai* in Chinese) as one of the three most important things for children to learn in preschool. As Merry White (1987) and John Singleton (1988) point out, Japanese view learning perseverance as the key to character development. Lois Peak (1987) describes how Japanese preschool teachers cultivate perseverance in children by urging and cajoling their charges into dressing and undressing themselves and by steadfastly refusing to assist them with the task. Peak argues that the pedagogical purpose is less teaching how to dress oneself than cultivating the ability and willingness to persevere. Japanese parents and educators clearly are very concerned with children's educational achievement, but this concern leads not to an academic curriculum in the preschool, which most Japanese believe would be inappropriate and counterproductive, but instead to fostering a positive attitude to school and cultivating skills in thinking, studying, and getting along with others that will promote educational success later in life (Peak, 1986).

Although Americans give great emphasis to the importance of academics in preschool compared to the Japanese, compared to the Chinese, Americans are laggards: only 22 percent of Americans compared to 37 percent of Chinese respondents chose "to give children a good start academically" as the top reason for a society to have preschools. Sixty-seven percent of the Chinese who filled out our questionnaires listed academics as one of the three top choices. The reasons for the Chinese emphasis on academics are multiple, including a Confucian cultural tradition of highly valuing early and strenuous study and a Cultural Revolution legacy that though it is antiintellectual is even more profoundly antifrivolity. To the degree that the legacy of the Cultural Revolution continues to hold sway in China, the effect on preschools is largely to discourage nonideological, frivolous play and to encourage the learning of skills needed to be a productive member of society—reading, writing, computation, memorization, and clear speaking. Another effect of the Cultural Revolution is the "compensation mentality" it has produced in urban parents whose education or careers were disrupted when they were sent to labor in the countryside. Many of these parents look to preschools to provide their children with the educational opportunities they missed. Frustrated in their own careers, they tend to be very serious about those of their children.

Although two-thirds of our Chinese respondents emphasized the importance of academic learning, another third did *not* list "to give children a good start academically" as one of their top three reasons for a society to have preschools. Our interviews in Beijing and Shanghai suggest that especially in urban centers, particularly among child-development specialists and intellectuals, a less academically oriented, more balanced social-skills-and-play preschool curriculum is gaining favor. Ministry of Education authorities and normal school professors of preschool education, looking to the West, are working to rebuild and reform a preschool system left in tatters by the Cultural Revolution. In Chinese normal universities, a new generation of preschool education students is being exposed to the Western educational model of balancing academic learning with social and emotional development. Following graduation, these students are dispersing to preschools throughout China. New educational and play materials are also being developed and widely distributed. Papers calling for more classroom freedom and for a less narrowly academic approach to the preschool curriculum are appearing in academic and popular journals.

American scholars who visited Chinese preschools during the Cultural Revolution and then again in the 1980s generally are enthusiastic about the dramatic turnabout they have observed in classroom mood, curriculum, and pedagogy (Sidel, 1982; Stevenson et al., 1982). We also have been impressed with much that we have seen on our recent trips to China. But it will take many more years before these changes can saturate China's more than 170,000 mostly rural preschools. Preschools observed by foreign visitors are nearly always of the more urban, sophisticated, progressive minority, obscuring the fact that in much of China, particularly in rural and provincial areas, preschool is school, or just group baby-sitting. We must also keep in mind that what is seen as progress by some is reactionary change to others. There is a deep division in Chinese society between intellectuals and antiintellectuals that predates the revolution. Today, the liberal intellectuals whose views of child development are familiar and attractive to most Japanese and Americans hold sway in China, but other powerful, less liberal currents of thought continue to flow beneath the surface.

In the United States a similar battle is being waged in early child education circles—in this case between those who believe that "play is children's work" and those who believe that "work [academics] is a form of children's play" (Kagan and Zigler, 1987). The "play" advocates see the function of preschools as promoting emotional growth, interpersonal and social skills, and cognitive development (Robison, 1983; Feeney et al., 1987). The "work" advocates see young children as avid, able learners, ready to read, count, and learn about science, computers, foreign languages, and fine arts if only adults would raise their expectations and stop holding children back (Montessori, 1912). American parents, often ambivalent, confused, or naive about the implications of choosing a preschool program that emphasizes academics, play, or a mixture of the two, find themselves torn between wanting to give their children an academic head start and worrying about the dangers of hurrying them (Elkind, 1981).

The egalitarian thrust of the Communist Revolution in China, the post-occupation, democratic educational reform movement in Japan, and, in the United States, the twentieth-century diffusion of the middle-class dream of upward social mobility through education have meant that a majority, rather than, as in the recent past, only an elite minority of families in all three cultures, has come to view education—beginning with pre-school—as the most sensible of parental investments. Realizing that there will not be room at the top (or even in the middle) of the economy for every family's children, parents in China, the United States, and Japan are anxious to give their offspring a fast educational start in preschool if not earlier. Yet this temptation to hurry children is tempered, especially in Japan, by the fear that children pushed too hard too early, as, for example, in high-pressured academic preschool, will suffer from educational burn-out before reaching the end of the educational race. In general, academic instruction is stressed more in China, play is stressed more in Japan, and the picture is mixed in the United States. But in all three cultures pre-school staff feel a similar and increasing pressure from parents to prepare children for academic and economic success.

Spoiling

Chinese parents, preschool educators, and child-development experts are very worried about the problem they call the "4-2-1 syndrome": four grandparents and two parents lavishing attention on one child. Chinese respondents (at 12 percent) were more than five times as likely as their American and Japanese counterparts to list "to reduce spoiling and make up for deficiencies of parents" as one of their top three reasons for a society to have preschools. But spoiling is not only a Chinese concern. In all three countries there is a strong feeling that contemporary home-reared children are at risk of growing up lacking the self-reliance they will need to make it in society.

In all three cultures preschools have a mandate to correct the excesses of parental overindulgence and to make children more independent and self-reliant: 80 percent of Japanese respondents, 67 percent of Chinese, and 66 percent of Americans chose "to make young children more independent and self-reliant" as one of their top three reasons for sending children to preschool. To Americans accustomed to thinking of Japan and perhaps China too as cultures of dependence these figures may be surprising. But the independence expected of children in preschools in all three cultures is less related to individualism, which is clearly an American and not a Japanese or Chinese cultural value, than to the ability to dress, feed, and control oneself, which is required in all cultures.

The term *spoiling* in the United States and Japan has meanings that include but go beyond the Chinese notion of spoiling (*ni-ai*) as parental and grandparental overindulgence and failure to discipline a child. Assistant Principal Higashino told us that Hiroki, the bad boy of Komatsudani, was spoiled (*amayakasu*) as a result of receiving too little rather than, as the Chinese hypothesized, too much love and attention at home as an infant and toddler. Japanese child development experts associate the problem of spoiling less with parental overindulgence than with the kind of narcissistic, overinvolved maternal investment in children common in areas, such as new housing developments in commuting towns, where mothers are isolated and emotionally needy and look to their children for gratification otherwise lacking in their lives (Lebra, 1984; Imamura, 1987). In the United States, spoiling is often blamed on parents who are too busy with work or too preoccupied with their own problems to pay appropriate attention to their children, but who instead buy the children off with material goods, sweets, and television. The divorced father who once a week takes his young child out for ice cream, toys, and a movie is the figure in contemporary American popular culture most clearly associated with spoiling.

Although spoiling covers a somewhat different range of meanings and is blamed on different parental flaws in China, Japan, and the United States, all three cultures view it as a major hazard of modern parenting and see preschool as a proper venue for corrective action.

Parental Investment in Urban-Industrial Societies

Beneath the controversy surrounding questions of academic readiness and spoiling lies a more basic ambivalence about parental investment in children. All parents want their children to be happy and to love and respect them. At the same time they are anxious that their children be able to compete in what the parents perceive to be an increasingly competitive world of school and work.

The profound economic and social changes brought by the industrial and postindustrial revolutions in Japan and the United States from land to capital and knowledge-based economies, have made it vastly more complicated for parents to pass on wealth and privilege directly to their offspring. Although China is by no means postindustrial, the revolution of 1949 has had a similar effect. These socioeconomic changes have affected parent-child relations in all three cultures in complex ways. As Cowgill and Holmes argue in *Aging and Modernization* (1972), parental authority decreases as parents' ability to bequeath power and wealth to their heirs diminishes. As the filial piety characteristic of societies organized by the logic of primogeniture declines in contemporary capitalist and communist economies, parents need to cultivate feelings of filial love and obligation in their children.* With cash and land difficult to bequeath, parents invest instead in their children's emotional development and education, struggling to give their offspring the personality attributes, social connections, and knowledge they will need to compete in the wider world. Thus, many parents of preschoolers find themselves torn between their desire to nurture, indulge, and bond their children and the pressure they feel to instill in them the qualities of self-reliance and perseverance.

In Japan this ambivalence is expressed in the ongoing debate surrounding an exam-dominated, high-pressured education system that most Japanese as citizens deplore yet most Japanese as parents implicitly support and even fuel in their eagerness to see *their* children succeed. In China, where most families these days have but one child, parents believe it is more important than ever before that their child succeed academically and thus socially and economically since this single child may have to provide for two aging parents and four grandparents down the road. In the United States and Japan a dwindling supply of factory and farm jobs and a "crisis of rising aspirations" are driving increasingly large cohorts of parents to push their children into the academic fray. Although very different culturally, economically, ecologically, and historically, urban China, Japan, and the United States, as low-fertility, educationally competitive, industrial societies, have come to hold similar beliefs about family, education, and parental investment in children.

When compared to the full array of the world's cultures, moreover, a study of China, Japan, and the United States covers only a small range of the approaches that can be taken to child care (Whiting and Edwards, 1988). Cultures make different sorts of investments in children in part because of the differing environmental, ecological, and geopolitical pressures they face. In subsistence agricultural societies with high infant mortality (the pattern common to most human cultures until the past hundred years or so) families tend to have many births, to concentrate energy and resources on keeping infants alive during their vulnerable first eighteen months, and to avoid giving infants and toddlers the kind of highly stimulating verbal and visual attention that would lead them to develop into

---

*See, for example, Bernheim, Shleifer, and Summers's paper called "The Strategic Bequest Motive" (1985) and Wu's discussion of filial piety (1987).

emotionally demanding children (LeVine, 1983). Once children in these high-fertility cultures reach three or four years of age, parental investment in them emotionally and economically decreases as parents turn their attention to keeping the next infant alive and the whole family fed.

But in urban China today, as in Japan and the United States, birthrates are low. Secure in the knowledge that their one or two children are unlikely to die in infancy, parents in these cultures can afford to invest themselves emotionally in their children from birth through higher education. Uneducated children in low-fertility urban-industrial societies, unlike their counterparts in agricultural societies, are an economic liability. Parental resources in these societies, therefore,

> are concentrated on the prolonged development and education of a few children at a cost that is enormous and continually growing, no matter how it is calculated. Child-rearing is labor-intensive, capital-intensive, and time-intensive for parents, and the qualitative aspects of development replace the number of offspring as a parental goal. (LeVine, 1983, p. 51)

LeVine argues that whereas parents in high-fertility cultures do a lot of soothing and not much stimulating of their infants, parents in low-fertility cultures do a lot of stimulating and not much soothing, and "this produces more active and less tractable babies and toddlers, who expect increasing rather than decreasing attention to their needs over the preschool years" (p. 52).

This expectation for attention is precisely the "spoiling" that is worrying social planners in one-child China. Having moved from a moderately high to an extremely low level of fertility in just a few generations, Chinese society has had to develop strategies for coping with the attention-needing, intensely demanding, self-centered children characteristic of low-fertility, education-oriented, competitive societies. When Chinese say they are worried that their children are becoming spoiled, they are saying, among other things, that their children, for better or worse, are becoming like Japanese and American children.

The individualistic ego structure that is the goal of American parenting is one the Chinese find attractive as a tool of modernization but fear as a threat to the communist social order. David McClelland (1961) suggests that the first step in the economic development of any culture is an increase in individual achievement motivation in young children. Achievement motivation is stimulated by formal schooling and also by a parenting style that promotes independence, "activism," and initiative.

This explanation of modernization has been labeled psychologically reductionistic and universaling by anthropologists (LeVine, 1973; LeVine and White, 1986). These critiques are well taken, yet McClelland's suggestion that economic modernization must be preceded by character change and thus by change in child socialization is a kind of reasoning consistent with revolutionary Chinese thought (J. Lewis, 1965), which sees complex causal links between a society's mechanisms of production and its family structures.* Zhou Nan of Beijing Normal University writes:

> In China we place great emphasis on children passively acquiring existing knowledge. . . . We overemphasize development of memory and performance and do not fully develop creativity. In China when the teacher speaks, the children memorize. Our kindergartens are like this and so are our primary and secondary schools. But this method of education is not compatible with what our society needs now in order to forge new directions in science, technology and economics management. In the area of preschool education, this means we must strive to develop creativity and imagination. (1985, p. 6; also quoted in Press, 1987, p. 385)

But the strategy recommended by Zhou and other intellectuals of using preschools to produce a cohort of imaginative, creative children who will lead China to modernization carries with it the undesirable side effects of individuality and egotism. McClelland points out (again in terms many Chinese find sensible) that the achievement-oriented ego style that is a prerequisite of economic development tends to encourage selfishness and thus to pose a threat to social cohesion if it is not corrected by an emphasis on "other-directedness" and "collectivity" in the education system. Similarly, in her 1987 paper on "Early Childhood Development and Education in the People's Republic of China," Billie Press offers the

> opinion that much of the recent political turmoil in China revolves around the fundamental question of whether the Chinese can succeed in rearing a generation (or, at least, sufficient numbers) of creative thinkers who are, almost by definition, "individualistic" in their thinking but who also retain the *social* values prized by Chinese families and by the State. (p. 380)

By the time the single or single-siblinged Chinese, Japanese, or American child enters preschool he is already likely to be very different in character from his multisiblinged counterparts in agrarian, high-fertility cultures. Much of the structure of Chinese, Japanese, and American pre-

---

*It is also consistent with the thought of radical American scholars of the family, such as Chodorow (1978) and Zaretsky (1973, 1982).

schools can be understood as an accommodation to the special needs, abilities, and character of these children of low-fertility, high-competition societies.

Children's need for attention and stimulation is both met and corrected by preschool. Preschools correct this need not by attempting to stamp it out but by channeling it. In all three cultures' preschools children are taught to find satisfaction in interactions with people other than parents, to draw attention to themselves by exhibiting competence rather than neediness, to take turns in the limelight, and to find stimulation in self-motivated, solitary play as well as in the company of friends and the group. Preschools are institutions created to provide children with levels of attention, stimulation, and achievement motivation that parents in low-fertility, competitive, urban-industrial societies want their children to have but these days themselves cannot provide. At the same time, preschools must balance the socially centrifugal effects of emphasizing individual achievement and individualism with a socially centripetal strategy of discouraging selfishness and encouraging other-directedness.

The Narrowing World of the Child

The family has shrunk unmistakably and dramatically in China in an era of officially encouraged single-child families. But even in Japan and the United States, where the government has no clear position on family size, single-child families are becoming more common, and the three- and four-children families that were the norm just a generation ago are becoming rare among the middle and upper-middle classes. China's single-child family policy strikes many Japanese and Americans as harsh and even cruel, but the two-child limit that is currently being self-imposed by a majority of middle-class Japanese and Americans would have seemed equally harsh just a generation ago.

In all three societies, parental energy, concern, and resources that would have been diluted across four or five children and across many years of parenting are now concentrated on just one or two children and collapsed into a handful of years of caring for young children (Imamura, 1987). The family in China, Japan, and the United States is also shrinking in ways beyond a decreasing birthrate. Many Japanese feel that the postwar urbanization and middle-class homogenization ("embourgeoisiement"; in Japanese terms, "my-homism") of Japan, a movement from vertically and horizontally extended households in the countryside to a mother, a mostly absent father, and two children living in a small apartment in an urban-ring commuting town, presents children with a world far less rich and complex than the one their parents and grandparents enjoyed as children. With grandparents left behind in the countryside and uncles, aunts, and cousins scattered across urban industrial centers, many Japanese children grow up isolated from their extended family (Fuse, 1984). In Japanese suburban communities, as in the American suburbs of the 1950s and 1960s, the rise of mothering as a full-time occupation and even as an identity, when coupled with the physical isolation of women and children in their single-family homes, increases the likelihood of maternal overinvestment in children and thus of spoiling (Hendry, 1986; Imamura, 1987). In an era of shrinking families, the perception that the world of the child is narrowing leads parents, educators, and social planners to view preschools as more necessary than in earlier eras, when children spent less time at home alone with their mothers and were the focus of less intense parental attention and concern.

Keith Brown (1987) suggests that the ubiquity of the "new" Japanese family has been overestimated and that in rural areas in particular extended families with three or more children and relatively little academic pressure remain the norm. But this does not change the basic structure of our argument: whether or not the world of the child in fact has significantly narrowed, many Japanese believe this to be the case and act accordingly, enrolling their children in preschool to expand their world. Similarly, in the United States it is the popular perception of an educational crisis that places pressure on preschools to teach more reading and writing. In China it is the perception that single children are spoiled, and not empirical evidence supporting this belief, that leads Chinese to look to preschools to make up for the deficiencies of parents.

In a world they believe to be less friendly, manageable, and safe than the idealized past in which they grew up, parents in Japan and the United States are hesitant to allow their children to venture outside the home without adult supervision. In all three cultures, but especially in the United States, the perception if not the reality that social cohesion and community-shared responsibility for the well-being of children have significantly diminished has made parents reluctant to turn their children loose in the neighborhood as parents did just a generation or two ago. In Japan, the perception of decline of the *kinjō* or *chiiki*, the community of concerned others, especially in urban areas, has made parents hesitant to allow their children to enter the public arena alone.

In all three cultures, children's chances of enjoying unsupervised, spontaneous neighborhood play also are affected adversely by a decline in fertility rates. The lower birthrate means that both older siblings with whom a preschooler can tag along on trips to the park or store and neighborhood friends he can meet on the street corner are less available than before. Even if the neighbors next door are parents, they are likely to have only one child, who may be the wrong age or sex to play with or whose mother works, so that he attends preschool, leaving him available for neighborhood play only late in the afternoons and on weekends. In the contemporary United States and Japan parents who do not put their children in preschool find that providing opportunities for them to interact with peers increasingly requires planning and effort.

Widening Children's Worlds

Preschools provide contemporary children in all three cultures with their best opportunity to interact with peers, to make friends (and, equally important, to fight with enemies), and to interact with adults who are not their parents. Seventy percent of Japanese, 42 percent of Americans, and 25 percent of Chinese respondents chose "to give children a chance to play with other children" as one of their top three answers to the question, "Why should a society have preschools?" Twenty-four percent of Japanese, 18 percent of Americans, and 7 percent of Chinese chose "to provide children with a fun place to go each day" as one of their top choices. Why are there such large cross-national differences in these scores? One explanation may be that the metaphorical walls surrounding the nuclear family in China are less formidable than those that isolate Japanese and American children from the outside world. Postrevolutionary China remains a society of street life, public meetings, public squares, and open markets, a society where children not enrolled in organized play groups or preschools still have many opportunities to enjoy spontaneous and varied interactions with peers. The notion of "providing children with a fun place to go each day" also may have struck many of our Chinese respondents as too frivolous a reason for an economically strapped society to invest in preschools.

Conversely, in rich, driven, educationally pressurized Japan, parents who themselves are struggling with the "leisure problem" (Plath, 1969) feel it is important for their children to learn from a young age how to relax and have fun. The educational pressures that await children in primary and especially in intermediate and high school lead Japanese parents and teachers to see play and fun as appropriate and even crucial functions of the preschool. Valuing interpersonal skills as a key to economic success as well as to personal happiness, Japanese parents see providing children with the chance to play with other children as essential to the mission of the preschool.

Americans also believe in the utilitarian value of learning from a young age how to get along with others and how to have fun and relax. Middle-class American children growing up in a society of automobiles and widely spaced suburban homes are more physically isolated from other children than are their counterparts in Japan or China and thus even more in need of preschools as a setting for peer-group interaction.

The opportunity preschools offer to get away from home and to play with peers liberates children from the smothering maternal attention and love Chinese associate with the dangers of spoiling in the single-child family and Japanese and Americans associate with the loneliness and neediness of full-time, isolated mothers. In Japan and the United States the walls around the nuclear family have grown taller, with children and often their mothers left trapped inside. Preschools offer children and nonemployed mothers a daily release from their too-intense dyadic interactions and from the isolation of their overdomesticated lives. For children of employed mothers preschools offer an environment richer in possibilities for peer interaction than they are likely to find with a baby-sitter or in a group-care home.

Preschools and Group Feeling

Sixty-one percent of Japanese respondents chose providing children with a group experience as the single most important reason for a society to have preschools. Ninety-one percent of Japanese respondents made this one of their three top choices. Neither Chinese nor Americans gave groupism so high a priority, but still 44 percent of Chinese respondents and 62 percent of the individually oriented Americans selected giving children a group experience as one of their top three answers. Why did so many Americans value learning to be a member of a group? Perhaps one reason is that though Americans value individuality, the reality of their everyday life is not so different from life in Japan or China: in all three societies children and adults spend much of their school and work days in groups, and thus it is crucial that they have group experiences in preschool.

Chinese respondents, more patriotic than their Japanese and American counterparts, were far more likely to list "to start young children on the road toward being good citizens" as an important reason for a society to have preschools: 30 percent of Chinese compared to 18 percent of Japanese and 14 percent of Americans chose this as one of their top three answers. Clearly, citizenship is more widely viewed in China as something important to teach than in Japan and the United States.

We have chosen to discuss "experience in a group" and "learning to be a good citizen" together because we see both as conceptually part of the more encompassing concern that young children be taught to identify with something larger than themselves and their families. This is perhaps *the* single most important function of preschools in China, Japan, and the United States since in all three cultures it is the lesson hardest for parents to teach at home.

At home Japanese children learn to love and to be loved, they learn the ways of dependence (*amae*), they learn dyadic interpersonal skills, and they learn to have an ease in spontaneous interactions in the bosom of their families. But to learn to enjoy ties to peers, to learn to transfer some of the warmth of parent-child relations to other relationships, to learn to balance the spontaneity enjoyed at home (*honne*) with formality (*tatemae*), emotion with control, and family with society, to learn to become, in other words, truly Japanese, the child must be given a chance to move beyond the walls of the home to more complex social interactions. In today's Japan, for most children, these more complex interactions are found first in preschools.

In China, beneath the warnings that parents are spoiling their single children lies a broader concern about balancing the personal and the communal. Children belong to parents *and* to society. As parents, Chinese naturally have a great desire to cherish and protect their children, particularly their single children. But as citizens, Chinese want to see their children grow up identified with their nation and its struggles, not just with narrower individual and familial concerns. The period of the Cultural Revolution is understood by many Chinese to be an example of the danger of allowing the social to totally dominate the individual and familial. But the other extreme (most often labeled selfish, self-centered, bourgeois) is widely believed to be dangerous as well, in allowing the personal and familial to dominate the greater social good. Chinese preschools, and the ongoing debate surrounding them, reflect this search for balance.

Although American folklore celebrates the loner, the iconoclast, the rebel, and the self-made man and looks with scorn on the joiner, the organization man, and the "ant-colony mentality" seen as characteristic of group-oriented cultures, some Americans worry that in our celebration of individualism the threads that bind people to one another have been stretched too thin and that as a result the fabric of American society, already frayed on the edges, has begun to unravel. Some Americans, questioning the free-market, Adam Smithian notion that if everyone pursues his economic and personal self-interest the society will be wealthy and strong, are looking to government, church, and community organizations —including preschools—for direction and for a sense of shared purpose and identity.

In all three cultures preschool is playing an increasingly important role as a focus where parents' and society's differing aspirations and concerns for children meet, compete, and are resolved. Children enter preschool belonging to their parents and leave with more diffuse, more complex ties to a world still centered on, but now much larger than, their families.

Working Mothers

In the United States increasing numbers of single-parent families, like China's single-child families, present children with a narrowed world. Single parents (usually single mothers) need child care at a minimum for the hours they are at work. Many single working parents use group-care homes instead of preschools, since home care is generally cheaper and allows them greater flexibility in drop-off and pick-up times as well as providing evening, weekend, and sick-day care unavailable at most preschools. In Japan, where single parents are much rarer than in the United States, their problems may be even worse. Thousands of Japanese mothers who work evenings and nights in the "water trade" (bars, brothels, and the like) place their children in unlicensed, unregulated "baby hotels" whose existence has been barely acknowledged by Japanese child-care authorities (Fuse, 1984).

The percentage of working mothers of young children is over 90 percent in the People's Republic of China, 60 percent in the United States, and 40 percent in Japan. With aunts and grandmothers as well as mothers of young children employed, paid child care is a growing need. Yet only 8 percent of Japanese and 25 percent of Americans chose "to free parents for work and other pursuits" as one of their top three responses to the question, "Why should a society have preschools?" The figure was 48 percent in China, but this is still low for a society where virtually all women work outside the home and child-care alternatives are limited. Why didn't more respondents view freeing parents for work as a legitimate and important reason for a society to have preschools?

Perhaps, especially in China, where everyone works and thus every family with a young child needs some form of child-care assistance, freeing parents for work may strike respondents as so intrinsically bound up with the meaning of preschool—"a place where children go while parents work" —that they see no need to list this as a distinct function.

In Japan and the United States, where mothers are often erroneously and unfairly thought of as *choosing* to work (and thereby neglecting their children), this aura of choice brings with it the problems of defensiveness, shame, self-doubt, and guilt. Perhaps parents in the United States and Japan who feel guilty about having to place their children in child care longer or from an earlier age than they would ideally like may defend themselves from this guilt by rationalizing that the most important reason for placing the child in preschool has to do with the child's developmental interests rather than with their own financial need or professional ambitions and desires. Other respondents, for reasons having nothing to do with guilt, may agree that preschools do free parents for work and see this as worthwhile, but not as important as preschool's other functions.* Alternative forms of child care, including paid home care and leaving children in the charge of relatives, also free parents for work, but there are other functions preschools alone can provide that better justify their value to society.

The relationship between women's work and child care has been affected significantly by the dramatic drop in the birthrate experienced in a single generation in all three cultures. Preschools can thrive and even flourish in times of falling birthrates if, as cohorts of children shrink, the percentage of young children enrolled in preschool rises. This is just what is happening, or has happened already, in China, Japan, and the United States. Although it may seem counterintuitive, as women have fewer children, preschool becomes more rather than less likely.

In eras when women had four or more children, pregnancy and child rearing consumed a great deal of their energy for a significant portion of their adult lives. Where large numbers of children are the rule, women work hard, but rarely in jobs that preclude their ability to care for, or supervise the care of, their young children. As the number of children women expect to bear drops to only one or two, the equation changes dramatically: for example, an American woman planning to have only one child is unlikely to decide that her child will need full-time attention and care long enough to justify sacrificing the lifetime emotional satisfaction and earning potential of a career. Or the cause and effect of this reasoning can be reversed: a woman who highly values her career may decide to have only one or two children on the basis of a calculation of how much time and energy she can afford to divert from her job to parenting without jeopardizing her future employment. A woman with a four-year-old child and a baby is likely to conclude that, as long as she is home anyway, she might as well keep her four-year-old home with her and save on preschool tuition. For a woman with a four-year-old and no baby it would make better economic sense to enroll the child in preschool in order to return to work.

For American women with low-paid, unsatisfying jobs, the equation is even more brutal. At the minimum-wage level in the United States, the cost of even inexpensive full-time preschool care for one child will eat up

*See Craig's discussion of schooling as consumption versus investment (1981).

more than a third of her annual earnings. With two or more preschool-aged children the cost ratio makes working for minimum wage and putting children in preschool an unattractive option. Salaries have to rise dramatically above minimum wage before putting two children in child care makes much economic sense. But there is a further complication, as women earning considerably more than minimum wage will rarely be satisfied with or qualify for the least expensive preschool programs. Some American women who stay home with their own children supplement their families' earnings with a paid home job, which often means caring for a working neighbor's child. But for women who want or need to work full-time, having two or more children can be an overwhelming financial hardship. The story is much the same in China, where, as Tao and Chiu write, "Two children make a mother a slave to the household" (1985, p. 155).

Some women (and men) place children in preschools to free their time for pursuits other than work. In the United States, nonworking women who can afford to do so often put their children in preschool for their own emotional well-being as well as for their children's. For example, an American mother we spoke with told us "I'm a better mother if I don't have to mother all day." Another said "I need some time of my own each day to avoid going crazy." In the United States it is not uncommon for parents of preschoolers to themselves still be in school, finishing college or working toward an advanced degree. American women (and men) anticipating a career often choose to spend several thousand dollars a year on preschool as an investment in their future earning potential and life satisfaction. Again, this kind of investment becomes less likely with two or more children. When parents balance the cost of paid child care against the loss of earnings and jeopardy to a career, it is almost always the wife's and not the husband's earnings and career that are at stake, since full-time house-husbanding remains an unpopular family option even in these supposedly liberated times.

What is the cost of children? In the United States the expense of preschool education at the beginning of parenting and college education at the end are parental concerns significant enough to affect parents' decisions about how many children they feel they can afford to have. To have a third child means to many parents not having enough money to care adequately for the first two. A third child might mean spending on preschool money that otherwise could be used toward a down payment on a first home or the beginning of a college savings fund. Just as the first two children are finally old enough to be in free, public, elementary school, having a third child might mean struggling for three more years on one income (the husband's) at a less than desired standard of living until the youngest child is old enough to begin preschool and free the mother for work.

In China it is society as a whole, facing staggering population pressures, and not just individual families that cannot afford more children. Chinese parents are urged by social pressures and economic disincentives to have only one child because if families had more, the nation as a whole could not prosper, and indeed, many might starve. As a society China makes a covenant with young parents: "You do the right thing by having just a single child, and we will make sure your child is healthy and well educated." Providing preschool education is one important way Chinese society keeps up its end of the bargain.

In Japan, where many women in urban and especially suburban neighborhoods are full-time, unemployed mothers, space and parental energy, as much as money, are important concerns affecting decisions about family planning. For parents living in apartment complexes, a third child would mean even more crowding. In his study of bank employees Thomas Rohlen (1974) points out that since young couples live in cramped company apartment buildings precisely during the years they are having their children, this acts as a powerful control on family size. In *The Value of Children: A Cross-National Study* (Arnold and Fawcett, 1975) the problems of housing was found to be Japanese respondents' second most commonly chosen disincentive for having an additional child. Financial concerns were first. A third child might mean that a mother working part time to help save for a down payment on a home for the family would have to give up this work, sentencing them to several more years of cramped, inadequate government- or employer-provided housing. A third child might mean a dilution of the maternal energy needed to tutor, monitor, and encourage the first two children's educational careers (M. White, 1987). Many, perhaps even most, Japanese parents are not committed wholeheartedly to pushing their children into and through "examination hell," but there are many parents who commit virtually all of their spare time, energy, money, and even space in their home into directly or indirectly subsidizing their children's academic careers (Vogel, 1971).

The nonworking mother of preschool-aged children, rare in China and a shrinking minority in the United States, is still common in Japan. But with only two children per family and housework becoming streamlined, how long will Japanese women continue to conceive of mothering and housewifery as careers? Historically, all but the richest of Japanese women have worked hard, mostly in agricultural work. It is only in the past thirty years or so, with the emergence of the new middle class, that the nonworking mother has become the norm (Steinhoff and Tanaka, 1987). There are some indications that this is changing. Young women are becoming increasingly reluctant to give up their jobs when they marry, or even after their first child is born (Holden, 1983; Carney and O'Kelly, 1987). With housework rapidly becoming less time-consuming and the number of children per family shrinking, it is becoming harder for Japanese women to conceive of mothering as a full-time, lifetime job.

Currently, approximately two-thirds of Japanese children are enrolled in half-day nursery school and kindergarten programs (yōchien), one-third in full-time day-care programs (hoikuen), which serve working mothers. With the birthrate falling, some Japanese preschools will have to close, and a gradual shift in women's life-styles from full-time mothering toward a more job- or career-centered orientation seems to favor survival of hoikuen over yōchien in the long run. In all three cultures, a decline in birthrate will mean that for more and more women, mothering will cease to be a career, and full-day preschools will be more needed than ever before (O'Conner, 1988).

Preschools and Parents

It is not only children who are served by preschools. Although parents are naturally reluctant to think of themselves as needing support, correction, and education, these are important functions of the preschool, albeit functions prioritized differently in China, Japan, and the United States.

In China, where preschools are expected to correct the mistakes and deficiencies of overindulgent parents, the role the preschool plays vis-à-vis the family is explicitly political and ideological: preschools, as society's representative, have the right and responsibility to socialize children away from a narrow identification with family toward citizenship, selflessness, and communal identity (LeVine and White, 1986). In China preschool teachers do not work for parents; they work for society, and as public employees with a governmental mandate, they carry authority into their interactions with parents. This is expressed clearly on the walls of some boarding classrooms, where slogans state, "Teachers are even better than parents."

In the United States, the relationship between preschool teachers and parents is variable and often ambivalent. Some parents treat their children's preschool teachers as employees, as modern, institutionalized versions of the nannies and tutors parents in the West have retained and ordered about for centuries. In wealthy neighborhoods, where parents' income and social class is likely to be well beyond that of the poorly paid preschool teacher, the "upstairs, downstairs" feel of parent-teacher interaction is especially pronounced. For other American parents, their relationship to their children's teachers is more nearly equal but still adversarial, as they try subtly or not so subtly to get teachers to teach more (or less) reading, to move (or not move) their child into a special program, or to use a stricter (or less strict) form of discipline to deal with their child's misbehavior. Believing that they know what is best for their child, optimistic about their chances of influencing teachers' approaches to instruction and classroom management, but aware that their influence and power over teachers are tenuous, many American parents engage in an ongoing dialogue with other parents, with teachers, and with preschool directors in school hallways, at parent-teacher conferences, and in other formal and informal gatherings. Most American preschool teachers and administrators seek parents' involvement in their school and want to hear their concerns, but feel, in most cases, that they know children's school needs best and that when differences of opinion arise they should listen, explain, compromise, but never just give in.

With some other parents, American preschool teachers play a role that is nurturant, supportive, even therapeutic rather than subservient or adversarial. Many American preschool teachers speak of the great neediness, loneliness, and desperation they sense in many parents' lives. American parents, overwhelmed by economic pressures, by separation and divorce, by the daunting demands of single parenting, by anxiety about their children's emotional, social, and academic well-being, and by their feelings of inadequacy as parents, turn to preschool teachers for friendship, advice, referral, crisis intervention, and emotional support. Teachers, generally sympathetic to these needs, but untrained in the skills required to respond adequately, do the best they can to be helpful and supportive in the few minutes they spend with parents in classroom doorways at the beginning and end of the school day. In a world many Americans find increasingly anomic and uncaring, a preschool can be an oasis of care and concern, a place children and parents turn to in hopes of finding advice, appreciation, and nurturance (Kagan et al., 1987).

Japanese nursery schools (yōchien) play a role vis-à-vis parents that though not as manifestly ideological as the role of preschools in China is nevertheless ideological and though not as manifestly therapeutic as the role of preschools in the United States is nevertheless therapeutic. Japanese nursery schools provide the prophylactic, community–mental health function of responding to the anomie, isolation, and confusion that confront many young Japanese mothers. Profound social and demographic shifts in postwar society have changed the shape of Japanese marriage and parenthood, creating a cohort of women in need of the camaraderie, support, contact, and counsel that in the past they would have received from relatives, friends, and community. Declining family size, the increasing nuclearization and isolation of families caused by the migration of young people from the countryside to the city and from center city to suburbs, and the reduced participation of women in work other than child rearing and housekeeping which have accompanied the rapid postwar rise of the middle-class life-style—these factors have combined in contemporary Japan to leave a vacuum of meaning and structure in many young mothers' lives, a vacuum that preschools help to fill.

Many young Japanese families live in sprawling apartment complexes in newly created communities an hour or more from the city center. Young wives spend their days in a world of women and children, where everyone is like them in age, income, and situation and yet no one is bound to others by blood, common history, or years of acquaintance or friendship (Imamura, 1987). It is especially in commuting communities of this type that preschools can assume the therapeutic role of bringing isolated mothers together around child-centered tasks and activities, giving a young woman who feels very much alone in her child rearing a place to go each day and a sense of pace and structure to the weeks, months, and years (Higuchi, 1975; Lebra, 1984). Yōchien often offer activities for mothers including PTA meetings, talks on child rearing, and "mamas" volleyball teams. Many also offer late afternoon and Saturday *juku* (special classes) in art, music, and English conversation for preschool children, giving young mothers a chance to meet and socialize with other like-minded women while their children's lessons are in session (Imamura, 1987).

Yōchien are ideological in the sense that they function to prescribe women's role behavior, to teach them their socially defined duty, their place in their separate sphere, and at times subtly to censure those who deviate too far from their appointed path. Preschool PTA officers in Japan are far more likely to attempt to bring into line a wayward mother than a wayward teacher or administrator. Yōchien mothers who fail to attend "optional" events at school or to send their children to school properly dressed and equipped are subjected to subtle and not so subtle pressure to come around. "Preschool mother" is a clearly defined role in Japan, an identity based on an easy-to-read script telling young women how to dress, act, speak, and rear their children.

What we are calling the therapeutic and political functions of preschools vis-à-vis parents are two sides of the same coin: Japanese nursery schools provide mothers with structure that is simultaneously supportive and restrictive, concerned and intrusive, reassuring and limiting. Compared to preschool in China and the United States, and even compared to Japanese hoikuen, yōchien both give more to and require more of mothers. But in all three cultures, in one way or another, preschools serve parents as well as children.

The Qualities of a Good Preschool Teacher

Chinese, American, and Japanese responses to the question "What are the most important characteristics of a good preschool teacher?" show more similarities than differences, but the differences are interesting (see table 5.3). The most striking can be seen in the choice "good at making children study hard," which was chosen as one of the top three characteristics of a good preschool teacher, by 35 percent of the Chinese as compared to 1 percent of American respondents and no Japanese respondents. Before their educational careers are over, most Japanese children and many American ones will have studied hard, but in Japan this studying is unlikely to begin in preschool, and in Japan and the United States it is parents and the child himself rather than teachers who are most likely to be the driving force behind this educational effort.

In all three cultures, "understands and likes children" was seen as an important characteristic of a good preschool teacher. This was the top response for the United States and the second choice among Japanese and Chinese respondents. "Affectionate and warm" ranked second in the United States, and first in Japan and China, but differences across cultures on these two items were not great. There were significant differences in ratings of the importance of tolerance, however. Only 16 percent of Americans and only 2 percent of Chinese chose tolerance as an important characteristic in a preschool teacher as compared to 63 percent of Japanese respondents. One might argue that Japanese preschool teachers, with thirty students per teacher and very high levels of chaos permitted in the classroom, have no choice but to be tolerant. Chinese believe that teachers should like children and be warm, but should be more firm than tolerant. Press (1987) suggests that Chinese "barefoot" (untrained) teachers are often selected from among the ranks of their fellow factory workers on the basis of their being patient. But patience should not be confused with tolerance. Chinese teachers work patiently (persistently, diligently) to correct children's behavior, but they do not tolerate misbehavior. Expecting preschool teachers to correct the excessive indulgence (the overtolerance) of parents, Chinese do not especially value tolerance in teachers.

The relative importance respondents from the three countries gave to teachers' being knowledgeable of subject matter, experienced, and devoted reflects realities of staffing patterns in their preschools. In Japan, where, by government regulation, all teachers have degrees in either early childhood education or child development and most preschool teachers retire after only three or four years to marry and start families, "knows subject matter" was seen as twice as important as "experienced." The figures are just the reverse in China, where, in the aftermath of the Cultural Revolu-

Table 5.3   *"What are the most important characteristics of a good preschool teacher?"*

	China		Japan		USA	
	FIRST CHOICE	TOP THREE	FIRST CHOICE	TOP THREE	FIRST CHOICE	TOP THREE
Affectionate, warm	51%	66%	42%	78%	18%	77%
Communicates well with parents	3	23	1	12	2	32
Knows subject matter	1	8	5	22	4	19
Experienced	3	27	1	10	3	1
Devoted and conscientious	3	13	7	22	10	41
Creative	4	42	5	37	0	31
Understands and likes children	34	84	24	54	57	82
Good at making children study hard (a firm taskmaster)	1	35	0	0	0	1
Tolerant	0	2	16	63	3	16

tion, trained preschool teachers are still in short supply and untrained but experienced teachers are plentiful. Preschool teachers who have experience but little formal training might be expected to see experience as more important, whereas teachers with college degrees but little experience might be expected to give greater importance to knowing the subject matter.

In the United States, where preschool teachers may lack experience, training, or both, "devoted and conscientious" was seen as a more important attribute of a good teacher than either experience or knowledge. American respondents were twice as likely as Japanese and three times as likely as Chinese to choose "devoted and conscientious" as one of their top three characteristics of a good preschool teacher. Perhaps in China, where teachers are assigned to jobs for life, and in Japan, where teacher turnover is predictable and orderly, devotion is less a concern or a problem than in the United States, where teachers devoted to their school and their profession are relatively rare, as reflected in the large numbers who change schools or even leave teaching each year.

Preschool Teaching and Gender

In contemporary Japanese, Chinese, and American preschools, talk of innate male-female differences in ability or temperament is out of favor, and the notion of purposely treating young boys and girls differently is discouraged. And yet preschools in all three countries remain highly gendered worlds.

The importance of gender is most evident in staffing patterns. Few social institutions are as sexually segregated as preschools. Most preschool teachers and aides and a majority of preschool directors in all three countries are women. And in all three, the higher one looks in the preschool hierarchy, the more likely one is to find men: male teachers are exceedingly rare; male preschool directors and university professors of preschool education are more common; government officials overseeing preschool education more often than not are male.

Preschool teaching's relatively low status compared to teaching older children makes it a low-paid women's field. In the United States full-time day-care teachers usually earn the minimum wage or a little higher. Their yearly salary is approximately half that of an elementary school teacher and a third that of a plumber. Nursery school teachers, who usually work less than forty hours a week, earn even less. In China and Japan preschool teachers' wages are closer to, but still lower than, the salaries paid to elementary school teachers. In China, where wage discrimination on the grounds of gender is explicitly prohibited, preschool teachers nevertheless continue, on the average, to earn less than their counterparts in traditionally male fields. In Japan, where sexually differential treatment in the workplace is still widely accepted (see, for example, Susan Pharr's 1984 "The Revolt of the Tea Pourers"), teachers at private yōchien and hoikuen receive very low wages; only publicly employed preschool teachers, who are paid according to city or prefectural wage guidelines, earn a decent living. In all three cultures preschool teachers' pay is low, but only in the United States do they routinely earn less than women workers in other sectors of the economy.

Preschool teaching, like mothering, is supposedly intrinsically rewarding, and like mothering, it is viewed as requiring not so much special training or knowledge as goodheartedness, common sense, and warmth, with which women are believed to be naturally endowed. In China, where men and women are officially equal, there are virtually no male preschool teachers because women are still believed to be naturally more patient in dealing with children (Korbin, 1981). In the United States, women who have been successful in mothering are often attracted to child care as a profession, and in Japan younger women often choose early child education as a college major and a short-term career in anticipation of making a good marriage and dedicating their lives to mothering.

In all three cultures the preponderance of women in preschool teaching reveals a persisting link in people's minds between preschool teaching and mothering. Although most preschool teachers reject the suggestion that they are motherlike in practice or demeanor or that they fulfill motherlike roles, the low pay, low status, ambiguous professionalism, and absence of men in the field suggest that the link to motherhood and women's separate, unequal sphere remains strong (Finkelstein, 1988).

Preschool, although a relatively new institution, thus reflects long-standing values and traditions of sexual inequality and gender-based distribution of labor. Although preschool teachers in all three cultures may try to minimize sexually stereotyped play among children and to treat the boys and girls in their charge equally, the absence of male adults in the daily life of the preschool presents children with a world that is female-dominated and dissimilar for boys and girls: boys lack an opportunity to interact with same-sex adults in preschool, girls the opportunity to interact with adults of the opposite sex. As Nancy Chodorow (1978), among others, has argued, whether at home or at school, this is the perfect recipe for reproducing gender differences in character.*

The Socioeconomics of Preschool

Preschools in China, Japan, and the United States reflect economic as well as social and cultural realities. In all three countries the quality and availability of preschool programs are a function of parents' and government's ability and willingness to pay for child care.

Much of what our informants did not like about Dong-feng had as much to do with poverty as ideology. Dong-feng, although an excellent facility by rural and provincial-capital Chinese standards, is dark, underequipped, shabby, and behind the times by American, Japanese, and Beijing standards. Beijing teachers and early childhood education experts criticized us for not having chosen a better preschool to represent their country. Yet many of these same Chinese teachers informally acknowledged that we could easily have found a much worse, much poorer, much less sophisticated preschool had we ventured farther into the countryside.

Preschools vary from program to program and city to city in all three countries, but this unevenness is most striking in China, where urban-rural differences in preschool education are enormous. For example, a 1985 comparison of urban and rural districts of greater Beijing reveals striking differences in preschool attendance (75 percent in the city, 34 percent in the countryside), in student/teacher ratios (22.7 students per class in

---

*For a discussion of the origin of gender differences in varied cultural settings, see Beatrice Whiting and Carolyn Edwards's *Children of Different Worlds* (1988).

urban districts compared to 35.2 students in rural areas), and in staff training (only 15 percent of preschool directors in the countryside had more than a junior high school education, whereas a majority of urban preschool directors had high school diplomas or better). Although China's eighteen normal universities have reopened and graduates are being placed throughout the country, in a nation with 170,000 preschools it will take many years to close the gap. Rural Chinese preschools today are often dirt-floored, poorly equipped baby-sitting services staffed by inadequately trained or even illiterate women too old for agricultural work.

In a country based on an ideology of equality, such elitism and urban-rural differences are serious problems for preschool education. Preschools serving children of party leaders, soldiers of the People's Liberation Army, city workers, university professors, hospital staff, and government bureau-crats on the average are much better funded, more professionally staffed, and better equipped than preschools run by neighborhood associations, factories, farm cooperatives, and rural villages. Thus despite the fact that officially there is no longer a class system in Chinese society, elitism is creeping back into child care. Although not officially sanctioned, nannies (*amah*) are again becoming common in Beijing, Shanghai, and other large cities where country girls come to live au pair with urban families and care for infants and toddlers. Where there are significant differences in wages and standards of living, as between urban and rural China, the care of young children tends to both reflect and contribute to these differences.

Compared to China, with its great differences between urban and rural preschools, and to the United States, with its great differences in child-care options available to the rich, the poor, and the middle class, there is more uniformity in child care in Japan. The government sets a national curricu-lum, licenses preschool teachers, and subsidizes preschools, contributing to a nationwide system of preschools similar in approach and quality.

Ninety-six percent of Japanese children have at least one year in pre-school before entering elementary school. Tuition is much higher in Japan than in China, but Japanese preschools are inexpensive by American stan-dards. Throughout Japan sliding-fee scales are available in public pre-schools, so that parents pay no more than they can afford.

Student/teacher ratios most Chinese and Americans would consider unacceptable help keep down the costs of preschool education in Japan. Yōchien operate with as many as forty children per teacher, hoikuen with as many as thirty per teacher. These classes are too large even by Japa-nese standards, and the extra ten children per class over the number most Japanese would consider ideal are a form of built-in tuition subsidy. Career paths of preschool teachers also work to keep Japanese preschools affordable. In Japan, where salaries in almost every field are linked quite closely to years of service, the short (four- to five-year) careers of most preschool teachers keep down personnel costs, which are the costliest line item in most preschool budgets.

The Japanese system of public and private preschools supported by a combination of government subsidy, parental tuition, high student/teacher ratios, and relatively low staff wages works, but not without problems. A decline in the birthrate and dramatic population shifts have meant that preschools in some areas of the country are being forced out of business while in other regions there is a shortage of preschool slots. The gap in quality and reputation between hoikuen, which traditionally have served the children of blue-collar, working mothers, and yōchien, which traditionally have served the children of wealthier, more gentrified, nonworking mothers, is narrowing, but still exists. Battles for control of preschool education between Mombushō (the Ministry of Education) and Koseishō (the Ministry of Health and Welfare) loom as the missions of the yōchien and the hoikuen grow more similar.

The social-class distinction between yōchien and hoikuen that has characterized Japanese child care for the past eighty years is in the process of being replaced by a distinction between upper-middle- and lower-middle-class hoikuen and yōchien. In urban and suburban communities private hoikuen and, more frequently, yōchien, offering enriched programs including classes in swimming, tennis, piano, ballet, violin, and English conversation, are competing to attract an aggressive, upwardly mobile clientele willing to pay a premium for their children's preschool education. The significance here is less that one group of children is getting a better preschool education than the other than that a process of sorting out has begun. Families intent on helping their children over the examination hurdles that must be cleared on the way to the top begin with their choice of a preschool to distinguish themselves from families unable or unwilling to compete on this level. Most enriched preschool programs offer less a fast academic start than an introduction to upper-middle-class life. Enriched preschools, like *jukus* (cram schools; M. White, 1987), *yobikō* (post–high school university-preparatory schools; Tsukada, 1988), and private elementary, intermediate, and high schools (Rohlen, 1983), represent attempts to circumvent the egalitarian effects of the postwar educational reforms (W. Cummings, 1980) and thus to restratify Japanese society.

In the United States there is a striking lack of government support for preschool education (Hewlett, 1986). Unlike culturally similar Western European democracies, the U.S. government has failed to provide more than token support for child care. An exception is Head Start, a federal-

and state-supported program for children from disadvantaged homes. But at current funding levels Head Start has slots for less than 5 percent of the children it could potentially serve.

The absence of government support for child care, coupled with the great income and wealth differences that characterize American society, has led to a system of child care split along class lines. Sixty-seven percent of American families with yearly incomes over thirty-five thousand dollars have their young children in preschool as compared to 40 percent of middle-income families and less than 5 percent of families earning less than ten thousand dollars. The well-to-do can easily afford good preschools while the middle class struggles to pay tuition and the poor most often are left with second-rate proprietary child centers, family care homes, and inadequate makeshift arrangements.

Most American studies show that though there are no demonstrably negative effects on children who participate in good-quality preschool programs, mediocre or poor-quality group care can have negative short- and long-term effects on children's emotional, social, and cognitive development (Belsky et al., 1984). The absence of subsidized child care thus relegates children of the poor to a second-class start and works to replicate class distinctions from generation to generation.

Preschools: Conserving or Transforming?

In 1971 President Richard Nixon vetoed the Comprehensive Child Development Act, arguing that it would be a grave mistake to commit "the vast moral authority of national government to the side of communal approaches to child rearing over against the family-centered approach." As Sylvia Hewlett (1986) points out, right-wing hardliners in the United States for over fifty years have seen in the child-care movement evidence of a Bolshevik conspiracy to undermine the stability of the family and thus destabilize American society. But in the United States it is not only right-wing extremists who worry about the implications of institutional child care and not only conservative politicians who vote against or veto child-care legislation. Moreover, some conservatives have come to see the wisdom of governmental support, at least on a small scale. In 1987 Sen. Orrin Hatch of Utah, formerly an opponent of institutional child care, proposed a bill to expand private and public day-care programs: "I believe that it is far preferable for parents to care for their own children, but I have been persuaded by the facts that our policy choice must be to enable citizens to work without fear for the safety and well-being of our children" (Kantrowitz and Wingert, 1988). But Hatch's bill (which calls for only $250 million a year) and more ambitious Democratic child-care bills will travel a difficult road in a society still deeply ambivalent about supporting institutional day care for young children. As parents, many Americans worry about the long-term emotional and cognitive effects of sending their children to full-time day care, and as citizens many Americans view day care for young children as a radical and disturbing departure from the family (maternal) care and attention American children received in the idealized past (see, for example, Bronfenbrenner, 1981).

Similar concerns can be heard in Japan, where some critics argue that the ubiquity of preschool education is heralding if not hastening the breakdown of the traditional family and community (for example, Yanagita, 1957). In Japan, as in the United States, critiques of day care as a dangerous, radical innovation are usually coupled with attacks on women for working outside the home and forsaking their responsibility as mothers.

In China, during the era of the Cultural Revolution, preschools were accused of fomenting counterrevolutionary tendencies and promoting recidivistic, bourgeois ideology in young children. But in contemporary China these charges are rarely heard. Many Chinese would agree with Japanese and Americans that institutional day care for young children is a radical change from home care. But in China the past is remembered bitterly rather than romanticized.

In all three societies, the rise of preschool is viewed, for better or worse, as a radical departure from traditional modes of caring for young children. And yet our interviews and observations lead us to view preschools more as agents of cultural conservation than change. We would argue that in the United States and Japan the truly radical social experiment has been not the preschool but the "cult of domesticity"—the enshrinement of the full-time, nonemployed, middle-class mother-housewife as the child-rearing ideal. The full-time mother enjoyed her greatest popularity in America in the 1950s, an era in which large numbers of men returning from the war and needing jobs pressured society to endorse an ideology that would justify the expulsion of women from the work force.

In Japan until the economic boom of the late 1960s, only women in wealthy families could afford not to work while their children were small, and since these women could also afford servants, they rarely raised their children alone. Thus the full-time Japanese mother, endlessly available to care for her one or two children until they reach elementary school age, is less a traditional Japanese mode of child rearing than an invention of modern urban and suburban Japan.

Japanese preschools function not to destabilize or transform traditional Japanese child rearing but to compensate for features of traditional family and social life lost in the unsettling changes of the postwar era. Japanese preschools provide children with a fictive version of the community of concerned others (the kinjō) in which children enjoyed growing up in the past, and they provide isolated suburban mothers with links to others missing from modern commuting communities. Japanese preschools are conservative in giving children a chance to develop a traditionally Japanese sense of self difficult if not impossible for them to learn in their radically narrowed modern worlds.

What is labeled "traditional" in contrast to "Western" in Japan often has little to do with historical reality. Values held by conservatives are, de facto, believed to be traditional. For example, large class size and high student/teacher ratios usually are considered to be traditionally Japanese, whereas small classes with low ratios are considered Western. But the system of large classes currently typical throughout Japanese education actually reflects a relatively recent Japanese borrowing from the West. The contemporary Japanese school system was developed little over a hundred years ago, in the early Meiji era, and was based on Western educational models of the time and revised, under American direction, in the Occupation period. Japanese education, before it was influenced by the West, emphasized small classes, individual tutorials, hands-on training, and learning through apprenticeship (Dore, 1965; Rubinger, 1982). Thus the contemporary system is traditionally Japanese less in the sense of being a legacy of the distant past than in the sense of promoting what many Japanese believe to be important traditional values. In an era in which family size has shrunk and extended-family and community networks of kin, neighbors, and friends are feared to be unraveling, large class size with large ratios and letting children fight a little in preschools are important strategies for promoting what is believed to be the traditionally Japanese value of groupism and for combatting what is believed to be the danger of Western-style individualism.

In China, preschools are frankly conservative, conserving not the familial and social structure of the pre-1949 era but the values of the revolution. In freeing mothers as well as fathers to work, preschools serve China's need for labor as it struggles to modernize. In giving young children the chance to interact in groups, preschools begin educating them in the civic virtues that lie at the heart of the revolution. In countering the spoiling that Chinese view as endemic to the single-child family, preschools function to conserve rather than transform the character structure fundamental to a communist society.

In the United States, for all the fears of the extreme right and the concerns of moderate Americans that preschools present a threat to the traditional American family, we see the role played by preschools as conservative rather than destabilizing or transforming. Preschools in the United

States are not changing the family; they are responding to changes that have already occurred.

The history of the American preschool movement reveals a consistent conservatism. As Eli Zaretsky argues in his 1982 essay "The Place of the Family in the Origins of the Welfare State," early-twentieth-century progressive social theorists like John Dewey and Jane Addams saw preschools and other new social inventions as an antidote to the anomie and social disintegration characteristic of modern industrial-capitalist societies: "In [the progressives'] view, the rise of industry had destroyed the self-sufficiency of the old, petit bourgeois family, making it necessary to develop other institutions, particularly schools and neighborhoods, to perform many tasks once performed by the family" (p. 207).

In the contemporary era this same conservative progressivism is most apparent in the services preschools provide, not, as they did a century ago, to children of immigrants, but to children from single-parent families. Single parents and other parents feeling overwhelmed by the economic and emotional pressures of simultaneously providing for and caring for children look to preschools to give children some of the stability and continuity, the attention and stimulation, and the values and character children are believed to have received from their nuclear families, kin, and neighbors in earlier eras.

Preschools, although a relatively new invention, are more a force of cultural continuity than cultural change. Preschools work more to instill than to subvert the values parents in China, Japan, and the United States wish to pass on to their children. With family size and patterns of women's work dramatically changing in all three cultures in the last twenty years, Chinese, Japanese, and American parents look to preschools to play the essentially compensatory and conservative role of minimizing the undesired effects of these wrenching changes on the lives of young children.

References

Addams, J. (1910). *Twenty years at Hull House*. New York: New American Library.

Ainslie, R. (Ed.). (1984). *The child in the day care setting*. New York: Praeger Press.

Alvino, J. (1986). *Parent's guide to raising a gifted child: Recognizing and developing your child's potential*. New York: Ballantine Books.

Arnold, F., & Fawcett, J. T. (1975). *The value of children: A cross-national study*. Honolulu, Hi.: East-West Center.

Asch, T., Conner, L., & Asch, P. (1983a). *A Balinese trance séance* [Film]. Watertown, Mass.: Documentary Educational Resources.

————. (1983b). *Jero on Jero: A Balinese séance observed* [Film]. Watertown, Mass.: Documentary Educational Resources.

Belsky, J. (1982). The ecology of child care. In M. Lamb (Ed.), *Nontraditional families: Parenting and child development*. Hillsdale, N.J.: Lawrence Erlbaum Associates.

————. (1984). Two waves of day care research: Developmental effects and conditions of quality. In R. Ainslie (Ed.), *The child and the day care setting*. New York: Praeger Press.

Belsky, J., Lerner, R., & Spanier, G. (1984). *The child in the family*. Reading, Mass.: Addison Wesley.

Benedict, R. (1946). *The chrysanthemum and the sword*. Boston: Houghton Mifflin Co.

Berger, D. (1988). *Play as a medium for learning and development*. Portsmouth, N.H.: Heinemann.

Bernheim, B., Shleifer, A., & Summers, L. (1985). The strategic bequest motive. *Journal of Political Economy, 93*(6), 1045–1075.

Bettelheim, B. (1967). *The empty fortress*. New York: Free Press.

Bowlby, J. (1980). *Attachment and loss: Vol. 3. Loss, sadness and depression*. New York: Basic Books.

Breiner, S. (1980). Early child development in China. *Child Psychiatry and Human Development, 11*(2), 87–95.

Breitbart, V. (1974). *The day care handbook: The why, what and how of community day care*. New York: Alfred A. Knopf.

223

Bronfenbrenner, U. (1974). *A report on the longitudinal evaluation of preschool programs: Vol. 2. Is early intervention effective?* (DHEW Publication No. OHD 74–24). Washington, D.C.: Office of Child Development.

————. (1981). Children and families: 1984. *Society, 18*(2), 38–41.

Brown, K. (1987). Farm life in a Japanese village. *Japan Society Newsletter, 34*(5), 2–5.

Carney, L., & O'Kelly, C. (1987). Barriers and constraints to the recruitment and mobility of female managers in the Japanese labor force. *Human Resource Management, 26*(2), 193–216.

Cazden, C. (1988). *Classroom discourse.* Portsmouth, N.H.: Heinemann.

Children's Defense Fund (CDF). (1986). *A children's defense budget.* Washington, D.C.: Children's Defense Fund.

Chodorow, N. (1978). *The reproduction of mothering.* Berkeley: University of California Press.

Chu, G. (1985). The emergence of new Chinese culture. In W. Tseng & D. Wu (Eds.), *Chinese culture and mental health.* Orlando, Fla.: Academic Press.

Clarke-Stewart, A. (1982). *Daycare.* Cambridge, Mass.: Harvard University Press.

Clarke-Stewart, A., & Gruber, C. (1984). Day care forms and features. In R. Ainslie (Ed.), *The child and the day care setting.* New York: Praeger Press.

Clausen, J., & Clausen, S. (1973). The effects of family size on parents and children. In J. Fawcett (Ed.), *Psychological perspectives in population* (pp. 185–208). New York: Basic Books.

Clifford, J. (1983). On ethnographic authority. *Representations, 1*(2): 118–46.

Conner, L., Asch, T., & Asch, P. (1986). *Jero Tapakan: Balinese healer.* Cambridge: Cambridge University Press.

Cowgill, D., & Holmes, L. (1972). *Aging and modernization.* New York: Appleton-Century-Crofts.

Craig, J. (1981). The expansion of education. *Review of Research in Education, 9,* 151–210.

Cummings, E. (1980). Caregiver stability and day care. *Developmental Psychology, 16,* 31–37.

Cummings, W. (1980). *Education and equality in Japan.* Princeton, N.J.: Princeton University Press.

Dahrendorf, R. (1979). *Life chances: Approaches to social and political theory.* Chicago: University of Chicago Press.

DeVos, G., & Wagatsuma, H. (1973). *Socialization for achievement: Essays on the cultural psychology of the Japanese.* Berkeley: University of California Press.

Doi, T. (1974). *The anatomy of dependence.* Tokyo: Kodansha International.

————. (1986). *The anatomy of the self.* Tokyo: Kodansha International.

Dore, R. (1965). *Education in Tokugawa, Japan.* Berkeley: University of California Press.

Elkind, D. (1981). *The hurried child.* New York: Addison Wesley.

Engel, J. (1982). *Changes in male-female relationships and family life in the People's Republic of China* (HITAHR Research Ser. 014). Honolulu: University of Hawaii.

Featherstone, J. (1970, September 12). Kentucky fried children. *New Republic,* 12–16.

Feeney, S., Christensen, D., & Moravcik, E. (1987). *Who am I in the lives of children?* (3rd ed.). Columbus, O.: Charles E. Merrill.

Fein, G. (1982). The informed parent. In E. F. Zigler & E. W. Gordon (Eds.), *Day care scientific and social policy issues*. Dover, Mass.: Auburn House.

Fein, G., & Clarke-Stewart, A. (1973). *Day care in context*. New York: John Wiley.

Fein, G., Moorin, E., & Enslein, J. (1982). Pretense and peer behavior: An intersectoral analysis. *Human Development, 25*, 392–406.

Finkelstein, B. (1988). The revolt against selfishness: Women and the dilemmas of professionalism in early childhood education. In B. Spodeck, O. Saracho, & D. Peters (Eds.), *Professionalism and the early child practitioner* (pp. 10–29). New York: Teachers College Press.

Fitzgerald, J., & Brackbill, Y. (1976). Classical conditioning in infancy: Development and constraints. *Psychological Bulletin, 83*, 353–376.

Fraiberg, S. (1977). *Every child's birthright: In defense of mothering*. New York: Basic Books.

Freedman, M. (Ed.). (1970). *Family and kinship in Chinese society*. Stanford, Calif.: Stanford University Press.

Freud, A., & Dunn, S. (1951). An experiment in group upbringing. *Psychoanalytic Study of the Child, 6*, 127–168.

Friedan, B. (1983). *The feminine mystique*. New York: Norton.

———. (1985). *It changed my life: Writings on the women's movement*. New York: Norton.

Fuse, A. (1984). The Japanese family in transition. *Japan Foundation Newsletter, 12*(3), 1–11.

Gentry, J. (1981). Early childhood education in the People's Republic of China. *Childhood Education, 58*(2), 92–96.

Harlow, H., & Harlow, M. (1962). Social deprivation in monkeys. *Scientific American, 207*(5), 136–146.

Harper, J., & Richards, L. (1979). What will become of the children? In *Mothers and working mothers* (pp. 110–186). New York: Penguin Books.

Hawkins, J. (1983). *Education and social change in the People's Republic of China*. New York: Praeger.

Hendry, J. (1986). *Becoming Japanese*. Honolulu: University of Hawaii Press.

Hewlett, S. (1986). *A lesser life: The myth of women's liberation in America*. New York: Warner Books.

Higuchi, K. (1975). The PTA: A channel for political activism. *Japan Interpreter, 10*(2), 133–140.

Hinze, R. (1987). Childcare in Hawaii: Oversight or challenge? *Hawaii's Private Schools, 1*(2), 58–62.

Ho, D. (1986). Chinese patterns of socialization: A critical review. In M. Bond (Ed.), The psychology of the Chinese people. Hong Kong: Oxford University Press.

Holden, K. (1983). Changing employment patterns of women. In D. Plath (Ed.), *Work and life course in Japan* (pp. 34–46). Albany: State University of New York Press.

Hsieh, J. C., & Chuang, Y. C. (1985). *The Chinese family and its ritual behavior.* Taiwan: Institute of Ethnology, Academia Sinica.

Hsu, F. (1975). *Iemoto, the heart of Japan.* New York: John Wiley.

Imamura, A. E. (1987). *Urban Japanese housewives: At home and in the community.* Honolulu: University of Hawaii Press.

Iritani, T. (1979). *The value of children: A cross-national study: Vol. 6. Japan.* Honolulu, Hi.: East-West Center.

Kagan, S., and Zigler, E. (1988). *Early schooling: The national debate.* New Haven: Yale University Press.

Kagan, S., Powell, D., Weissbourd, B., and Zigler, E. (1987). *America's family support programs.* New Haven: Yale University Press.

Kantrowitz, B., & Wingert, P. (1988, February 29). The clamor to save the family. *Newsweek,* 60–61.

Kessen, W. (1975). *Childhood in China.* New Haven: Yale University Press.

King, A., & Bond, M. (1985). The Confucian paradigm of man: A sociological view. In W. Tseng & D. Wu (Eds.), *Chinese culture and mental health* (pp. 29–42). Orlando, Fla.: Academic Press.

Kiplinger Report (1987). *A special Kiplinger report: Child care benefits for employees.* Washington, D.C.: Kiplinger Editors.

Korbin, J. E. (Ed.). (1981). *Child abuse and neglect: Cross-cultural perspectives.* Berkeley: University of California Press.

Kuroyanagi, T. (1982). *Totto-chan: The little girl by the window* (D. Britton, Trans.). Tokyo: Kodansha.

Lake, A. (1974). The day care business. In V. Breitbart (Ed.), *The day care handbook.* New York: Knopf.

Lappé, F. M. (1975). *Diet for a small planet* (Rev. ed.). New York: Ballantine.

Lasch, C. (1977). *Haven in a heartless world.* New York: Basic Books.

————. (1979). *The culture of narcissism.* New York: Norton.

Lazar, I. (1982). Lasting effects of early education: A report from the Consortium for Longitudinal Studies. *Monographs of the Society for Research in Child Development,* 47(2–3, Serial No. 195).

Lazar, I., Hubbell, R., Murray, R., Rosche, M., & Royce, J. (1977). The persistence of preschool effects: A long-term follow-up of fourteen infant and preschool experiments (Final Report, Grant No. 18–76–07843). Washington, D.C.: Office of Human Development Services, Department of Health and Human Services.

Lebra, T. (1976). *Japanese patterns of behavior.* Honolulu: University of Hawaii Press.

————. (1984). *Japanese women: Constraint and fulfillment.* Honolulu: University of Hawaii Press.

LeVine, R. (1966). Outsiders' judgments. *Southwest Journal of Anthropology,* 22, 101–115.

————. (1973). *Culture, behavior, and personality.* Chicago: Aldine Publishing Co.

————. (1983). Fertility and child development: An anthropological approach. In D. Wagner (Ed.), *Child development and international development: Research-policy interfaces.* San Francisco: Jossey-Bass.

LeVine, R., & White, M. (1986). *Human conditions: The cultural basis of educational development*. London: Routledge and Kegan Paul.

Lewis, C. (1984). Cooperation and control in Japanese nursery schools. *Comparative Education Review*, *28*, 69–84.

Lewis, J. (1965). Party cadres in communist China. In J. Coleman (Ed.), *Education and Political Development*. Princeton, N.J.: Princeton University Press.

Lian, Y. (1985). An epidemiological study of child mental health problems in Nanjing District. In W. Tseng & D. Wu (Eds.), *Chinese culture and mental health* (pp. 305–313). Orlando, Fla.: Academic Press.

Lu, H. (1956). *Selected works of Lu Hsun (Xun)*. Beijing: Foreign Language Press.

McClelland, D. (1961). *The achieving society*. Princeton: Van Nostrand.

Mahler, M., Pine, F., & Bergman, A. (1975). *The psychological birth of the human infant: Symbiosis and individuation*. New York: Basic Books.

Marcus, G., & Fischer, M. (1986). *Anthropology as cultural critique*. Chicago: University of Chicago Press.

Maynard, F. (1985). *The child care crisis: The real costs of day care for you and your child*. Ontario, Canada: Penguin Books Canada.

Montessori, M. (1912). *The Montessori method*. (3rd ed.). New York: Frederick A. Stokes.

Nagai, M., & Bennett, J. (1953). A summary and analysis of "The Family Structure of Japanese Society" by Takayoshi Kawashima. *Southwestern Journal of Anthropology*, *9*, 239ff.

Nagano, S. (n.d.). *Docility and lack of assertiveness: Possible causes of academic success of Japanese children*. National Institute for Educational Research, Japan.

National Commission on Working Women. (1985). *Child care fact sheet*. Washington, D.C.: National Commission on Working Women.

Newkirk, T. (1989). *More than stories: The range of children's writing*. Portsmouth, N.H.: Heinemann.

O'Connor, S. (1988). Women's labor force participation and preschool enrollment: A cross-national perspective, 1965–80. *Sociology of Education*, *61*, 15–28.

Orton, R., & Lang, B. (1980). What is government's role in quality day care? In S. Silmer (Ed.), *Advances in early education and day care* (Vol. 1). Greenwich, Ct.: Jai Press.

Osborn, D. K. (1980). *Early childhood education in historical perspective*. Athens, Ga.: Education Associates.

Paley, V. (1986). *Boys and girls: Superheroes in the doll corner*. Chicago: University of Chicago Press.

Parish, W., & Whyte, M. (1978). *Village and family life in contemporary China*. Chicago: University of Chicago Press.

Pasternak, B. (1985). The disquieting Chinese lineage and its anthropological relevance. In J. Hsieh & Y. Chuang (Eds.), *The Chinese family* (pp. 165–191). Taiwan: Institute of Ethnology, Academia Sinica.

Peak, L. (1986). Training learning skills and attitudes in Japanese early educational settings. In W. Fowler (Ed.), *Early experience and the development of competence*. San Francisco: Jossey-Bass.

————. (1987). *Learning to go to school in Japan: The transition from home to preschool life*. Ph.D. dissertation, Harvard University.

Pharr, S. (1984). The revolt of the tea pourers. In E. Krauss, T. Rohlen, & P. Steinhoff (Eds.), *Conflict in Japan*. Honolulu: University of Hawaii Press.

Plath, D. (1969). *The after hours: Modern Japan and the search for enjoyment*. Berkeley: University of California Press.

Poston, D., & Yu, M. (1984). Quality of life, intellectual development and behavioral characteristics of single children in China: Evidence from a 1980 survey in Changsha, Hunan Province. *Journal of Biosocial Sciences*, *17*, 127–136.

Press, B. (1987). Observation on early childhood development and education in the People's Republic of China. *Early Child Development and Care 29*, 375–389.

Provence, S., Naylor, A., & Patterson, J. (1979). *The challenge of day care*. New Haven: Yale University Press.

Robertson, J., & Robertson, J. (1952). A two-year-old goes to hospital: Young children in brief separation. I, *Kate* (1967); II, *Jane* (1968); III, *John* (1968); IV, *Thomas* (1971); V, *Lucy* (1976). [Films]. London, England: Tavistock Child Development Research Unit.

Robinson, N., Robinson, H., & Darling, M. (1979). *A world of children: Day care and preschool institutions*. Monterey, Calif.: Brooks/Cole.

Robison, H. (1983). *Exploring teaching in early childhood education*. Newton, Mass.: Allyn and Bacon.

Rohlen, T. (1974). *For harmony and strength: Japanese white-collar organization in anthropological perspective*. Berkeley: University of California Press.

————. (1983). *Japan's high schools*. Berkeley: University of California Press.

Rubinger, R. (1982). *Private academies of Tokugawa, Japan*. Princeton, N.J.: Princeton University Press.

Ruby, J. (1982). *A crack in the mirror*. Philadelphia: University of Pennsylvania Press.

Shigaki, I. (1983). Child care practices in Japan and the United States: How do they reflect cultural values in young children? *Young Children*, *38*, 13–24.

Shoji, M. (1983). Early childhood education in Japan. In G. Lall and M. Bernard (Eds.), *Comparative early childhood education*. Chicago: Charles C. Thomas.

Sidel, R. (1972). *Women and child care in China*. New York: Hill and Wang.

————. (1982). Early childhood education in China: The impact of political change. *Comparative Education Review*, *26*(1), 78–87.

————. (1986). *Women and children last*. New York: Viking Penguin.

Singleton, J. (1989). *Gambaru*: A Japanese cultural theory of learning. In J. Shields (Ed.), *Japanese education: Patterns of socialization, equality, and political control*. State College: Pennsylvania State University Press.

Smedley, A. (1976). *Portraits of Chinese women in revolution*. New York: Feminist Press.

Solomon, R. H. (1971). *Mao's revolution and the Chinese political culture*. Berkeley: University of California Press.

Spitz, R. (1965). *The first year of life*. New York: International Universities Press.

State Education Commission (SEC). (1986). *Achievement of education in China*. Beijing: People's Education Press.

Steinhoff, P., & Tanaka, K. (1987). Women managers in Japan. *International Studies of Management and Organization, 16*(3–4), 108–132.

Stevenson, H., Azuma, H., & Hakuta, K. (Eds.). (1986). *Child development and education in Japan.* New York: W. H. Freeman.

Stevenson, H., Lee, S., & Stigler, J. (1981, summer). The reemergence of child development in the People's Republic. *Society for Research in Child Development Newsletter,* pp. 1–5.

Stevenson, H., & Lee, Y. (1986). *Learning to read Japanese.* In H. Stevenson, H. Azuma, & K. Hakuta (Eds.) 1986.

Suransky, E. (1982). *The erosion of childhood.* Chicago: University of Chicago Press.

Taniuchi, L. (1984, November 26). *Interrelationships between home and early formal learning situations for Japanese children.* Paper presented at the meeting of the Comparative and International Education Society, New York.

Tao, K., & Chiu, J. (1985). Psychological ramifications of the one-child family policy. In W. Tseng and D. Wu (Eds.), *Chinese culture and mental health* (pp. 153–165). Orlando, Fla.: Academic Press.

Thompson, V. (1974). Family size: Implicit policies and assumed psychological outcomes. *Journal of Social Issues, 30*(4), 93–124.

Thorne, B., & Yalom, M. (1982). *Rethinking the family: Some feminist questions.* New York: Longman.

Tobin, J. (1989). Visual anthropology and multivocal ethnography: A dialogical approach to Japanese preschool class size. *Dialectical Anthropology* 13 (2).

Tseng, W. S., & Wu, D. (1985). *Chinese culture and mental health.* Orlando, Fla.: Academic Press.

Tsukada, M. (1988). Institutionalized supplementary education in Japan: The *yobiko* and *ronin* student adaptations. *Journal of Comparative Education* (England), *24*(3).

U.S. Department of Labor, Bureau of Labor Statistics. (1985). *The United Nations decade for women, 1976–1985: Employment in the United States.* Washington, D.C.: U.S. Department of Labor.

Vogel, E. (1971). *Japan's new middle class* (2nd ed.). Berkeley: University of California Press.

Wang, N. (1984). *Socialization of the only child in China: An investigation into kindergartens.* Paper presented at the Conference on Child Socialization and Mental Health, Institute for Culture and Communication, East-West Center, Honolulu, Hi.

Weikart, D. (1982). Preschool education for disadvantaged children. In J. R. Travers & R. J. Light (Eds.), *Learning from experience: Evaluating early childhood demonstration programs.* Washington, D.C.: National Academy Press.

Westinghouse Learning Corporation. (1969). *The impact of Head Start: An evaluation of the Head Start experience on children's cognitive and affective development.* Athens: Ohio University Press.

White, B. (1985a). Foreword. In F. Maynard, *The child care crisis: The real costs of day care for you and your child.* Ontario, Canada: Penguin Books Canada.

———. (1985b). *The first three years of life* (Rev. ed.). New York: Prentice-Hall.

White, M. (1987). *The Japanese educational challenge: A commitment to children*. New York: Free Press.

White, M., & LeVine, R. (1986). What is an Ii Ko? In R. Stevenson, H. Azuma, & K. Hakuta (Eds.), *Child development and education in Japan*. New York: W. H. Freeman.

Whiting, B., & Edwards, C. (1988). *Children of different worlds*. Cambridge, Mass.: Harvard University Press.

Wilson, R. W. (1970). *Learning to be Chinese: The political socialization of children in Taiwan*. Cambridge, Mass.: MIT Press.

————. (1974). *The moral state: A study of the political socialization of Chinese and American children*. New York: Free Press.

Winget, W. G. (1982). The dilemma of affordable childcare. In E. F. Zigler & E. W. Gordon (Eds.), *Daycare scientific and social policy issues*. Dover, Mass.: Auburn House.

Wolf, A. (1985). Chinese family size: A myth revisited. In J. Hsieh & Y. Chuang, *The Chinese family and its ritual behavior*. Taiwan: Institute of Ethnology, Academia Sinica.

Wolf, M. & Witke, R. (Eds.). (1975). *Women in Chinese society*. Stanford, Calif.: Stanford University Press.

Wu, D. (1966). *Cong Renleixue Guandian Kan Muqian Zhongguo Ertong Yangyu* (An anthropologist looks at Chinese child training methods). *Thought and Word* (Taipei), 3(6), 741–745.

————. (1981). Child abuse in Taiwan. In J. Korbin (Ed.), *Child abuse and neglect: Cross-cultural perspectives* (pp. 139–165). Berkeley: University of California Press.

————. (1982). *The Chinese in Papua New Guinea 1880–1980*. Hong Kong: Chinese University Press.

————. (1983). *Child-rearing in China*. Paper presented at the Annual Meeting of the American Anthropological Association, November 16–20, Chicago.

————. (1985a). Child training in Chinese culture. In W. S. Tseng and D. Y. H. Wu (Eds.), *Chinese culture and mental health* (pp. 113–134). Orlando, Fla.: Academic Press.

————. (1985b). *Jiating Xiandaihua Xiade Zhongguo Ertong Yangyu* (Modernization, changing family, and the issues concerning Chinese child rearing). In C. Chiao (Ed.), *Proceedings of the conference on modernization and Chinese culture* (pp. 31–39). Hong Kong: Chinese University of Hong Kong.

————. (1988). *Zhongguo Renkou Zhengce yu Dusheng Zinu de Jiaoyang* (China's population policy and the rearing of single-child). In C. Chiao et al. (Eds.), *Proceedings of the second conference on modernization and Chinese culture*. Hong Kong: Chinese University of Hong Kong.

Xu, T. (1985). Child mental health and elementary schools in Shanghai. In W. Tseng and D. Wu, *Chinese culture and mental health*. Orlando, Fla.: Academic Press.

Yanagita, K. (1957). *Japanese manners and customs in the Meija era* (C. Terry, Trans.). Tokyo: Obunsha.

Zaretsky, E. (1973). *Capitalism, the family and family life*. New York: Harper & Row.

————. (1982). The place of the family in the origins of the welfare state. In
B. Thorne and M. Yalom (Eds.), *Rethinking the family*. New York: Longman.

Zha, Z. (1986). The psychological development of supernormal children. In
J. Freeman (Ed.), *The psychology of gifted children* (pp. 325–332). New York:
John Wiley.

Zhou, N. (1985). Drawing from experiences of developed nations toward reform
of our preschool education. *Yale-China Association Update*, 5(2), 5–6.

Zigler, E., & Gordon, E. (Eds.). (1982). *Day care scientific and social policy issues*.
Dover, Mass.: Auburn House.

Zigler, E., & Lamb, M. (1983). Head Start: Looking toward the future. *Young
Children*, 38(6), 3–6.

Index